Dear A,
Happy
Love
Richard and Shirley

Make a Skyf, Man!

Make a Skyf, Man!

Harold Strachan

Way Up Way Out – what they said:

"A shamelessly engaging and utterly refreshing look at South Africa and South Africans. A truly memorable gallery of characters. Harold Strachan´s book will delight all lovers of South Africana with its acerbic wit and elegant prose."
– Athol Fugard

"In the environment we live in today, it is very easy to forget what happened to Lawrence Gandar, the former editor of the Rand Daily Mail *when he dared to publish the words of Harold Strachan reminiscing about his prison experience. Strachan was arrested and sent back to Pretoria Central for his pains."*
– Pallo Jordan, Freedom Day Speech, 2004.

Make a Skyf, Man! – what they are saying:

"Quite simply one of the most ruthless accounts of what it was like to be alive in old South Africa if you happened to have a bit of that old-fashioned thing called a conscience. He spares nobody – least of all himself as he takes you on a journey that at one moment has you staring at the page with horror, the next splitting your sides with laughter or trying hard to swallow the lump in your throat as the pain of those years stands full-frontal naked in front of you. And then of course there is again that extraordinary gift for story telling which in my opinion makes him the rightful heir to the Herman Charles Bosman crown of our time. But what you also know by the time you reach the last page is that this book, like his earlier one, could only have been told by a man who passionately loves his country and its people."
– Athol Fugard

"Harold Strachan was condemned to a lengthy term of imprisonment for his activities as a member of the underground resistance to the apartheid regime. In Make a Skyf, Man! these episodes in his life are described with a mixture of fury and high spirits that is unique to him. His ear for the varieties of South African English speech is unfailingly sharp; so is his eye for cruelty, pretension and bad faith; so is his readiness to honour generosity and fair dealing whenever he comes across them. Aside from Strachan's earlier account of his boyhood, Way Up, Way Out, I know of no South African memoir as painful and witty as this one."

– Dan Jacobson

"Harold Strachan is a national literary treasure. Make a Skyf, Man! is a highly readable struggle and prison novel-cum-memoir that crosses boundaries in an inimitable South African way. Imagine a mixture of Herman Charles Bosman and Spike Milligan – sort of 'Verwoerd: his part in my downfall', but with Strachan's unique brand of sharp observation, agile language and rich irony. Strachan's account of his almost casual induction into underground resistance against apartheid is both gripping and funny. His efforts to assemble the ANC's first home-made bombs, aimed at launching the movement's foray into sabotage, emerge as equal parts courage and farce, high ideal and madcap invention – all fuelled with necessary amounts of stolen cherry liqueur. His description of capture, trial, imprisonment and eventual release is shaded darker: at times haunting, even tragic, but always utterly unsentimental and studded with satire and compassion amidst the madness and cruelty of prison life. Buy this book and help ensure that Strachan keeps writing: his crazy country still needs him."

– Sam Sole

One

THIS, BRU, WAS AN ANGLER'S PLACE. A shad place. And weight for weight there's no game-fish in the waters of this world like the one called Saltatrix, the dancer, and dance she does. Never mind the tranquil dam and the romance of the mountain stream and all that, nor even the mysteries of deep sea, get to the tumult of the wild white Natal surf where this frenzied beast has its being and you'll know what hunting is all about. Maybe the only thing better than getting into a shoal on light tackle is to take a small one and put her alive on the big surf rod, and let her swim out a hundred metres and get taken by a barracuda the size of your leg. Hunter on relentless hunter.

And for some reason the shad liked Pattie's Groyne. The best place around Durbs, easily.

The problem was getting out to the end of it, where the water was good and deep. This being about the nastiest coast in the world, as I've heard mariners say, with waves building up to sixty feet out there in the Agulhas current, the height of a six-storey building, man, and on occasion getting into phase so as to make a Hole in the Sea of ninety feet which has been known to swallow a ten thousand ton ship without trace; even though we got only the left-overs at Pattie's, I tell you brother the sight of such waves heaping up way out there was a thing of primeval horror at times. As when watching the wake of a torpedo; they took so long to arrive and where the hell to turn and run to, and should I risk my existence for this?

Well of course it wasn't always as wild as that; sometimes it was dead flat, but you'll understand what that sign on a creosote pole at the base of the pier meant, I'm sure. It said **EXTREMELY DANGEROUS KEEP OFF** and it wasn't just the state of the sea it was talking about. Pattie's was a random jumble of ten-ton concrete blocks and demolition rubble dumped in the surf by some unimaginable mechanism to save the beach from erosion and the palm-trees, high-rise hotels, Kentucky Chickens, the lot disappearing forever 'neath the wine-dark sea, like Atlantis. Back on the golden sands thus preserved stood another sign nailed to another creosote pole. It said **EUROPEANS ONLY** and went unread by us ouens of Pattie's Groyne. Come to think of it, I was the only ou with any of the Pure Unleaded Fluid squirting round my cardiovascular system, along with a bit of undeclared substandard stuff from the Middle East and the Kalahari, plus a few tablespoonfuls mixed in of that darkish tarry glop known around here as Huguenot Blood. The rest of us were just shad-sammies. We leaned our rods on the board whilst preparing for the dash across the groyne.

The trick was not to fall between the blocks and break your bones and drown if the tide was up and thumping, but your rod was eleven feet or so in length, and you could use it as a sort of rope-walker's pole, muster a bit of confidence and hop from top to top by building up a turn of speed. The fish cared not a fig for the preferences of human beings in the matter of wind and weather and conditions at the surface of the sea, nor the perils of rock-hopping. When the shad were there you had to be there too, or catch none. Not at Pattie's, anyway.

All this was okay. The holiday mob didn't come and tangle up our tackle. We worked together, you see, intuitively, though strangers. With a simple wooden centre-pin reel and quick-taper rod we could most cunningly bring the fish on the boil with a concentration of bait or flashing of spinners and locate the shoal and keep in touch and in reach.

Well, one afternoon at about three-thirty, with an incoming neap tide, and the half-moon in just the right place down the vertical and over to the left a bit, and the shad getting restless and a bit fierce, we there espied, those of us who were interested enough in such trivia, a figure in tennis shirt and shorts with a cardboard shoe-box under its arm, examining the approaches to Pattie's Groyne like Sir Edmund examining the South Face of Everest. To be accurate, I think I was in fact the only one to notice this citizen, because I had a freezer-full of fish at home anyway, and my friends had taken to crossing the street when they saw me coming because they knew I was going to unload more onto them. So I was there only to get a couple of nice fresh ones because folks were coming to supper, and I'd a lot of time for staring about.

Come to think of it, I was probably excluded from the ANC, not because of the above European Blood, but because I smelled of fish, like a pelican.

Lal was up on his rock. If you were bloody quick you could nip up on to this rock when he went for a pee or something, and have a turn there, but in the main he never moved from it, and if the wind was offshore he'd pee from the rock too. He had a big canvas pocket sewed on his raincoat, full of sardines and pinkies and fillets of shad, their own cannibal kindred, for bait, and one of his numberless laaities behind him with a mealie-bag for the fish. Lal was there for protein, being unemployed, and having one of those extended Indian families to feed, so extensive and packed into the family house so tightly they must have slept standing up, or perhaps with a coat-hanger in the pyjama jacket, hooked on a nail in the wall.

Lal was not only the ugliest man I've known, with a complete set of black teeth, but also the best angler I've known, anywhere, fresh or salt water. He not only knew how fish species thought, he knew how to think like an individual of the species, which he could see even in white water, and buggered if I know how he did it. He never explained how he did it. He never spoke. He was also the most silent man I've known.

So here I am with all these sammies, plying our skills for sport and protein and working out a lot of male hunting needs the while, when I observe this pioneer making his way over Pattie's the way Hillary made his way over the Goddess Mother of the Earth, by climbing up and along each block, with this shoe-box under his arm, and all without ropes or pitons.

When he gets a bit closer I notice that the thing in his hand is in fact a wee tiny river rod, and when he eventually arrives, against all probability, I see that the shoe-box contains ill-assorted tackle which some shlock in Point Road has had in stock in his Vakansie Tee-kamer along with yesterday's meat pies and Souvenirs of Durban such as Ghanaian ju-ju masks made with a kitchen knife just over the hill in a Zulu mens' hostel. This gent is completely kitted out for catching zilch, zero, ifogololo except maybe an inexperienced frog in a drain somewhere.

He smiles a smile of boundless innocence and calls me his brother and tells me he is from Brakpan and wishes to try Natal surf angling, of which he has heard great tales. Man, in almost every skill, art, science or sport, a beginner needs the best equipment, and the more the experience, the easier the improvisation with cheap tools. So I think What the Hell, since I'm crafty enough at this thing to regard his dreckishe tackle as a challenge, I'll see if I can actually catch a fish on it, well, the two of us together, that is, so he doesn't go home empty-handed. Somehow I feel I owe it to someone so dedicated.

I take from his cardboard box this horrible little fixed-spool reel with plastic gears, and I fix it on his toothpick rod and thread the line through the runners, and all of this he views with the utmost excitement, and exclaims Hel, hei! with each new event, especially the part where I get from my box the bung and the three-oh hook with the steel trace, and sharpen it on a little whetstone and knot it on the line and tie on the sardine with bait-cotton.

I fling this lot into the sea on the outward surge of a wave, and hand the rod to him and say Nou moet jy wakker wees, jong, want hierdie vis het 'n helse aai kjoe, i.e. one must be quick-witted with this species, and know that the bung bobbing about means your shad is having a sniff and a taste, but when the bung is seen to disappear entirely beneath the surface you must strike fast, and hard. Timing is all. And as the rod arrives in his hand the most uneducated shad in the salt sea takes this sardine and swallows it so totally that when ou Brakpan does get round to striking to set the hook it is already somewhere around its giblets.

He hauls it out of the water, deadweight, over the rocks, and is enthralled, as indeed he should be; I myself am enthralled by such good luck, and to drag it over the stones like that too. A fish! A Natal shad! His! Never mind that he's standing in his shirtsleeves under this salt waterfall; as I get the pliers out and cut loose the steel trace sticking from the mouth with the needle teeth still slashing about, because there's no way to get the hook from down in its gut, and put the fish in my bag to die with all this apparatus still lodged in its innards, this ou says Hei aai'm doeing orraait! How many fishes you think this koelie here has got hei? Krish, how many fish you got, you? I call. Seven, Krish here on my other side replies, and he has to count them, because he's not really into tallies. He's been going a couple of hours to get his seven, but he's not really watching the time either.

Seven. That's okay, I've been going five minutes and I've got one, so in an hour's time I should have twenty, this ou thinks. Well, all great Neptune's oceans do not contain a second shad as onnosel as the first, and I try to explain this to ou Brakpan as he gets anxious now, because he's lost three sardines to the shoal in following casts and missed each time. Relax, I tell him, enjoy it! You're very lucky to get a shad at all, as a beginner, really you are, I try to explain.

But he can't relax, so I say Here let me get a nice long cast for you, and I take his little stick and throw in another sardine, and I hang on to the rod a bit, pretending to adjust the reel, and as the first shad chops the bait I hit him hard and straight and get the hook well set, then I release the bail of his little reel so the line goes slack and the fish has got nothing to fight against, and gets confused and dithers about just below the surface, and the bung comes to the top again. I re-engage the line and hand the rod to ou Brakpan, and he doesn't know at all there's a fish on it. After a few seconds the fish feels the pull at his mouth once more and goes bananas, dives deep and darts about bedonderd down there, and Brakpan is doing something similar up here and he's wild and excited and shouting and happy again.

But not for long.

I wonder why he's so upset about losing sardines, since I'm providing them. Another three, I suppose. Every time he misses a strike he curses and crinkles up his brow and swears upon his oath something's wrong. How many fish has he got now? he asks. Hey Krish, how many this time, you? Nine. NINE! Shit, and I've only got two! He shakes his head and mutters about mathematical injustice while I try to console him about the wasted sardines. At about sardine six he gets into a fish, though I don't know how, the way he's flailing about in his desperation. He's going to be happy now, for sure, with three nice four-pound shad to take home after his first outing. But disaster! Disaster! He loses it. Crisis. He looks the other side of Krish at Lal on his rock. How many fish has that one got, you think?

Lal, man, I call, how many fish you got, you?

Twenty-seven, me, calls Lal over his shoulder.

Anguished, dismayed, Brakpan flings his rod down on the rocks, shoves his hands in his pockets, frowns hideously and snarls That's the bloody trouble, so waar! The vokken Indians take all our fish, man!, as if I'm with him in his rage and the fish all belong to us, according to government policy, maybe, or perhaps we hold them in some ancient inalienable fiefdom which disallows poaching. He yells things for all to hear, standing there dripping wave water, his hair all streaming down over his eyes, as I watch his shoe-box fill up from the last big one and the glue of its corners all dissolve and the whole thing open up like a daisy on the rock where it stands and all his tea-room tackle slip out of sight over the edge.

After a bit Lal hands his rod to his laaitie and gets off his rock. He makes his way over to Brakpan. Not European Ocean this ocean! he.says; Indian Ocean! Why you don't fuck off you? Go to Vaaldam, catch barbools, you!

Jis, my heart only sinks now, man, because Brakpan just wants to fight, hay?

Catching barbel is only one up from catching paddas, though I'd have to think about it a while to be absolutely sure. Brakpan is young, and well-muscled too, but there's a hell of a lot of skinny charras around, and fierce nogal, with nasty septic-looking bait knives, and while he takes these factors into account, plus the decisive one that he's not really on the best surface for defensive footwork, I come up close to him and say, sort of avuncular, Ou boet, moenie met hierdie ouens hierso kom droogmaak nie, jong; hulle sal jou w'ragtig in die water gooi! And they would too have thrown him in the water, with just a bit more of his bullshit, because the Natal coast is Injun Territory, man, by traditional occupation, and if ever you want to see God, soon, just get between a Natal angler and his shad.

I take his arm and turn him away from the scene of his sorrow, and thread his fish on a piece of line and put them in his hand and point him homeward and watch him make his wet way over the Himalayas to his holiday flat and a sullen supper of bitter fish, salivating sweet eventual revenge with each mouthful.

I suppose up at the top of the racialist structures one could have a cheery uncomplicated life with one's fingers sunk deep in the honeycomb of big profit and the big big slush funds of the régime, and really gigantic governmental fraud, not to mention of course the Ultimate Additional; getting your name in the Book of National Heroes, along with the Shepstones and the Freres and the Milners, as do indeed all these new anti-apartheid aspirants these days, who've come up from the Other Side, the North Face. To be sure, the slush funds where they have come from are slushier and deeper, and as limitless as the Okavango swamps. But the people I saw about me, the plundered and the privileged both, were chronically ill with envy, guilt, revenge, arrogance and superstition. Superstition especially. Blessed are they who can slide out from under this ten-ton block.

Bring me headache, that fellow, says Lal.

Two

THE DURBAN CONGRESS OF DEMOCRATS in the mid-Fifties was like the Royal Family. Ah yes, these were yet the staunch early days of Commonwealth, and Queenie was still with us first time round, quite new and shiny too, though I can't honestly say pretty, this being obviously beyond the reach of any Windsor. But ja, as I say, we were like them, in that we had to be sure never all of us to travel together in the same vehicle, in the case of the Congress of Democrats a Morris Oxford. There might occur a dreadful unlucky traffic accident and we could all get wiped out and the lineage become extinct.

We would congregate twice a month or so at the socialist home of the Hawthornes, Margaret and Michael, a family of doctors. A merry band, we. There was much tea, then there would be minutes, which seemed like hours, of the last meeting, and then we would sit and sigh, and bend our brows, and furrow our foreheads, and take more tea, and ask ourselves and one another cosmic questions. Wheretofore? and Whenceforth? we would ask, and What are we doing here?, and hope that maybe David Evans from the Liberal Party would happen by and perhaps add a bit of non-ideological sparkle to the funereal evening with political scandal about the Régime, which all could enjoy, and perhaps even a few jokes about the Gummint or something, who knows?

Even the next time, after an Evans visit, there would be a bit of residual adrenalin left in the old veins, perhaps, for we'd all sit about and say with a gasp or two of disbelief, in fact of shock, how curious it was that one as intelligent as he could take such a naive non-Marxist view of the struggle. But when the thrill was over and our usual cemetery demeanour had returned, after the second long silence and maybe third tea libation, somebody would breathlessly blurt out, illogically enough, Why don't we just pack up here and go and join the Liberal Party?

The only thing to meet such heresy with is stony silence, and we always met it with that, though there were never reprimands, for we all cherished such treason in our hearts, somewhere, and we each one of us knew that one day our time would come and our piano-strings would snap, and we too would blurt out this capitalist abomination.

I have heard that Japanese find Americans smell of meat, like the cat-cages at the zoo, which may be true, the number of cows they get through in a year, and I often quite seriously wondered if perhaps there was something similar that was wrong with us whites, that we weren't allowed to join the African

National Congress straight, but had to sit in a corner over there by ourselves, like carnivores in a vegetarian restaurant. Received wisdom was that we would frighten country folk in the ANC, as indeed Indian and Coloured congresspeople would, but to me we seemed rustic enough ourselves, or whatever the urban equivalent might be.

I don't mean we were dumb or anything like that, Lord love you, no, for we had to be able to decide what our secretary would say when he went to local joint meetings of All the Congress Secretaries; from the Indian congress, the Coloured congress, the African congress and, of course, ours, the White congress, called the Congress of Democrats because being White was unfashionable, sort of, in the Struggle; what he would say when he arrived in our Morris Oxford, known as Oxfam because of the poverty of its appearance and performance.

Hell, man, sometimes our secretary would actually go to Johannesburg, to the Vatican itself, and actually touch the hem of the robe of the Main Ou of the Actual Party, and actually kiss the ring, and actually feel the flesh after wiping the sweating palm with a tissue damp with Peoples' Olie Kolonie, whilst lesser Monsignori of the Peoples' Selfless Struggle smiled brotherly smiles, and indeed sisterly smiles, for these are enlightened people, hey?, and watch the chimney for perhaps a sudden puff of this or that coloured smoke to rise and announce increased opportunities Selflessly to Serve the Toiling Masses from a rung higher up. Or two. Come to think of it, somebody even has to be at the Top.

Not one of the sisters, naturally, but of course these were entitled to watch the chimney anyway, as observers, and each maybe as cheerleader for a favoured Monsignor, though I wouldn't want to be misconstrued here and thought to be suggesting the sort of cheap cheerleader one might see at an American football game, with a crude fluffy military-type thing on her head and those coarse sexist high-heeled boots and that embarrassingly contrived skirt that showed her excessive buttocks and thighs and the very form of her labia in whatever minimal lingerie contained them, every time she kicked up her nubile legs, and why does she have to kick up her legs so anyway; she's not having a go at goal, is she?

No, the type of cheerleader I have in mind here is the Mother of Africa type of cheerleader, with ethnically-patterned flowing robes of Democratic Africa. Nigeria, say now, though maybe I should prefer an ethnically patterned flowing robe from an African Country of True Socialist Sensibility, and if you give me a minute or two I shall think of one, but then again, is it important to stick on such detail when we have a tale of the class struggle to get on with?

But I do blunder so! Now I have suggested a matronly figure, when I meant a maternal one. Yet once again I've got it wrong! What I mean is a mum, a fragrant soft enclosing presence for the innocent young, a reassuring mama for the confused uncared-for kids of this land.

Well, let's get on with the story then.

No, honestly, I mean I have seen, in fact personally met, those from the Actual Party who have achieved sainthood in their own lifetimes, such was their sacrifice. Jack Hodgson came to one of our meetings whilst in Durban on secret organisational business. Business had always to be secret, obviously, even going to the Greek shop for a pack of fags, for the security police were of such cunning that any smallest bit of information they could glean about you they might well use to imply that you had pulled some libidinous coup with a comrade's wife, or bled party money or something, and destroy your reputation and your credibility in the Movement, forever, although one's comrades were people of breadth of mind, it goes without saying, who in truth had there own little peccadilloes, as it were.

Then again, of course, the manifestation of one's skill at secrecy allowed one's comrades an insight into one's earnestness of purpose in this Class War, and they might understand perhaps how a little unsought fame may have fallen upon one's shoulders, as it were.

Jack Hodgson was a man of sorrow, for he had been obliged to abandon his family hitch-hiking on the side of the yellow-brick capitalist road, and make his way solo through the dreadful hazards and minefields of the revolution, seeking neither reward nor acclaim nor status, in accordance with his principles and his dedication.

Like the body of Saint Francis, the body of Jack Hodgson bore the signs of rigour. He could not walk too far, for the state of his lungs would not permit it. He was obliged to leave his mouth open most of the time, for breath, closing it in fact only briefly, about four times to the minute, upon a cigarette, or in order to wipe his lips on the back of his hand after coughing something up and spitting it down the lavatory bowl, or out of a handy window. This unfortunate condition of Jack Hodgson's respiration was the consequence of smoke, which it was necessary for him to inhale continuously, in order to find relief from the continual unbearable hardship and the sacrifices he had perforce to accept in the course of the struggle, I mean Struggle.

Like one of Saint Francis' children, Jack Hodgson was obliged not to sit, but to perch upon a chair in order to eat his supper, or attend an awfully important unlawful meeting. This was because of his haemorrhoids. Haemorrhoids are the affliction of revolutionaries who eat only perfunctorily in the course of their unrelentingly hazardous daily life, and who endure unremitting anxiety in consequence of such hazards, Jack Hodgson explained, and these were anxiety haemorrhoids. The curious squatting posture had caused to develop down there a great bunch of muscadel grapes, as the poetic image employed by Jack Hodgson had it when describing his symptoms to cdes yet unaware of the degree of his selfless tribulation. I know you university cdes prefer long intellectual words like Psychosomatic, but please don't make the ignorant mistake of thinking these haemorrhoids less real for having appeared originally in the mind, said Jack Hodgson.

However forlorn our meetings may have been, the Durban Congress of Democrats had an air of privacy about it, and meetings were restful enough, if not downright soporific, due to the humidity of the city, and a local tradition of slow movement and unhurried thought, known as febris natalensis, or Natal Fever. Such slowness makes for conservatism, I suppose, so Jack Hodgson appeared as something of an incongruous gymnogene sticking his beak into our peaceful nest. Oh ja, he had in addition to other remarkable attributes this great cucurbitine hooter on his face, with enlarged pores, and which seemed no longer to have a function of breathing, since it it was all blocked off with some sort of endogenous putty, on account of the smoke. This was why Jack Hodgson had to leave his mouth open all the time.

Shame, poor Sarah, one of our number, had a bad marriage. It was a matter of sympathy between her and the rest of us. I mean, she knew we were all available for support by way of a shoulder to lean on, an ear to listen, and a tissue or two for the moist eye, and if ever these aids to distress were needed, well, they had only to be asked for. Of course such sorrows in these modern days are no longer buried or secret or suffered alone in the long silent hours of the night.

I want to tell you what Lenin said about marriage problems, spake Jack Hodgson to Sarah, whereupon, squatting upon a dining-room chair, he spake to all present the Party Prescription for Marriage and Related Family Problems, as propounded by Vladimir Ilyich himself, in the room opposite the sausage factory in Zürich perhaps, whilst Comrade Helpmeet Krupskaya dashed it all down on the back of a hastily-grabbed envelope, urgently, so as not to waste any of the wisdom and subtleties contained therein.

A bit like K. Marx himself walking in Hyde Park hand in hand with his cheery daughters, I suppose, and giving them the original Marxist Interpretation of Shakespeare, you know, straight from the horse's mouth, man, and what a horse! An interpretation available unbowdlerized and straight also from the mouth of Jack Hodgson, who had this too on his list of available topics. Should one need it at any time, one had only to ask, so ready was he to oblige his cdes with insight into life and art. In fact, so ready was he, he would bestow such insight upon one without one's needing it at all, just in case one might have need of it later on.

Ja, so he lays on Cde Sarah what Cde V.I. himself had to say about marriage problems, including hers, because they're all the same really, you must realise, arising from the same definable and predictable contradictions in the class struggle. Like causes have like consequences, I want you to understand, and to

Hell with psychotherapy, what do you want that boodjwar garbage for when there's good stuff written by good party people, and if you can't get your hands on copies of these works, why, it is my pleasure and duty to give you a resumé of them all, right here and now, for

I am Sir Oracle,

And when I ope my lips let no dog bark,

and no, no more tea thanks, I mean please!

We've just had a cup, man, and how do you cdes drink so much of the stuff? It will affect your health.

I sit there then reflecting on two things; first, that the Like Causes bit sounds to me, a non-party man, like homeopathy; second, that maybe it would have been interesting to hear Krupskaya's view of marriage, not sitting on the edge of the marriage bed there opposite the sausage factory, but perhaps after a couple of nice beers down at the Beach Hotel in Durbs, out on the verandah watching the dolphins beyond the white water, just the two of us, and getting mellow and a bit silly perhaps and intimate after Lager #2. No, I think Pilsener is nicer of a late summer's afternoon, well in Durban anyway.

But I must say it all does poor Sarah a power of good, for as I watch her dabbing her eyes with tissues, I realise that these are not the tears of sorrow we have seen on occasion recently, but tears of suppressed mirth. But always a Lady, Archie, always a Lady, in spite of Hell and Transmigration. Why brawl with Jack Hodgson, caricature or not, even if he happens not to know that I, Sarah, myself am a psychotherapist, and a pretty good one, by my record of success?

Vera, now, didn't give much of a hoot about the ladylike bit, nor had she a very ladylike presence, being all skinny and twisted up from spinal tuberculosis as a kid.

I feel uneasy talking of Jewish women as Jewesses, like actresses or poetesses, some alternative version of the real thing, you know what I mean. Potatoesses. Vera was an alternative version of nothing, thank you, but straight from the East End of London, dockland, herself, complete with the accent and the insubordination that go with the indefinable working class of London. Her voice was like a nail coming out of a plank.

Ar piss off, Hodgson, you silly prick! says Vera.

But never submit to such dismissal, man! Don't even by innuendo or the grace available in friendship ever concede anything! I mean, it's not only the Security Branch who are cunning. The Movement is a Byzantine place, you mumble when you're all alone in bed and the lights are out, so nobody can perhaps see your lips mouthing such cynical thought, and if rumour gets back home from Durban, aspirants back there, or those ahead up here might say; Ye-e-es. A good man, but short of theory. SHORT OF THEORY, hear what I'm saying: That, my mate, is your LOT! You will be able to make your contribution down at the bottom, licking stamps or taking up arms or getting hanged, but you will NEVER join the VANGUARD of the VANGUARD!

Jack Hodgson goes to the lavatory and gets some more contact adhesive from inside his system and deposits it in the pan. Then he goes to the washbasin and flings water on his face and takes time drying it, and combs his hair. The total performance takes five, maybe ten minutes, the time it takes for real tension to build up out there in the meeting. I mean, that's how long it has taken in the past.

Others will hear of this indiscipline! he exclaims as he emerges from the bog and takes his jacket from the back of his chair and folds it carefully and places it over his arm in preparation for leaving.

Stupid bloody git, says Vera, this isn't even a Party meeting, for fuck sake! So.

Our meetings were not normally interrupted by such Sturm und Drang. Peace generally prevailed, if woebegone. Come to think of it, I was Treasurer of the Congress of Democrats, though I don't remember much money ever being about, nor any other treasure, except the treasure of friendship, of which we were replete. Friendship appeared to be something distinct from Comradeship.

At about this time some imbecile wordsmith decided that Apartheid sounded more genteel than Baasskap as a name for a whole set of shiny new laws putting a police state in position for our shiny new programme of social engineering. But baasskap it remained, and after twelve years of moralistic bullshit the shining had got a bit much, and the short-circuit switch was due to trip. The fuse had to blow.

Well, Sharpeville was the spectacular that blew it, of course. Police action there was no more than the usual, in fact. The sort of thing one had grown to expect. But the seventy-two corpses this time, and the pictures! The photographers had known it would happen, and they were there. The media gave us the symbol, the emblem and the slogan: Remember Sharpeville!

Zealous marchers descended on the cities: shanty dwellers, slum dwellers, township dwellers, poor folks instinctively outraged, spontaneously joining along the way, here and there a political person, a Robert Sobukwe, up ahead.

A fearful spectacle! Every upwelling of desperate fury in the past had been in the nature of a Bambatha Rebellion; send in Colonel McKenzie and his true soldiers and mow the buggers down with shellfire at a place called Dobo, and when Bambatha flees almost naked send Loyalist Natives in pursuit, and when they find him far away escaping up a stream to leave no tracks, slam an assegai in his body.

But this was no peasant Jacquerie, my mate. It was no tribal Pondo uprising. This was our workforce. Maybe the Security Branch is right, perhaps these are proletarian revolutionaries, and what THEN, hey? The endless column winds its peristaltic way from Cato Manor into Durban. Mostly men, they carry sticks, fighting sticks, and sing as Africans sing. And let me tell you, when Zulus sing it is not like a soccer crowd at Wembley, matey. It gives you the chicken skin. It adverts the mind to Isandlwana, the prospect of twenty thousand of this lot spilling out of the Nqutu gorge and hissing through the yellow grass to fall upon the horrified 24th Regiment of Foot.

Deep, controlled, musical, menacing. The fearsome menace of malehood. With here the mindless roaring racket of Harvards overhead; reporting what to the Saracen armoured cars on the ground? There's nothing to report, you can see it all from ground level. The Harvards are there for intimidation. The Saracens block off the Cato Manor road. The marchers filter away to the sides and reassemble behind them. They do it again at Toll Gate, and again there's a waving of sticks and a filtering off down the side streets.

At the bottom of Berea Road the police make a stand: Saracens across the road and armed men down the side streets. They open fire there. Jess and I are on our way home to lunch, the art school closes early on Friday. In front of us a guileless slightly-built bloke with a bag of cheap Granny Smith apples strolls across the road into Syringa Avenue and takes a bullet through the back. His apples fly about the road. He dies.

It all looks like a Ben Shahn painting: his blue denim jacket rucked up round his neck, his green apples and their purple paper wrappings against the grey gravel under a violet-stemmed rubber-tree in the full glare of the subtropic summer sun. And the thin trickle of blood across to the storm-water drain. How irreverent, to think about painting at a time like this. But Ben Shahn did a great one of an American marine shot to hell on a Pacific beach, and there was also a trickle of blood, says Jess. Why don't you do a painting of it? she asks, and I do, but years later, when things have settled into sullen stasis.

Well the marchers are much thinned out now, as you can imagine. Alas, they are not purposeful proletarian revolutionaries, they are after all a bullied and confused and desperate rag-tag, living out the fag-end of their culture a hundred years after the purposeful destruction of their nationhood by other, British, tyrants.

A residual five hundred or so make their way to the Central Prison to bang on the great oak door with their sticks and demand the release of their leaders who are locked up in there without trial. We follow them. A lunch-time crowd of white office workers turns out to stare. The Saracens pull up and a platoon of police with a captain march up in column of route, army style. They are armed with Sten guns, a nasty crude bitch of a weapon, likely to go off of its own volition if you jar it the wrong way. Prison warders line the top of the wall, with rifles.

The marchers pull back, the captain draws up his men in single rank between them and the wall. He looks at his watch... Will all those white people up there go away, he says, there's going to be shooting here. I give everybody else two minutes to disperse, he says. He orders his men to cock their weapons. PANIC! The spectators scramble, the marchers stay put, and what do we do now?

He looks at his watch again. One minute. Come, I say to Jess, and do the most bloody stupid thing I've ever done, and I've done plenty. Don't say a single word to anybody, I say, or somebody's going to say we're giving orders, and we walk up and stand in front of the demo. If the presence of whites will inhibit things maybe we can prevent another Sharpeville. Fold your arms in front of you, I say, and don't look round. A nut political figure called Anthony de Crespigny comes and stands next to us and folds his arms. An Indian attorney called Bhagwandeen joins us. We stare at the wall, and the captain stares at his watch.

A sour-looking fucker in civilian clothes steps up to Jess scowling and points his Sten at her guts. Nobody can put the ice on people like Jess. She gives this fucker the Medusa look and he shifts his glance over her shoulder before he turns to stone, and points his Sten at somebody else back there. Dogs do it when avoiding a fight.

The crowd grumbles and slowly starts to drift off. It's over the two minutes. The captain is dithering about killing a few folks or something, as a matter of pride. We deftly duck in amongst some parked cars and from the other side of the street see him looking for us. Bad luck, boet, we have no political image, nobody will recognise us from any photograph.

But the hunt was on. Of course we had organised it all; black people don't know how to march all on their own.

And lo, a month after all this a letter arrives, from the Air Force, instructing me without delay to present myself in Pretoria as a member of the Special Reserve, so I can go and fly round and round in a Harvard and tell policemen in Saracens what people are doing in the street. After another month another letter arrives, explaining that I have no choice in the matter, and so on for a year, getting more and more vexed until somehow they get hold of my mother's address, and write explaining to her that if her son doesn't report instantly he will have his epaulettes, wings, buttons, badges and moustache torn off on a parade ground in front of all his comrades, and flung in the dust and trampled underfoot. He will then be cashiered disgracefully. So please send us urgently his present address.

The present address, says my ma, is Pretoria Central Prison.

Sharpeville sent us into a political spiral and an ensuing State of Emergency. An emissary from the Vatican up there on the Highveld appeared amongst us at sweaty sea level, to assess and evaluate our attitude to revolution, and to gauge our probable response to a call to arms. A grue, a sort of frisson, rippled through the congress community: the conclusion of such revolution would be predictable and inevitable, our Marxist theorists assured us of that, and now it seemed the starter's pistol was about to be fired, but what about the bit in between? What perils and heroism would our grandchildren read about our personal selves in the history books?

You would think, wouldn't you only, that a rewarding life teaching art would be enough to keep any young fellow out of trouble with any government of any country, especially a lad as hesitant as myself, and timid by nature, for the profile I may present of self-possession and great guts is but of cardboard: it is not bravery you're looking at, but bravado, all silhouette, no substance. But I mean you would expect even a brave being to apply a bit of common sense to the proposition, and stay within the blade wire, and find the adventures of life in the hunting of shad, and the pursuit of zizipompom with the pretties of the art world.

But not me! God bless you no! I mean our big indigenous capitalists have no need of racial restriction in employment because it obstructs the important business of profit-making, and we have a labour movement simply burgeoning, man, in spite of racial laws disallowing it, and intent on the important business of wage-making regardless of persecution, and if you can think of a more potent couple of unlikely bedfellows than that in the defiance of a racist mystique, please write and let me know.

V.I. Lenin was never a pal of mine, and in the new ANC, after the leadership had been captured by the Leninists in the Fifties and the territories of Albert Luthuli colonised by the new zealots, I had an uncomfortable feeling that Ol' Vladimir there was looking over my shoulder all the time. Yet at the one moment when I really did need the sod to look over this shoulder and say into my dinky pink Hold it, Matey, this is adventurism!, at that moment he was out of town, and remember, whatever sort of social bastardry V.I.L. was good at, there was one thing he was specially good at, and crafty, and that was revolution.

Nuncio Hodgson arrives from Joeys then, with a carton of capitalist Camels and authority from Comrade Yoshke to invite us to consider the ideological correctitude of starting the Peoples' Armed Struggle now that the white supremacist fascist regime has thrust its iron heel on the throat of the People in their Gandhian Phase of struggle and there's nothing left now but the Armed Phase.

Yoshke Slovo is the Main Ou in the Actual Party.

So the Congress of Democrats, Durban Branch, drinks further tea, and ponders this revolutionary proposition like anything. But being all sweaty and slow of thought in our lousy climate, we haven't got through our pondering by a long chalk, we aren't even halfway done, in point of fact, and we're really working at it, when Jack H. disappears as suddenly as he came, leaving a trail of stompies behind him so he can find his way back when suitably tinted smoke has risen from the Peoples' Democratic Chimney-pot, to tell us whether R-day is on or not.

Detention without trial, and our lad shouldn't get it, that's the crisis that has snatched J.H. away. He's wanted for Deep Party Thought at the Top.

People have been four months in detention by now, maybe five, and maybe it'll be forever. For Jess and me there's a warrant of arrest in somebody's hands, on a charge of riotous assembly. My nice new missus is a very riotous art teacher who assembles with people in front of prisons where these folks are detained.

Matter of fact, there's a warrant out for almost everybody's arrest, such is the drama of the time. Not exactly: I mean there's a piece of paper about anybody who's somebody, who's almost nobody, like us, telling the Security Branch that this citizen can be detained without warrant.

Orders, not legality. That's what the story was about.

We pack our unironed laundry and a few working books into a rucksack and take ourselves off to Issy Benjamin's place at Isipingo Beach. Issy B from Issy Pingo is his name in the architectural community.

Every morning Issy brings us into town, and along the way to the Art School he drives past our nice new house to see if the garden rake is lying on the front lawn. We have invited one of my senior students to occupy our house rent-free, rates- and telephone-free. The other half of the deal is that every evening he will place this rake on the front lawn, and take it inside again in the morning. If the SB come at their usual four a.m. he will not take it in. A fail-safe system.

So after about three weeks we see the rake on the lawn at seven forty-five or so, and Issy turns round his Wolseley and drives us back to Isipingo. The SB ask the student called Iain McSomething what he's doing in our house and if he knows our present address, and this same MacStudent soon thereafter sells our furniture, all of it, even the knives and forks, and fucks off to Amsterdam on the proceeds, explaining to anti-apartheid commissars there that political life in South Africa is now so hazardous that his nerves are shattered, and will they supply him with some money for rent and a bursary for interrupted studies, please?

Issy turns the Wolseley around once again when we get back to Isipingo. We chuck in our unironed clothing, and a lot of petrol, and shmeitz to Swaziland, there and then. Issy makes sure of getting through the border post before the Security Branch instruct the soporific boere at the boom to put down their cups of coffee and hou dop for fleeing verraaiers.

Three

WE PULL IN AT THE WHITE REFUGEES' CENTRE, two big adjacent flats in the middle of Mbabane, Swaziland, no co-habitation in a British Protectorate, eh?, and we sit there for three months listening to the Refugees' Central Committee bellyaching about the quantity of meat the black refugees are devouring daily over at the Lutheran mission station out of town, and for which we have to do the bookkeeping with a World Council of Churches budget, and about the lack of dedication to cooking displayed by some of the comrades back here in the white refugees' refuge, who can't even get a gravy recipe right for the rolled roast, and how the hell will they ever understand Marxist theory if they can't understand the theory of gravy, i.e. how you have to get a sachet of Turkey Broth dehydrate from the supermarket to boost up this populist dressing, and this revolution is going to take a bloody long time with the sort of raw material coming up to us from the boodjwazie, I want you to know, and mark my words comrade.

There is this big jaap Afrikaans communist here called Piet or Koos or something, I forget, with dewlaps down to his clavicles and great grey hammocks under his eyes, and he's something of a miracle and a hero in the Struggle because he's not in the security police where Afrikaners are supposed to be, though in my humble opinion he might as well be there, because his only contribution to any debate or disagreement is Yiss! I only want to YIT you man!

Then there is Jack Hodgson, forsooth, I mean just our fucken luck to have him along here, hey?, with his hooter and his haemorrhoids, who announces his intention to deliver a series of dialectical materialist lectures after the Sunday roasts when everybody was looking forward to a curl-up under the eiderdown, on how our species shot straight up the evolutionary ladder from being a sort of pitiful degenerate lungfish which slopped about eating mud and learning to breathe air, to being sort of peoples' poets after the dictatorship of the proles and the withering away of the state. All work will be done by electrical robots. All over on green lawns will be Jack Hodgsons walking about with pointy toes and small clipboards, writing poetry, all day.

But he never gets beyond the hunter-gatherers and life in the caves for shortage of time in this educational programme, because this is still a British Protectorate, don't forget, Cde, and it is important to the refugee community that we should be on good terms with the authorities, and Jack Hodgson and Piet (or Koos, that is) must go guinea-fowl shooting with dogs and shotguns and eat supper afterwards with the District Commissioner, and spit out lead shot into a special Regency English shotgun-pellet spittoon, decorated with a pheasant motif, and afterwards listen on the newfangled stereophonic gramophone to big 120-decibel Beethoven concerti which they don't understand but the DC is a cultured Tory like Edward Heath so we'd better sit and emote a bit whilst we privately think on next Sunday's roast with the turkey broth gravy.

At Central Committee meetings they emote about our penetration of the secret plans which the British have for us, and we all know about Perfidious Albion, and suchlike assorted platitudes.

I have this nasty sceptical streak in me, handed down by my pa, who was a Scot and real mean. He used to say It runs in the blood, like a wooden leg. So it does occur to me, I must confess, that it would take a specialist surgeon and specialist anaesthetist and an operation to get these two out from where they're lodged in the anatomy of the District Commissioner.

Then also on the Refugees' Central Committee is this big bulbous Jewish bird like one of those force-fed geese in the French death-camps, called Doris or Mavis or some sort of -is, I forget, though Tochis seems apt enough to me, thinking back, but she's known as The Lily of Pine Valley because of her dancing Swan Lake barefoot in the early pearly dew of the morn 'mongst the pines of that valley, after the pachydermatous thumps and grunts of her hippo humping with Piet Whomever, all night. She knows this ballet technique, man, how to cast eyes down and arms up, with her wrists bent all inwards and her fingers all fancy, as if about to take a draught of the true blushful Hippocrene with Tchaikovsky by first light of the nipple-pink dawn.

She too has these great grey drapes under her eyes, like the velvet curtains in those old-time bioscopes, or the Palace of Versailles maybe. With the eyes downcast and the dark mauve of the lids added to the general murk of the orbits, one understood why westerners are known in Hong Kong as Ghost-Eyes.

When the state has withered away, all over and in amongst the male comrades with pointy toes writing poetry on clipboards on the lawn, will be lady comrades dancing Swan Lake with pointy toes, maybe Giselle too, even if that isn't Russian music, but we're all broadminded around here, and where have you been, comrade, we're internationalists, aren't we?

She isn't into the guinea-fowl shooting with the smelly dogs and all that brutality and blood, of course; her specialty is home-made strawberry ice-cream with real fruit, which she home-makes in the kitchen of the District Commissioner's Lady Wife, well okay, her maidservants, out on the farm there, and she's demure and ready for the men when they return home with the trophies of the hunt. None of your Red Army female Lieutenants around here, none of your babushkas piloting the gantries in the steel mill!

About a third of us whites were committee members, now that I come to remember it, and all from Joeys. The toptop ones were vulgar Rosebank allrightniks and the bottom ones were dreck and followed orders, unless one were famous for something, anything, farting through a keyhole in the Gulley Jimson manner, perhaps. Then one might get a smile from time to time, or even a dissertation about the Marxist Interpretation of Keyhole Farting, time permitting, after the Sunday roast.

I remember just one big personality for these folks, cut up into segments like a pizza and each one getting a piece. I do remember that they were good at Theory. But other than that, nothing much. I remember too our sense of urgency to get away from under this great mound of Talmudic Marxist compost.

So I send a telegram to my sus in Maritzburg and she packs up for me certain items of my camping things, not the miniaturised mountain tents and lightweight back-packer's utensils, but the surf-angling big square canvas sail, big enough to go right over one's car as a windbreak with various gear stuffed underneath to counter the draught, and leave a comfortable sleeping and cooking space in its lee. A lot of rope too, for stretching this sail tight tight between the wild trees of the shad-beaches of the Natal coast, especially down there south of Umtentweni, where for unexplained botanical reasons one could find nice little open patches of grass in amongst the jungle of dense dune bush. All the pots and pans and the like for life inside this pozzie she packs up too, being a woman of sense.

We recruit from our commune this no-good deviationist refugee bum called Fletcher, also from Durbs, which is why he's such a shlof, and we're down to the depot to await the camel train of South Africa, the South African Railways bus, a kolossaler German chassis with a moerse big SA body built on it, towing this huge brute trailer with another set of the coarse rock-busting tyres, as on the bus.

After a two-or-so-hour wait – for this is not your Nineteenth-Century English train we're waiting for, full of gentlefolk taking a dish of tea with anchovy sandwiches from an osier hamper since it is now eleven o'clock, and by whose passage at any point along its rural route one could set one's watch – eventually then we see this dust-storm approaching from the south. Odd, because the wind is easterly, and not much of it, but we straightaway realise, of course, that this is the bus, five miles off and approaching fast.

It heaves to with a brutal blast from the compressed-air brakes, the terminal gasp of a ninety-foot Blue Whale down below the harpooneer up there on his gunnery platform; thank God the suffering's over, and life has been sweet.

She has hauled in downwind, finally, and there's a minute or so while the following cloud overtakes her and we hold hats and tissues over our noses and the locals hold their breath for the ninety seconds, not bad for a schnorkeller, in fact, but these folk are used to it. Around here they're like Japanese pearl-divers.

The fowls in their hoks way up on top of the bus are all Rhode Island Reds, we note. This is curious to us, because that is a fairly specialised breed, plump clucky sort of birds, while your average Kaffir Fowl, alias Zulu Chicken, to be proper, is just about any colour except blue, and these birds up there have anyway the physiology of ostriches, on a 1:10 scale of proportion, with those big bare velociraptor thighs for athletic escape and the hunting of locusts, and no big puffy fluffy mummy feathery bellies for warming eggs. It's hard to imagine T. Regina laying an egg, and same here.

We ponder this as passengers come groping their way down the steps of the bus. They are the same colour as the Rhode Islanders. Their eyebrows are Gaelic red, as are the hairs of their noses, and the old mens' beards, and everybody's hat. They feel their way over to where certain entrepreneurs have ready-waiting drums of sorghum beer. The driver has to be white, by law, beneath his earthen mask. He steps over to a bar for a good shot of dop, he needs it.

Nobody really gives a shit about chickens, except in the matter of recipes, so it's a gentle deed indeed for the SPCA to insist that poultry in transit must have protection from slipstreams and dust and distress there atop the bicycles, Primus stoves, big bags of beans, mattresses, tins of paraffin, what else peasants carry about. Nameless bundles all roped down, and over them all the festoons of slipstream-shredded plastic of the poultry protection. Now that the ordeal is forbye the strips all dangle down like the locks of Whoopi Goldberg, only earth red.

The first apparatus I ever saw for windscreen washing whilst in motion was on this bus. The driver had available a great pedal like those for quadriceps development in a gym, which would squirt water on the screen from a ten-gallon reservoir. Other than this bit of windscreen everything and/or/anything/body of beast/and/or man/woman/child was full Burnt Sienna all over, bow to stern, topgallant fowls to keel.

We get our bundle of campstuff away from the marketplace bus terminus and thump it a few times up and down on the grass, standing upwind, then away up the big hills beyond Mbabane, a thousand and a half feet above. It's hard to be accurate about altitude after all these years, but I tell you it's a stern haul, and there up top we dust out each item with kicks and billowing six-hand flaps down the clear mountain breeze. We sit about in between, taking deep breaths, and draughts of World Council of Churches Chianti poured from an Mbabane Bottle Store half-gallon wickered fiasco hooked with the thumb over the shoulder, in the best Italian Christian manner.

The geomorphology is curious up here: strange hemispheres and rounded-off obelisks of igneous rock sticking ten, twenty feet up amongst the tussocks of rough yellow grass and wind-seeded young wattles sprung in a random grove amongst the stones, in a little valley in the hills. Not very far off stands a group of family houses, wattle-and-daub with single-pitch roofs, and pumpkins doing their bit in holding down the corrugated iron, along with various rocks and a bicycle; there's no way you're going to steal a bicycle off a tin roof without letting the world know. There are no nails, nor the sort of roofing timber into which you could hammer a nail. The iron sheets rest on wattle poles.

We rig up the canvas sail taut and trim amongst the junior wattles, with a tight tight rope between two of the older ones to make the ridge of a double-pitch roof, and under there we get our canvas house in order, both senses of the expression.

Jess has been but poorly recently, and we wise males put it down to Womens' Problems, which to be candid she does too, for she's been to a gynaecological specialist in Musgrave Road back in Durbs, who assured us her suffering was in consequence of excessive sexual pleasure without benefit of Christian vows and the slim gold band, would you believe it; that's what comes of mixing science and faith.

Well, she's got the gold band now, she's had it six months, more, but the distress continues, and if anything the sexual excesses have diminished in consequence, and Fletch and I bundle her up in my 'Berg bag all tight and cosy with a cuppa, and we set about constructing a cunning stove and braai-place there in amongst the interstices of the strange geological rock forms.

The theological vino produces marvels of imagination between us, in the matter of civil engineering. We have some nice bitey-looking cuts of goat, butchered with traditional weapons in the ancestral mode behind the bus station down there, and here we construct this flue-driven barbeque amongst piled stones in the hillbilly grove. A young black-haired coloured man with a lock hanging over his right eyebrow comes to us with a hospitable lump of pumpkin for our supper. The left shoulder-strap of his dungarees hangs loose over his chest. We introduce ourselves. His name is Abner.

Fletch is a union man. He is a SACTU organiser. SACTU is a fairly primitive general workers' union, but bejasus it's got guts in its confrontation with the régime. Fletch is not confrontative by nature, though, he's a friendly soul. Security policemen therefore take pleasure in bullying him. Now that we have a State of Emergency which permits such things, it is their delight to take him off to detention without trial, at a whim, perhaps simply on a chance meeting in the street. Black labour unions are unlawful, of course, and it's information they want about this sinister employment of Fletch. He sleeps in a police cell as often as he sleeps in his own bed in a cheap rooming-place.

Well, if they can't get evidence out of him that will convict somebody up top, and they can't even collect enough dribs and drabs and odds and sods to get a conviction of Fletch himself, at least they can get him out of the way, along with the bonus of some additional sport, so they stick a banning order on him which disallows his union work, of course, along with a host of other restrictions, big, small and petty.

Talking to anybody at all is one, except for such necessities as the buying of food and consultation with one's defence lawyers, for Fletch is always going to need one as much as the other around SA.

He is not allowed to have any social intercourse, as the Banning Order so elegantly puts it.

Much later on, years, I myself get one of these orders, served on me by a silly grinning twit of great police power, who requests my signature in the matter of receipt of these pages of typewritten restrictions.

Mr Wessels, I ask, What is meant by Social Intercourse?

Nee, says Ou Wessels, baring the hundred or so teeth he stores in his great gob, That's when they don't do it for money.

Then there's this long list of places you're not allowed to be in. It includes almost everywhere, you wouldn't believe it; think twice before entering a newspaper office to advertise the sale of your old roller skates, you are preparing something for publication. You are also on premises where publication happens, so that's already two contraventions of your banning order. If you still have enough spirit left in you, and if, of course, you are still eligible enough to have such enterprise in mind, and there were yet a spark of romance left in your disheartened heart, you might ask this nice lass at the Classifieds desk there to come for a bite of lunch with you, and you might just get away with it, because if and when you both appeared in court, you as the accused, she as state witness, she theoretically might say you were there for social purposes, and you would then say it was for business, which is not social, and it would be oath against oath, and any element of doubt must always go to the benefit of the accused. So generally you can get away with talking to one person at a time.

Two people, though, make corroborative evidence. They are a Social Gathering.

You can talk to your neighbour about the joint management of the bougainvillea hedge between your properties, that's business, it's OK, but he can't come to look at said hedge from this side, because you are allowed to receive no visitors on your premises. It's dodgy, but you learn the tricks. When you're smart at it it doesn't make a jot of difference to your life, except when you hear strangers about you talking of strange cultural experiences they've had, like the movies.

Nonetheless, the network of things you can't do for fear of the five years' maximum for contravention, and the extent of it, is such as to break the morale of many a sterner soul than Fletch, and Fletch is what I would call definitely not a stern soul. They hound Fletch into submission by way of obstruction to any chance of employment, until this desperate wretch applies for an exit visa, one-way out of South Africa, forfeiting everything, becoming an Unsouth African, forever.

They thought it would all last forever. I often think these days it would be interesting to meet them again.

They give Fletch this process now that his union work is over, intimidating any, everybody who offers him work, until he withdraws into the servant's quarters of Rosie Eaglestone's house, and gets into bed there, and pulls the bedclothes over his face and disappears, coming to life now and then to eat the food she brings him, and to perform other such biological functions.

They've had experience of this behaviour from other susceptible souls, naturally, but they have something special for Fletch. They know he's going to break, eventually. When he does and applies for his exit visa they give it to him straight away, so he's off with money from pals to get his seat booked on the London plane, and collect his papers from the Department of the Interior. All set! Can anything go wrong?

Yes.

Back there in colonial days some surveyor-general got one of his lads with a theodolite and a pith helmet to place a survey beacon in the middle of the great mosquito-hatchery south of Durban, where the Umlazi River flowed into a majestic vast wetland full full of creatures great and small, statuesque immobile herons and small fidgety fish, wee frogs and crustacea and goggae and nuni, in amongst the myriad species of reed and floating flora, where today stand the reeking fractional distillation towers of the Wentworth Refinery and a bloody big chimney burning off twenty-four hours of each day something that smells like an old sleeping-bag from the Iraq War.

Here it had been, then, this beacon in the middle of the swamp, and it marked the easterly apex of a long acute triangle of land that was part of the Magisterial Area of Umlazi; a County, I suppose, in English terms, or a Shire in Australian, but soon enough demarcated and classified here as a Homeland. Part of a bigger and better Homeland, that is, called KwaZulu, spread about like old Kleenex tissues on the map of Natal, but a Homeland, jong, and it was not part of the Magisterial Area of Durban. Come to think of it, it wasn't even part of South Africa. No, on second thought, it was, since the Chief Minister of this place never accepted independence from South Africa, it never became a Bantustan, on principle; but you may here just get a notion of the complexity of it all.

Well, at this point in my telling the story, not only the Wentworth Refinery is there on drained ground of the bubbly froggy chirpy marsh, this great apparatus pumping in its Brent Crude from the offshore mooring buoy a mile out at sea from a quarter-million-ton tanker.

Durban International Airport also is there. The swamp was canalised into a dead-straight concrete chute cutting through the half-mile of seventy-foot coastal dunes to dump all living marsh-dwellers in the surf, for the delectation of musselcrackers and stumpnose and Zambezi sharks, for a brief season.

The desiccated mortal remains of them as couldn't make it to the stumpnose bellies lie unto the last trump under a metre or two of steel reinforced concrete of the main, only, runway of Durban International Airport, on which now thump down great Airbuses and Boeings, sucking up with their turbojet intakes the new colonisers of this frontier territory; the kiewiets and dry grassland bird species, which go in pretty with feathers and things all sleek, and come out cooked, atomised, nothing more than a nice brief puff of braaivleis aroma in amongst the blistering blast of burnt paraffin, which is what these monsters drink.

The point here is: Fletch doesn't need to go through that baggage counter at Durbs Airport, nor wait at the suitcase roundabout at Heathrow, for he's wearing all his earthly possessions, excepting spare socks and underpants and a shirt, which are in his briefcase along with a few Union Christmas cards and other such gew-gaws. His passport is there, of course, along with his ticket. His spare trousers aren't worth the bringing along, and his jersey is tied round his waist.

He's away to liberty in the UK. His friend Dennis piles him into the Peugeot and they're off, singing old union songs. All is happiness. He didn't even have to climb furtively into the Peugeot this time; he's going with the knowledge and the permission of the Security Branch, indeed the encouragement.

Away down the main Pondoland road which takes one to the airport from the city, and as they get to the theodolitical line across this freeway connecting the theoretical trigonometrical beacon in the middle of the main runway to the rest of Umlazi, there stands a police roadblock squad seeking no thing nor body other than Fletch, and they haul him out of the Peugeot with his spare socks and stuff, and charge him there and then with contravention of his Banning Order, in that he did on such-and-such date leave the Magisterial District of Durban and enter KwaZulu without consent from the Chief Magistrate.

I mean he could have got to Departures by walking two miles along the beach and one up the banks of the Umlazi Canal and down the main runway a bit and along one of the taxi paths, and just arrived at the steps of the aircraft with his ticket in his hand and his jersey around his waist, if he didn't want to apply for permission to leave the magisterial area of Durban.

So why didn't he just apply then, to keep things simple?

Well, he DIDN'T APPLY, the decent lawful thing to do, surely. Then he came blatantly for all to see across the magisterial boundary, and THAT'S the problem. Otherwise all would have been just great.

As soon as he gets bail he climbs once again into the Peugeot and shoves off to the cheery refugee committee of Empire Buildings, Mbabane, Swaziland, and all his forwarded mail is now sent by his last scruffy old secret postal address lady Mrs McGee to Switzerland, for she has kissed his cheek, and taken his hand, and smiled wi' a wee teer in her ee as he left for liberty in Europe.

Mind you, they have some pretty weird names in Switzerland, like Reuti-Hassliberg mit Doubs, and maybe she thought Mbabane too was Schweizer Deutsch.

Thus we come to be living the three of us under the canvas awning in rock and pumpkin country.

After three months, then, we hear that this DC3 is going to fly in from some democratic place and rescue us all and take us to where all are soon going to be writing peoples' poetry and dancing on the lawn, all day, as described above, because The Withering Away Is At Hand over there and Prepare to Enter thy Nirvana, Comrade.

Meanwhile over there we males will be trained as commissar-soldiers, marching as to war, with the hammer and sickle of Brezhnev, or whatever clapped-out old Marxist/Engelsist/Leninist Iron-Law Megalomaniac Comrade was up there at the time, going on before.

Trouble is, the blokes who are going to chauffeur this Dakota want to know where there's a suitable secret landing-place, and neither Piet Iemand, nor Cde Jack nor The Lily of Pine Valley nor any nameless pizza-piece theoretician on the Central Committee has sufficient ideological wisdom to provide them with this information, nor know whether they've got to find a golf course or a tennis court or an undeveloped Heathrow. And though they've got on their muster the bloke who won WW2 by flying the bloody thing, namely me, they have to put into play a plan whereby spooks in Dar-es-Salaam will get this information through penetration of secrets kept by capitalism since 1936, the year of the design of this kite. They have their ways and means. Never doubt that we will go to the ends of the Earth to support your struggle, cdes!

They could have phoned South African Airways for this information at Jan Smuts Airport, matter of fact, if they didn't want to relinquish power to this unprole boodjore, namely me. SAA were still using Dakotas internally. Matter of fact, they could have employed SAA to fly us to wherever from the Mbabane airfield in one of them, since sanctions hadn't yet been laid on us.

Anyway, to cut short a long story of dismay, Jess and I decide that on balance we'd rather not march as to war in the cohorts of the Central Committee and their pals in Pointy Toe Territory, but thanks all the same. We decide to shmeitz back to S.A. furtively and separately and find some way to kick up shit there without the expertise provided in P.T.T., and maybe get a bit of a hand-out in the doing of it.

Fletch is as pissed off with the abject followership and the posturing leadership around here as we are, but there's absolutely no way he will agree to going back to the Union of South Africa. No way. We agree. It is not for us to persuade or dissuade.

But the critical thing just now is Jess's declining health, and one evening we decide it's just too critical, she is peeing blood and generally malfunctioning. We cook our porridge early in the morning and get her out of the bag and down the mountain to whatever rudimentary health care is available in this Protectorate for people without money.

There we see a nameplate in a street off the main drag, with a Portuguese name on the plate, and we reckon we're in a hurry and the queue will be shorter with a private practice doctor, and let's take a chance here and see if our pooled Christian money will pay for it. There's no queue in fact when we go in, it's too early in the morning maybe. Maybe there's not going to be much of a queue anyway, for after a bit a young Sephardic-looking guy comes out of the consulting-room who appears to be about fifteen and hasn't had his first shave yet. But the nameplate says he's qualified. At Wits, too.

Jess goes into the surgery with him and within the minute he's out again and asks me to come in with her, because he doesn't want to ask her to pull down her broeks without her husband being present.

It's better in the buttocks, he explains, your wife has bilharzia and we must now start a course of injections. He comes from Moçambique and he's probably the best in all of Africa and Asia, with his allopathic university skills and the nous of a Chinese barefoot doctor. Bilharzia he knows all about, man.

We tell him we'll be away soon, and he seems anxious; But get here for the next injection, he says, after that you must take this prescription with you wherever you go in the world, and don't miss one for twelve weeks. He seems really worried. I wonder why he takes on so; if you don't die of bilharzia in Moçambique, malaria is waiting for you. Then there's good old starvation, of course, but he seems not to have got used to the idea of death, strange for a doctor, even stranger for a Moçambican doctor. He seems to believe in life and in medicine.

Don't avoid exercise, he advises us, It's always good for the health. We smile and hand him some money which he brushes aside, and shake hands, and he sees us to the door. There still isn't any queue.

We examine various propositions and plans for our future as we trudge the streets of Mbabane on our way home to the hills, the trio of us, and just down the main drag from Empire Buildings we there chance upon a suave black dude leaning on the bodywork of a glitzy new Jaguar and scrutinising the bodywork of passing Swazi crumpet with great scrute, a real slick number. And as we come by I say to him Howzit, umfo?, and he says also Howzit, bru?

Fletch says to him You don't own that Joburg Jag, do you, and he answers No, I'm a freedom-fighter's chauffeur, still leaning on the headlamps there.

And Fletch tunes him What brings you here umfo? and he replies My man, I have delivered turkey broth and all that goeters to my madam, Missus Tochis, so as to make life in exile bearable: you know, smoked things and things in tins, that sort of goeters, and I am to return with certain copies of *The African Communist* stuck up a false exhaust pipe of this self-same Jag, but don't tell anybody about it, it's more than my job's worth.

It's more than his life's worth if the security boere get hold of him with that library up his tailpipes, and chuck him out of a tenth-floor window at Marshallplein and say he slipped repeatedly on an incidental cake of soap or something and fell out, but then again he looks educated enough to know that it could all rattle out of the false exhaust pipe or get stuck up a true exhaust pipe by mistake and get converted to charcoal before the SA border.

Keep your hand on it all, umfo, says Fletch in farewell. Always do, bru, replies the chauffeur.

The obvious place to head for is that volcano called Die Baai, where they have this 1: 50,000 scale model of the régime, into which every day they drive six-inch nails with a four-pound hammer, into the heart and the head and the scrotum, so that nicely bathed and Brylcreemed cabinet ministers in their metallic sheen Armscor suits are felled clutching their temples, waistcoats or Jockey Y-fronts in Parliamentary Session in the middle of the morning, shrieking that angina had struck, or the Big C has got them in the brain or the balls.

Where the hell else would an activist go?

Anyway Fletch, as I say, couldn't face going back. He decided to take his chance with the green lawns etcetera and the DC3, and later on died a profoundly drug-addicted National Health inpatient in a hospital in Maidenhead, Kent, unacclaimed, unrecognised, unsupported, unemployed, poor and totally lonely and rejected by everyone of sensibility amongst the Mission in Exile community of UK.

Well he didn't actually die in his hospital bed. He discharged himself from the place towards the end, and was later found dead in the street, full full of tabs and booze, leaking booze, oozing booze.

Don't be seen to hobnob with ignorant dissenters, comrade mate, whatever their excuses.

The only thing Fletch ever knew about Theory was that profit is made from workers' labour.

Four

SO THEN, JESS BORROWS A UNIVERSITY blazer and arranges a solo lift back to SA in two days' time with a couple of tourists from the U.S.A., who have been doing the game reserves, and just before leaving she will dye her hair black, while I arrange to go off right away to a Catholic mission station near the border, and cross it as a man of God in a God-collar with a couple of their blokes on the same day as the tourists, and we'll meet on the road on the other side. All is secret.

We pull in at the refugees' centre beforehand, as is our right. Coming down from the hills with our gear would slow everything up. We need decisive movement from now on. We abandon our campsite to the Abners.

The night before we depart, though, as Jack Hodgson sits perched on his chair at sundowner time, keeping his muscadels in position with his heels, he notices that Jess is now black-haired, and being a good party man he knows that's the first sign of conspiracy, so he puts the process on her and finds out what our intentions are.

He collects the other member of OGPU, Piet Iemand, for moral support, and they goose-step into the bathroom where I'm having a nice hot soak preparatory to leaving on the morrow, and tell me I am about to be disciplined for plotting my departure independently of the Central Committee.

I wasn't here when your committee was appointed, I observe, and thus Jou Ma se Committee. You didn't even have the discipline to report your scheming to us!, observes Hodgson. Indeed I didn't, for security reasons, I say.

Good God, man, you can't tell the Central Committee they're a security risk! Somebody alias Piet bunches up his fist and comes at me in my nice hot water there and says Man I just want to YIT you! and I stand up and step out of the bath and I'm all wet and glisteny and brown, and though I'm a skinny specimen, what have I been doing here in these boring three months but some useful marathon training, fifteen kays a day and forty-two each weekend, a standard marathon, and if I may say it myself, I look as if I'm composed of tungsten carbide. Most of Piet's 120-odd kg are composed of cellulitis.

Do it!

He backs off. One of the mistakes you must never make in this life is to get kicked in the gut by an ostrich or a marathon runner. Hodgson comes forward after some spitting in the basin and sticks his finger at my eyes and says I, I personally, on Party authority, will see that you never have a political function in South Africa! Ever again! Never!

Do it!

I lay a level gaze on him and he backs off.

I go for a hike the next morning, and when I'm sure nobody has noticed me I nip off the road and make my way forty-odd kays cross-country and local footpaths to the Catholics and work in their vegetable patch for two days and miss my nice new missus, for these are early days of marriage and a single bed is a dreary place.

Then we're up when it is yet dark, for this is what brothers in God and convicts do, and eat rusks with cafe latte, these being Roman Roman Catholics, and they're off to pray while I find a way to fix this back-to-front thing about my neck. We're at the border at mossiepoep, and there's only one boer there, busy scratching his armpits and ballas and yawning while he lights the Primus for his coffee, and he knows there's a vehicle coming because he can hear something, and he beckons us through without even looking round, and the driver priest doesn't have to brake nor drop a single gear as we whizz across the border.

I could have come by in the full formal dress uniform of a General in the Red Army of the Soviet Union, saluting beneath the four-square-metre red flag snapping in the slipstream above the turret of my T55 tank, and attracted no more attention.

My brothers in God drop me a few kays later, at the end of a long open stretch of road, so that approaching drivers can see the dog-collar and know this is no ordinary hitch-hiker here but a reliable moral person who might also be helpful in an emergency like a flat tyre or the like.

I go and sit in the grass and eat biltong and avoid all vehicles until I see way over there the blue-and-white rented Renault of the tourists, as described by Jess, and as it comes up closer I rise from the grass and the number-plate tells me okay and I thumb them down and they're really sentimental about helping out this priest. What a coincidence, they say, our other passenger here is also going to Pietermaritzburg, and they introduce me to Jess and we nod in greeting.

They are a New York couple from a vertical one-third brownstone house in Brooklyn, and they're tickled pink, as the saying goes, about playing Samaritan to this holy man.

I hear them speaking Yiddish after a bit, and I understand it because it's a bit like German, though they evidently don't realise this and are talking privately, just one to the other. And what they are saying is that priests are no longer what they used to be, insofar as they are acquainted with the Catholic community back in New York. I mean look at this one, ten minutes yet he's in the car, already he holds the shtikl's hand. But then the sentimentality prevails after a bit, and I notice she reaches out and takes his left hand off the steering-wheel and holds it too.

Five miles on and the husband looks in his mirror and sees framed there the heads of the priest and lady passenger engaged in molluscous kissing and running hands through each other's hair. I hear him say Move the mirror and fix your lipstick and while you're about it just take a glance what's going on back there, you wouldn't believe it. She does that and there's quite a prolonged silence now, of what? Perplexity in the main, I think. But sentimentality prevails again, which I can see turning to lust by the minute, for she's running her hands through his hair too, and not only on his head, but inside his shirt as well, for he's one of those hirsute Levantines and there's plenty of stuff on his chest to run the fingers through, and I get the impression she wouldn't mind if we got out for just a few minutes so they can have use of the back seat themselves, pulled up along here somewhere in the sugar-cane.

But social obligations and commitments prevail, and they push on to Maritzburg, though I notice the speed of this Renault increases in inverse proportion to the distance yet to travel; first all those writhing zoological couplings of the Kruger National Park, now all this human squirming within touching distance is too much, even over the slipstream noises you can hear it.

When we do finally arrive in Maritzburg and they drop Jess at her destination and then ask me Where would you like to be dropped, Father? and I say No, I think I'll just get out here too, they are both of them so jags, the heat of passion in their menopausal old constitutions is such that to this day I believe I did them a good Christian deed and they went off and screwed each other stupid in the first available hotel in Pietermaritzburg, probably the Crown in Commercial Road, and sorry it isn't there any more and got replaced by a discount bottle store, for from that day on I always regarded it as a shrine to Romance.

So we make contact with the family through a friend in Maritzburg and we borrow family money and take a train pulled by a great steam behemoth through places with names from the Anglo-Boer War, Ficksburg and De Aar and the like, places where De Wet the pig-headed old patriarch was too simple to know he was beat, and showed the Brits and the world some guerrilla tricks that the partisans of World War 2 could have learned from, and moving literally at the pace of the ox too, for he took his field-guns and wagons with him. Places of bitterness less than a lifetime old, and we're off to make some more.

We arrive in Die Baai a pair of total strangers in a totally strange place, luckily in the morning so we have a day to find ourselves a nest.

The nest we find is a flophouse down Summerstrand run by Mrs Garbutt, and it's a bit smelly from tomcats and that damp fermentation of upholstery that you get in beachfront buildings with a prevailing onshore wind. But it's on the beachfront! So I know that in between desperately trying to make political contact and desperately trying to find employment I will soon enough find time without desperation to get out of the sea for our supper a few of the silver steenbras for which this piece of coast is famous.

First thing though before the fishing experience is to find our way to the political scene without attracting the attention of the Security Branch. We scheme the best way is to approach some liberal in the art world and make our debut to PE there, with changed names. Jess remembers an old pal called Daisy who was good at art at school and came from PE and we take a long shot and look up her name in the phone book, and lo, there she is, who says there's no Santa Claus? and it's all going to be too easy, it seems.

We don't use the phone, though, for most liberals are bugged, and we have neither transport nor busfare, so we hike over to the North End where Daisy lives in an old row house with five other artistic young women.

We explain our predicament, and Daisy tells us never to worry, because she has met but recently an interesting ANC fellow at an exhibition of photography, and she'll invite him around to supper and we can come too, and meet him and talk about art and thus edge our way into the political life of Die Baai, sideways, as it were.

The furniture in Daisy's house is in the same condition of fermentation as Mrs Garbutt's, because, you know, it's blasted by the same southeaster, but in addition to the dry rot and damp rot it has much structural damage, and Daisy explains this is because of the vermiculous copulations of a pair of lesbian martial artistes who inhabit this house, and form a third of its community. The starboard arm of the sofa is missing, I notice, and many splinters of pine and shreds of fabric and twisted nails horridly appear there, as would the shoulder of Grendel after Beowulf had wrenched off his starboard arm.

Daisy explains that these two ladies are both very powerful of physique, and that their reflexive orgasmic kickings are such as to endanger any structure or human life within range. Quadrupeds are safe, however, for their centre of gravity is low, allowing of very rapid acceleration in any direction, as befits the life of the hunted.

So the night arrives, and the ANC fellow Max introduces himself at Mrs Garbutt's and loads us into his decrepit bakkie which drags its rear off-side mudguard and bumper like it's got poliomyelitis down there or been hit by a sniper's bullet or something. His big black dog stands in the bak, to guard the vehicle against theft by madpersons. His name is Footsack. We clatter our way over to Daisy's and pick up a bottle of scouring sherry along the way since it's not quite six yet, and count ourselves lucky to make it into the bottle store just in time, and be able to observe the social graces and offer a little contribution to the companionable evening before us.

There's a hell of a din at Daisy's when we arrive smiling with this bottle of baklei sjerrie, and Daisy explains it is because of the majestic love-wrangling of the Amazons which is happening at this very moment beyond the open door over there. Why don't you shut the door then, asks Max, so we can have a conversation? Furtive love-making is what men do, explains Daisy, and I must agree, however else you describe this sort of coupling, it isn't furtive.

Here they range through every arithmetical configuration between sixty-nine and eighteen hundred and twelve, and by and by, when the cannon-shot has been fired to the strains of the Imperial Russian Anthem, and the earthquake has done and the crustal plates settled down a bit, all within earshot and eyeshot and indeed noseshot of those making passage between the kitchen and dining-room, they join the rest of us settled affectionately around the dining-table.

This is always the best place for intimate conversation, over ashtrays and used dinner-plates and left-over bread rolls, it's part of trattoria culture, so we've managed to get some chat going, more or less, in spite of the rising crescendo of Sapphic glee coming from the open door. It has died down after a bit, as just described, and the ladies emerge to join us for supper. The smaller one wears navvy broeks and braces, but she's smaller only when standing next to the bigger one, who wears dungarees and army footwear and headgear that looks like that silicon equipment of Olympic swimmers, with the earpieces turned up. The big lady sits next to me, the lesser next to Max, opposite.

Max soon turns out to be a nice guy with a nice nature. He seems to be without aggression. Though not portly, he is nonetheless a man of comfortable body, a little this side of embonpoint, I should say, who would in the main rather sit in a sunny place and hum a small tune in his time off than get out on the road there and stiffen up his musculature with marathon running and all that ascetic obsessive stuff.

Themba Max, a strange name for an African. He has a ginger moustache, the only one I've ever seen on an African. He is a photographer. I like him, there and then.

Well we settle down and drink this sociable sherry, and get to know each other and feel amicable while Daisy prepares in the kitchen for the great moment when her Malay curry will appear on the table, a great moment because Jess and I know only Natal Indian curry, and this is going to be one surprise, man, what with all those sambals and Capie side dishes. The subtleties are in the variations on traditional Malay cooking, as came from the Malay slaves of the Cape in their new habitat with new ingredients for the familiar recipes. That sort of delicate stuff, to delight the taste buds.

We are going to start a Battered Womens' Centre, says Bigger here next to me.

Oh? says Max, interested. For or against?

JEE-ZUZ ! she chucks back her chair and rises with her fist balled, and her right-arm triceps and pectoralis major all set to feed Max this knuckleburger, and she's round the end of the table to get him, with me after her, and she's ready to slaat him fucken stukkend and kick him full of lumps with her beetlecrushers, and I grab her round the waist and dig in my heels, but to no avail, for this auntie is twice my size, man, and feels to the touch like an oaktree, or one of Horatio Nelson's ships of the line maybe, and she has spent the afternoon in her martial arts place nogal, all togged up in padded black leather bodywear and a mesh mask and knocking the living shit out of some similarly-clad auntie with a bamboo pole.

Lesser, dank die Here God, who is only one point five times as big as me, leaps to her feet as the big one comes round the end of the table dragging me behind her, and puts a free-style two-arm lock on her throat whilst reciting the code of ethics of their particular martial discipline, and sort of slows her up physically a little bit, which is all I want, really, so as to give Max a break. Max takes it and leaps over his fallen chair and runs like the clappers to his spastic motor vehicle and jumps in and winds up the windows and locks the door and starts the engine just in case.

Footsack bales out and thanks God it's night-time and he's black.

Fucking bastard! yells Greater, I'll come and kick your fucking windscreen in and drag you out and pull your fucking head off, I'll break you in half, you fucking bastard! Max avails himself of the advice implied herein and turns the bakkie around for a possible quick getaway. Not that this heap is capable of spinning its wheels, if you know what I mean, but at least it's pointed downhill now.

Needless to say, the evening was not what it might have been. We had our whack of Malay cuisine out of a plastic bag on the Summerstrand beach, opposite Ma Garbutt's flophouse with Max. It transpired later that Footsack had used the diverting hubbub to sneak into the ladies' bedroom and piss all over their furniture. He had always been a good dog, never known to do that sort of thing. Safer than biting, though, under the circumstances, and he done his bit.

But we had made close contact, Max and we, and were evidently very protective of one another. Max arranged covert introduction to the ANC. I on my part promised him a meal of braaied steenbras with baked spuds, the only delicatessen around here I was really confident of producing in the predictable future, with our present finances, for I would fetch it from God's great free-food outlet, the Indian Ocean. It would have to be on the beach, though, this braai: though the Group Areas act forbade only mixed residence, you wouldn't stay long in white lodgings if you brought a black bloke to supper.

In point of law, Max couldn't be on that beach either, for it was a White Beach, but at night nobody would notice, and the police would probably turn a blind eye if they did notice, maybe because Footsack was there, who might piss all over a policeman too, I dare say, if he didn't have his German Shepherd with him.

You can imagine how embarrassed Daisy had felt about the fracas in her home. In that curious way that embarrassment works, with its ingredient of guilt, she found herself in the rôle of saviour of Jess and myself. Within a week of our arrival in Die Baai, thanks to Daisy, I was employed as layout artist in a struggling sort of advertising agency, staying alive on two accounts, more or less.

Well, this firm stayed alive for another six months, and sufficient that was, from my point of view, as it unexpectedly turned out: it not only provided the means of buying a vehicle of even greater decrepitude than that of Max, if that's conceivable, but provided also good temporary concealment for the undercover life ahead.

The vehicle belonged to a gay colleague at the advertising agency called Basil, who lived with a chum in a block of flats called Bliss, a bit this side of Ma Garbutt's place on Summerstrand, where it wasn't so cheap and common and there weren't any of those coloureds trying for white.

You don't see a hell of a lot of faults in those you love or need, and I didn't see many in this thing, a Fiat 500 with a roll-back canvas roof and a hairline crack in the engine-block which nobody could locate, not that anybody put too much energy into locating it, but which nonetheless allowed overnight enough water from the cooling system to seep into the cylinders, and emulsify with the lubricants there, and provide a spectacular explosion and ball of blue steam from the exhaust pipe when the starter button was pressed in the morning. The tyres had no tread but good strong canvas, and there were assorted dents all over the bodywork, as if people had been dancing on it, which may well have been the case with Basil and his chum. Other than that and a few minor faults not worth the mentioning, she was all ready to go. I paid for her forty pounds, which is the equivalent of what you'd pay today for a pair of jeans, a shirt and a jacket. Chuck in a pair of shoes maybe.

I made a pair of tail-lights from beer cans and a cockpit light from a polystyrene toothbrush container, and put in new brake linings and made a neat hole in the roof to take a fishing rod, and invited Jess to take the air with me over at the Swartkops River mouth and eat a sentimental meat pie there with a bottle of lager, in celebration of our having joined the great motoring public.

There were three Baai laaities looking at the car in the morning when I brought out the hamper and ceremoniously opened the passenger door for Jess and placed the hamper on the floor at her feet: a small laaitie, a middle-size laaitie, and a big laaitie, the big one about twelve, I suppose. I did the normal cockpit check and pressed the starter button as normal and the normal reverberations shook the Fiat as the great mushroom cloud of carbon monoxide/steam from the exhaust system shattered the peace of the wondrous Sunday morning.

Ga poe stienk! said the little laaitie.
Hoer kontrepsjin! said the middle laaitie.
Sinkplaatse poes! said the big laaitie.

Down at Swartkops I extended a crafty little sort of navigator's table I'd rigged up between the two seats, and placed the feast of beer and pies and salad and afters on it.

As we were getting into the ice-cream, however, which was the climax of the feast, the mosquitoes arrived. Well one did anyway, and as we tried to locate its menacing zing, and squash the sod, we realised that the horizon of the sea was tilted left and our right-hand rear tyre was emitting this thin ugly sound and going flat and this was the reason for the vehicle taking the nasty list. Imagine our dismay on finding the canvas of that wheel pierced by the vertebral spine of a great fish bone, and we with no spare wheel either, and what to do?

Well I can tell you what not to do, and that's to let the ice-cream melt. We make a smart plan during the eating of it, and it has to be smart, for we have no jack either. We have a big screwdriver and a monkey wrench. So Jess stands by with some bricks and rocks people have used for a braai place nearby, and I give a great heave at the back and she shoves them quickly under the car. We dig the sea-sand from under the wheel with our hands and take it off with the bobbejaan spanner. There are plenty of leaves all around, from the Port Jackson willows they use to stabilise the beaches there, and some copies of *New Age* lying about the floor of the Fiat, so we wrench the tyre off somehow with the screwdriver and shove it full of these things, getting a fairly even stuffing all round so as to make the wheel more or less round, and how about that, she rides quite jauntily on this lot, if a bit bouncy as the stuffing beds down, for she isn't a very heavy car.

Thereafter, as the wheel became lumpy from time to time one could add further leaves or *New Ages* as available, and ram them in hard with the screwdriver, and maintain a fairly uniform pressure, as it were, and circular shape.

On one occasion we were stopped by a traffic policeman concerned at the extent of cloth showing on the tyre, who was quite nonplussed at realising that the law on depth of tread applied only to pneumatic tyres, and this one had no valve at all, nor any air inside, and thus no risk of blowout or puncture. There was, moreover, nothing to forbid one's using a tyre filled with leftist literature, which says something for residual democracy in the country at that time.

But she was a noble vehicle, and played her part later when all the big posh cars of the Umkhonto we Sizwe leader in charge of transport had disappeared with the big posh leader, and she ended up as a court exhibit, coated entirely inside with a thin film of highly floccable high-velocity explosive which we hadn't had time to remove. Or the means, come to think of it. She was driven away by a warrant officer of the Security Branch called Erasmus van Vuurwapen, who didn't know what all the silver stuff was. He was smoking a cigarette.

I must be careful not to jump the gun, though. This comes later.

Exactly coinciding with my new era of unemployment, to the day, came a decision by the ANC of Die Baai to induct me into subversion, which didn't actually constitute an underground as yet, but was sort of embryonic, something which could get really big as we gained experience.

The induction depended not on the depth of my Soviet Socialist theory, normally requisite for leadership in the True New Struggle, but upon the fact of my being white and thus camouflaged, as it were, and being also the sort of bloke who was prepared to give it a bash and see what happened. In this I was one of those freaks amongst whites in the struggle, who had no particular aspiration to status or acclaim in it.

But I had a certain craftiness, saichel, said they, which would come in useful for a life of cunning underground. The only cunning I had true experience of so far was that of the tongue, the lingus, but it's all the same thing in the mind, really, and I was ready for this new physical craft; the tricky production of an unregistered revolutionary newspaper, named *Izwe Lomze*, which was the purpose of this sinister enterprise.

I don't mean I had to write the thing, of course, but only to print it; it was written in Xhosa anyway, if you can imagine anything as impenetrable as Leninist German Jewish Philosophical Idealist sensibilities transposed into an African pastoralist language. The dreadful pogroms of Eastern Europe after the failed revolutions there a hundred years ago did strange things to this planet, exporting to the ends of the earth, along with the refugees, the scriptural mystiques of the failed revolutionists.

Our man in PE, our Engels to Govan Mbeki, the reigning Marxist presence, is the Lithuanian Anatoly Mallun, known and recognised as such only in his shoe factory and the regional business community, where he has considerable clout as a man of drive, but known to us low-calibre reds as Mister Moneybags, or Plumbin, his revolutionary nom de guerre on the analogy of Stalin, the man of steel.

To the big calibre Party guns he is known as Annie, and that should throw the Security Branch cement-heads off his track, for sure.

So. With suitable introductory buzzwords provided by Govan, I am visited by an unknown person who tells me to take myself off to the suburb of Walmer, which is about as respectable as you can get in PE, the equivalent of Hampstead Heath, I suppose. There Jess and I occupy a respectable house with a kitchen boy who turns out to be Max and a garden boy who is one Mountain, an ANC Youth Freedom Volunteer, who is going to be a sort of factotum whilst Max and I inside the house print this fiendish broadsheet and Jess struggles to remain pregnant through the terrible tension of it all and the remaining complications of bilharzia.

With ANC money we buy an SA Baroque table and chairs with ball-and-claw feet, and a matching divan and some ferns in pots and assorted mountain-and-cottage prints by Tinus de Jongh, just in case the neighbours pop in to introduce themselves. A few such things, you know what I mean, as cups with actual saucers and a tray to put them on and a little jug to put the milk in, instead of pouring the bloody stuff into our plastic tea mugs straight from a bottle at the open fridge.

The most majestic and by far the most important piece of furniture in the house, however, is a great farmhouse table, big enough for a family of eight at least, which we establish in the main bedroom, where nobody of any etiquette would ever venture, not in Walmer anyway, for the English have this curious prurience and furtiveness about bedrooms, and feel truly guilty when in any other than their own.

This table we stand on concrete blocks, so that one can sit under it in reasonable comfort on a coir mattress. The reason for this is that we have placed upon the mattress two top-technology Gestetner cyclostyle printers, the best in those primitive days, and somebody must be in there from time to time to supervise the working of these machines, and feed them paper and remove the wads of printed *Izwe Lomzes*. Around the sides and on top of the table we have packed five more mattresses, nothing better for absorbing sound-waves.

We set these things going non-stop, week after week, with doors and windows of this bedroom shut, stopping only to replace the worn waxed stencils with new ones, cut on a typewriter without a ribbon, and to top up with printing ink. Outside you can hear nothing of these goings-on, but inside the house everything submits to the insistent rhythm of these thrice-accursed Gestetners: one's waking, one's walking, one's breathing, one's chewing and the metre of the muscular waves shoving one's grub through the digestive tract. Jess keeps having untimely rhythmic miscarriage pains because of the insistent measured beat of these goddam machines.

We demonstrate the capitalist truth that you get maximum profit from your machinery with maximum working hours per day. We completely use up four brand-new Gestetners, finished, kaput, by running them non-stop throughout their entire mechanical lives, except for brief spells while we wipe them down roughly with toilet paper and meths, and squirt oil onto frictional surfaces.

In the carport we have this great individually-imported left-hand-drive vee-eight four-litre aircraft-carrier Oldsmobile with big slanted radar-deflecting fins at the stern, and the red rear-end lights there embedded in chrome-plated jet-efflux tailpipes. The radiator grille has sharpened chrome teeth in it, and it looks like some savage has got his fingers hooked in the corners of his mouth and he's stretching his chromium-plated lips six feet across.

Though it is registered in my nom de guerre, Lundie, this battleship was individually-imported by Plumbin and belongs to him. It strikes me he may have problems with his malehood, for it gives him great yichas to know that I have driven it at a hundred and twenty knots along the Uitenhage road with Govan and Yoshke and Walter from Joburg aboard, the wheels touching the tarmac road surface only intermittently as we get kind of airborne, and pursued in vain by the Security Boere at risible pace in a pitiful plodding police six-pot inline Chevy. But right now it stands in the carport as a Walmer status symbol.

Jess and I seek refuge and remission from the Gestetner by going to the corner shop in this Oldsmobile for groceries. The Greek there sees our approaching chromeware and calls his father, who asks if we want to open an account, which we do. His brother is in the clothing industry in a small beginning sort of way, and we can put any garments we need on the grocery a/c, classified by the bookkeeper as chocolates. I don't know how he did his stocktaking. Eventually we equip the entire sabotage strike force of the Baai ANC with dark blue overalls from this account. Black berets too.

Chocolates all.

The kitchen boy has Sunday afternoons off, and drives away in his Fiat 500, which is as it should be in liberal Walmer, where even kitchen boys have the goodies of life. His dark brown skin has gone sort of grey, and his ginger moustache pink, from too many hours indoors. From time to time he can be seen in the sunshine doing a bit of desultory weeding, moving at tortoise pace from weed to weed, with his big shady hat and dark glasses, like an albino with a feeble weeding fork.

Mountain is the luckiest of us all; he is off barefoot every afternoon at five with his guitar about his waist, which is as it should be amongst employers who vote for the Progressive Party. He is off to ANC Brass, since we don't use the telephone. He wasn't with us long. He disappeared as garden boys do, and the kitchen boy had to help out with weekend gardening for a bit of extra beer money, as the neighbours learned at the Greek shop.

Mountain had come with the first stencil, source unknown, also a rendezvous for the first delivery, and then disappeared according to plan; that was his single and only job, and enough contribution too, at a time when his behaviour could have earned him five years. I didn't ever know his real name, but nothing better than Mountain; I think it was a one-off for Max and me, and we never saw him again. As with that first stencil, I was at pains never to know where subsequent stencils came from, except they appeared in the boot of an unknown car. Ignorance was something more than bliss.

It had taken about a month to get everything installed and operating and oiled, and our tracks covered, and Mountain the only one link between our respectable selves and the ANC. Somebody paid our suburban rent, somewhere, but I never enquired who that was either.

Now the first issue of *Izwe Lomze* was bundled up and ready for delivery. The co-ordinates were simple and total and there was to be no phoning up for correction if they hadn't been understood: a single misunderstanding would dismantle the entire enterprise. Each one of us was a link that could instantly disappear from the chain.

Delivery was the dangerous part of the process, and the most punctilious: at a certain mileage along a certain road would appear an uncertain motor car with uncertain number plates and no driver, and its boot open as if begging for food, at ten pee em precisely, and I mean absolutely precisely. Inside this boot would be a piece of paper with the next co-ordinates on it, along with the next stencils. Urgent, but no space for mistakes: a series of straight sequential shots, good and simple.

Max wasn't allowed to know what the co-ordinates were for this first nor any later drop. We were disciplined ANC men. We were establishing an unlawful press, embryonic that's true, but if we had the craft to manage it, well, what limits were there to the enterprise? The drops were sometimes more than a half-hour from PE, but they were clear and no second driver was necessary for navigation. It took but five minutes or so to snatch the new sheets from the floor of the mystery boot, unload the boot of the Olds into this one here, and shove off.

I thought we had a fine infrastructure for an underground. To this day, as far as I know, nobody ever found out where the broadsheets were coming from, and we had the paper going for more than six months.

Five

WELL JESS CERTAINLY WASN'T DISAPPOINTED when the entire enterprise was called off without explanation. By saying that I don't mean I myself expected one: explanations were exchanged between the big gigabyte thinkers at the top, and though I wasn't as far down as tea-boy, at best I could define my mustering only as basement manager.

We found a nesty little flat, No. 11 Meyer Mansions, where Jess went into hormonal hatching mode, collecting fluffy and feathery things about her as she moved toward her time and became more and more ponderous with this great spinnaker before her, and sat down more than had been her habit, and gave up coffee and fags and other obnoxions.

Recent thought on contemporary childbirth, however, stressed the need for something more than food and warmth: one should also be physically as fit as possible, as is of necessity the case with other mammal mothers, in the interest of their unborn young by way of protection and escape. It makes a more athletic baby, of course, such as can flee the hazards of life amongst the carnivores and capitalists of this world after its birth.

So she's off to Fogarty's Bookshop on the main drag, and there she finds the most modern of all books for pregnant people, and it gives her something additional to this thing about physical condition for unborn babes. It has diagrams and graphics of good aerobic exercises for mums, and one of them is called "Polishing the Floor", good for the rectus abdominis and external oblique and related other muscles used for squeezing out these newcomers, and Jess being a woman of economical mind reckons What the hell about doing this exercise on a bed or carpet when the floor needs polishing anyway?, and gets out a bundle of rags and Sunbeam Wax in a tin, and sets about the floor like I've never seen it done outside of Pretoria Central.

This is the moment chosen by Yael Goshawk and New Dawn feminist pal to arrive. I mean these are not your old-time confused forward troops who would chain themselves to the railings of Buckingham Palace or fling themselves in front of the King's Racehorse and all that stuff; he's got plenty more horses to race with after we've broken this one's legs, and furthermore there'd have been good use for the brave soul who died doing it, what a waste, and then there's the matter of cruelty to the horse too.

These women go straight to the jugular and carotid with their sabre fangs, for they are Marxist feminists. Women are enslaved economically. They are allowed a corner of the culture where they give birth and cook nosh and polish floors and things, but forget about science and technology and finance and enterprise and the places of power and fame occupied by malekind. When they hit their Change of Life they're all used up, they don't even have a pension fund, it was too expensive, and they depend totally on this oaf who's busy out there shagging chicks with his feeble mid-life erection, but no problem, he's got the family money in his pocket to encourage these birds to feign orgasm.

When Goshawk and friend arrive they don't have to knock or ring or anything at the open door because it's a nice warm day and Jess needs the draught through the flat to cool her off at her floor-polishing. They stroll in all comradely and smiling and there find me lying unshaven on an unmade bed at eleven of a Sunday morning, and next to this bed is a glass and a half-empty bottle of cheap Chateau brandy which got half-emptied the night before in company with the woman here sunk in slavery, but who the hell needs to know that? This modest fling was the last, for benefit of the babe, but who needs to know about that either, since there I am for all to see, smoking fags with a sardine-tin ashtray balanced on my gut, and lazily paging through a personal history of the Great War by Robert Graves, and yawning and scratching the back of my left calf with the toenails of my right foot. I am still in my pyjamas.

I leave it to Jess to explain, but her belly is bloody nigh touching the floor down there when she's on all fours, and by the time she has piteously heaved herself up to a kneeling position the Goshawk nostrils have dilated and the Goshawk breathing has deepened and the comradeship has vaporised and the corridor outside the flat resounds to the sound of receding outraged sensible-shoe heel-stomps.

The reason why I am reading this personal war story is that I remember having seen in this book how the Germans towards the end were using bandages made of paper, such was their economic plight, and making trench-mortar shells out of jam tins, which they found means to propel over Allied trenches by the greatest ingenuity. There was this big jam-tin with a little one inside it. The space between was filled with assorted bits of found metal: old shrapnel, nails, any bloody thing which came to hand, as long as it was metal. The small tin was filled with something called Ammonal, and it wasn't for literary relish that I was reading war history.

Plumbin had phoned au clair one day at Walmer, which was a real shocker, I must say, considering the success we'd had with our secret subterranean newspaper, but he had said openly that Govan and he wanted Max and me at his flat for a meal, and we'd realised that there had been a change of strategy.

So Max and I and his new ginger moustache and his skin all nice and chocolate again get in the Olds and we go au clair to Plumbin's flat on the fifth floor of a ritzy block in central Baai. Govan's already here; it must be important. There is the sort of silence, when we arrive, which I think is called pregnant. Plumbin's nostrils are dilated, I note, and Govan's are anyway, what with his African shnoz, and I realise that something momentous is about to happen. Always read history according to the silentiae and the dilated shnozim.

The momentous thing about to happen is the industrial sabotage phase of the armed struggle. It seems achievable to Max and me, but we wonder and ask why we have been excavated from the underground which seemed to work so well. Our thing seemed to fit in so neatly with the M-plan, the Mandela plan of the 50s, which envisaged numberless small local ANC cells, and an always-replaceable local leadership, so that all the prisons of the country could be propvol, full to the cork of the bottle with droogmakers and shitstirrers, and the process would continue, unstoppable. We could eventually have a newspaper in every town, each totally independent of all others.

Short of fascism nothing was going to stop the trades unions either, and the industrialists and financiers of the country were not going to agree with any racist government in the matter of such fascism, so what a combination we had, hey? But anyway, if you still decide you want industrial sabotage when Karl Almighty Marx himself said socialism will first come to industrially advanced countries, why do you need us in it? Anybody can do it, and why waste us?

Plumbin takes the specs from his nose to remove the condensation which has formed thereon in consequence of the high temperature of his head, in which a mixture of brilliant thought and adrenalin is swirling about something wonderful.

Jock and Max, says Plumbin, I want you to understand about the historical materialist and dialectical materialist processes by which we have shot up the evolutionary ladder with but one set of rungs, and will further shoot, from being mere pulmonate osteichthyes floundering about ingesting quagmire and commencing to respirate oxygen from the atmosphere, to being fully moral people after the withering away of the state, when all will walk about with acutely everted and extended metatarsals on beauteous lawns, writing poesy, and hearing the ambient melodies of Lacus Cygni, all day.

Prokofiev and company are all right, but they've had their problems with dialectical materialism too, like you artistic comrades.

So he launches on this clarification of Max's and my confused thought, and after half an hour Max says excuse me I must pee and escapes, and I see it's clear Govan realises as I do that by the time Plumbin has got to the caves and the hunter-gatherers we'll all be twenty years older and our chance of revolution will have withered away.

Jock and Max, says Govan, with his gentle voice, we are about to create a revolutionary situation. We will create it with a vanguard, of ·which you comrades will be part. The armed struggle will be in three phases: the first will be industrial sabotage to show the big industrialists of the régime that we mean business, and to muster the masses behind our movement, and that's what we need you for now. Later will come the phase of urban guerrilla warfare: we won't make the mistake of rural guerrilla warfare where the troops of the régime can hunt us down, this isn't Kenya, we have options, and when that has made the entire country ungovernable we'll switch to full field warfare and take on a demoralised army.

Ja.

I don't actually see the big industrialists as part of the régime, but I defer to older men with more wisdom than I have. Max and I look at each other and hunch shoulders, and we let that one pass.

Ja again.

I have a brief recollection of my military days, my flying days, and of the awesome violence of even a single primitive old WW2 aircraft, a Hawker Typhoon maybe, with all its rocketry and guns going equivalent in firepower to an entire battalion of infantry, and wonder if the ANC has any plans for that.

But then I also remember something else, which was that the Communist parties in WW2 had been the central core of any resistance organisation in any country occupied by the Axis powers. Along with Italy, perhaps, or Greece, in Yugoslavia they'd been at their best. The partisans there had had such success, and captured such extensive territory and so many German aircraft, that they'd sent some of their lads for flying training with us in South Africa, and there was a fair chance of their having their own air force, except of course the Western Allies wouldn't have had that, they wouldn't have tolerated it.

So if you were looking for action rather than righteous declamation, the communists were your people all right. We'd had enough protest and demonstration.

A fairly uncomfortable silence follows, though, because I don't really see myself as a leader in an adventurist élite, vanguard of the vanguard, nor is Max good Che Guevara material, in my view. But Plumbin says we have the specialist skills necessary for it, Max being a photographer who knows about chemicals, and myself a trained bomber pilot who knows about bombs. He invites us to join the Communist Party and help start Umkhonto we Sizwe, the Spear of the Nation, the armed wing of the ANC, and all of these things he sees as one bundle, as I do to this day, though plenty of phoney bullshit was put out about MK being a separate spontaneous organisation and the ANC sharing only friendship with the Communist Party. How often I have been invited since that day to believe there was nothing kinky going on; they slept in three separate beds.

Max declares he knows enough about chemistry to put sodium chloride on a fried egg, and I observe that there may have been a war I haven't so far heard of in which bomber pilots flew about with wicker baskets full of bombs made in the kitchen, when the observer in some canvas kite would shout Look, there's a fat Boche on a bicycle down there, open the window and hurl one at him!, but it was less simple than that in war as I remember it.

This sarcasm is lost like rainwater off a dog's back, as my Oupa Van used to say, who lacked schooling.

We owe it to the Struggle and to the Nation, Plumbin tells us in a hushed sacred sort of voice, as if we are lucky to owe it to the nation, because we're the lucky few souls who are morally in the black, who will get the chance to pay it back. Like Henry Vee's lads on St Crispin's Eve.

Well Max doesn't seem to have much further employment by way of photography just now, nor do I by way of anything, and our printing press is shut down anyway, alas, so why not move in and give it a full-on dedicated bash and see what happens? It is in character with our order of inquisitive apes. It used to be called Experiment in the seventeenth century. It is what a chimpanzee does when he shoves a wand into a termite nest, to see what's stuck to it when he pulls it out again.

These days the true scientific community sets out by assiduous experiment to disprove its own theories. You can have your own intuitions, your own daydreams if you like, your own ideological motives, it doesn't matter where you start, it's this testing process that's decisive, truly scientific, rational, systematic.

So. Just don't come with spurious argument from the revolutionary scriptures if you fail, that's all, and a lot of misapplied scientific verbiage, to demonstrate success to your ovine followers, and make phoney propaganda for a gullible world, and keep yourself in personal power with such brilliant bullshit, at whatever cost to your integrity.

Remember Piltdown Man.

Max and I look at each other. We know each other pretty well by now. I suppose those who are not leadership material are a bit gullible in trusting those who have established themselves in leadership rôles. We have a fair share of adventurism in our personalities too, of course, so after a couple of days we go along with the new enterprise.

This is why I am lying in this foetid bed of a Sunday morning and scratching my legs with my toenails and reading Robert Graves.

I think it was Robert Graves, that is. It's a long time ago, and I'm not really sure.

We need a good incendiary device and some highish explosive and a timer/detonator to go with both, but most importantly, all devices must be so that ordinary unskilled people can make them, and from everyday cheap materials, too. Max and I feel we can produce at least some makeshift thing with an encyclopedia and a good public reference library and a bit of natural kop.

Revolutionists suck!

Max's best skill is in playing his guitar. His music is as idiosyncratic as the ginger moustache. He plays Xhosa folk melodies in whatever mode comes to hand: sometimes straight local, sometimes New Orleans, sometimes Country and Western, sometimes Boeremusiek. It depends how things have gone with present company.

Sometimes he puts the guitar down. He speaks to it the while: you just sit down there and shut the hell up, you, I'm going to sing my own song now, and he opens his mouth dramatically and sings really corny old English kak about Come into the Garden, Maud, or the like, for he was educated in a mission school somewhere which I forget, and sings these old Pom songs with some nostalgia, though he professes to see them as a load of garbage. Sometimes I am able to join him,

In springtime,
In springtime,
In springtime,
The only pretty ringtime
When birds do sing
Hey dingadingading,
Hey dingadingading,
Hey dingadingading,
Sweet lovers love the spring!

I say sometimes only because we hadn't much time in the ensuing months for the singing of songs. Most of our working time was in the strictest silence, and a lot in darkness, but there were the few spells of it when I'd haul out my old blues bekfluitjie and we'd invent our own music and songs. I suppose if they were anything identifiable they were a sort of African Calypso, with all the personal insult and political irreverence that goes with the Caribbean stuff:

I went from your tree to my tree,
Even to the lavatree,
En daar kry ek ou Yoshke sitting daar.

But this one comes later on, as the developing narrative will reveal.

We are inducted into a cell which is already two over the optimum of four, and with us in it it's now double strength, which is considered normally much too unwieldy and difficult to collapse and fold away in the attic in an emergency. But it seems to be the nexus of the PE system, for top party people, the decision-makers, are in it. So also is my dentist, who is as surprised to see the outside of my mouth as I am to hear him talk about something other than his bloody budgies.

Max and I are appointed to the District Committee as its Technical Sub-committee. Party people believe in committees, and love them. You know your thinking is right when the committee agrees on it, particularly when the agreement is unanimous, and most of our agreements are unanimous, what with the advanced thought coming from the minds of these top leaders in here. Union leaders are here too. I wonder about this. At what point do unions become soviets, and if not, at what point go into opposition after the revolution?

But such imponderabilia are for another time, man! The pressure of events upon us is such that we scarce get time to attend cell meetings. Comrades there wonder who we are and what in the wide world we're about since they never see us. Not even inside the cell do people know each others' total function.

Our function presently and immediately is to get ourselves a bit educated about explosives. The ammonal of Robert Graves is the only point we have to start from, and it's pretty rich with suggestions. It's pretty rich with danger too, clearly enough, because explosives cookery is not an art of intuition, where you may at a whim add soupçons of this and that to the brew and smack the lips accordingly.

Max and I talk long and earnestly about procedures in case of failed tests, and who's going to dismantle a set-up apparatus that has malfunctioned, because one thing we're sure as hell not going to do is leave this stuff standing where we left it, for some kid to play with or some passer-by to cop it when the thing goes off belatedly, by some chance that we haven't been able to calculate.

The surest way to get the masses not to follow you is to subject them to terrorism, planned or inadvertent. The mass out there is not a mound of mindless mieliepap that deserves no better description than the force by which it is attracted to the centre of the earth. No, that's weight, mass is inertia, a tendency to be immovable, but okay, however you define it, the word suggests that all they've got is physical presence, and no sign at all of judgement or mobility of mind.

It's condescension I like least in this world.

So there has to be some political content to what Max and I decide by way of chemical choice, and in the Eastern Cape we're the only ones able to decide it, and how in the name of Reason did a couple of artists like us, a photographer and an easel painter, end up having to make such choice?

Well you don't have to look long at the word ammonal to see what's in there. There's an ammonium salt in there and there's aluminium. We sit about and ponder the probabilities, and one of them is that the salt is ordinary farm fertilizer, otherwise how is it that explosives and fertilizers are so often made in one factory? But let's not talk about that when you kids are out there reading this lot, how's that for self-censorship?

The metallic aluminium content is obviously where extra energy comes from. I may not have made my own bombs in the war, but I do remember that during the big attacks on German cities powdered aluminium was added to the charges of the blockbusters, the Grand Slams, for this extra energy, and why and how?

It occurs to us to see how aluminium is gained from the natural ore, so we're away to the PE public library, and there in our uneducated way we find that the ore is called bauxite, and where there's a lot of energy available, and a lot of bauxite, that's where aluminium comes from. So the name Alcan comes to mind, and we realise that it's the vast availability of hydroelectric energy in Canada along with deposits of the ore that make this process profitable.

But coincidentally I happen to think of something else from the war, and that is the incendiary bombs that the Luftwaffe rained down on London. Everybody at that time knew that you couldn't put these damnable things out with water or sand or anything else, because they had their own internal source of energy, oxygen, and the best thing you could do was keep the surroundings cool and wet and contain the fire and let the bastardly thing burn itself out. I remember also that the bastardly stuff inside was thermite, a good old recipe from the Industrial Revolution, when railway lines and the like were welded with it.

So it's back next day to the library and the *Encyclopedia Britannica*, where we learn that thermite is iron oxide, ordinary old rust, plus aluminium, and suddenly it all falls into place: the energy, heat, given off by thermite, because aluminium is gaining oxygen from the iron, is the same amount of energy put into the bauxite ore to take off its oxygen in the first place, and leave the pure metallic aluminium, and that is one hell of a lot of energy.

Aluminium has a greater appetite for oxygen than iron has, as it were. So, if you put aluminium in the presence of the oxide of iron and heat it to start a reaction, it will steal away that oxygen and release the amount of energy needed to de-oxidise and purify the aluminium originally, and leave pure iron. That's how the welding worked.

We learn that the reaction starts, thermite burns, at three thousand degrees Celsius, and how to generate a temperature like that, I ask you with tears in my mince pies?

But a bit more Chateau when we get back from the library relaxes the mind of Max, and in the middle of Maud's coming into the Garden he suddenly blurts out Why don't we just ignite it with a fireworks sparkler? I give this a bit of reflection, and true's God, I can't think of anything whiter or hotter than that. We're off to an industrial chemist's in the morning in Plumbin's Oldsmobile, Max sits in it a couple of blocks away and I say I'm a science teacher, and I get there laboratory-grade pure iron oxide and aluminium powder, and we're off to the OK Bazaars for sparklers, which as luck would have it are on the shelves because Guy Fawkes night is approaching and this is still celebrated in the far-flung bits of the Empire, would you believe it?

We mix the stuff up 50/50 by volume, at a guess, because it's clearly a case of very simple combustion and it won't do any harm to have too much or too little fuel. We stick a sparkler into a jam bottle with this thermite in it, and light the sparkler and soon enough the thermite bursts into such brilliant deflagration that we realise if we look at it the ultraviolet light coming off it will injure our retinae as if we were looking at a welder's flame without dark goggles. Looking indirectly at surrounding places, though, we realise that the bottle has melted and the thermite is now on its way through the table, and that's all right because this table belongs to me, but soonish it's also going to be on its way through the parquet floor which belongs to Mr Meyer from whom I now rent this flat, and fall via the ceiling on him and his ever-loving worthy wife as they lie reading the Bible in bed, and that's a different matter, which I shall have to explain with the police and fire brigade present.

We rush like all hell and get a big kitchen pot full of water and shove it in the line of descent under the kitchen table, but what are we doing, man, we know this stuff will just cause one stunning steam explosion when it hits water, and scatter molten iron all over the place, we've read about it in the library. I grab the pot back taking care to spill nothing under the table, and Max leaps out of the front door because he's remembered seeing a fire-bucket full of sand on a rack in the corridor, such as was necessary in those primitive days, for fire-extinguishing; every landing has to have such a rack. He shoves the bucket under the table as I slide the pot away, and just in time too. The sand takes two twos to turn to glass, but Gott sei dank the thermite is all combusted half-way through.

We drink some more Chateau for the nerves, and after a bit have a nervous but also triumphant laugh.

We're away! We're not sure where to, but we've got a source of energy to start with. We drop the high explosive thing for now because the incendiary is the obvious one, and let's get one thing good and reliable in the two months' development time we have available.

We could have got the iron oxide from a hardware shop as red oxide for tinting concrete, and dry aluminium powder also is available there, for making one's own silver paint, easy, but for our tests we've used only the purest. Now for practical cookery we'll try another lot with these trade ingredients, a necessary thing because, let me again emphasize, there must be no part in this bomb industry that can't be got easily and cheaply past the cashier at a supermarket or paint place. A pharmacy might be okay, but only for everyday chemicals, nothing that might cause the person behind the counter to remember one's face.

This may be the big difficulty. Everything must be within easy reach and control. Techniques must be accessible to uneducated guys. Any ordinary citizen should be able to make this device.

As it turned out, the thing which gave us our big first nachis was the one which presented the first big tsoris. Sparklers are just great, but they're all over in thirty seconds, and pretty bright to the eye. If you could get one two yards long it would get you away from your secret placing of the device with three minutes in hand, which isn't much anyway, but what about the light, the illumination?

Intuition and imagination don't come easily to the hurried, anxious mind. We make an effort at relaxation and slow thought, and sing songs now and then as we get on with optimum proportions of red oxide and aluminium and find that 50/50 by mass is better than by volume, and suddenly an afternoon or two later, in the middle of Will ye no Come Back Again, a few things fall into place in my low-gear mind. Why should such an old-time sad rebel song bring to the imagination devices vital to this present rebellion? Coincidence, und Sigmund Freud.

I remember walking to work in Durban down Mansfield Road and whistling this same melody, and by strange process of association my whistling it now brings back to mind my finding at the Warwick Avenue corner outside the old Savoy bioscope there an ancient sangoma, such as is known to many of the uninformed as a witchdoctor, but who is in fact a pretty perceptive psychotherapist, with many a cunning stage device at hand to strengthen his patients' faith. I remember watching him at work on one of these patients, and having before him on the pavement a small pyramid of potassium permanganate, ground fine but still recognisable by its purple, stacked up like a little volcano less than an inch, about two centimetres high, and a little indentation at the top of the volcano, its crater, you might say.

Silent and nodding in the best therapist's style, when the patient came near to the climax of her personal story he produced from under his cowskin apron a small bottle of glycerine. This he waved around awhile with incantations, for whatever effect; a few drops then, dribbled into the little crater. He now made as if to go into a trance, necessary because he wasn't quite sure how long a certain reaction in the mixture here before him was going to take. When it did happen, though, he did his best act of all, falling over backwards with his big horny feet in the air and a startled cry of HAU!

I must admit I gave a roughly similar gasp myself, for the flash was so brilliant that I had bright violet counter-images as if printed on the insides of my eyelids when I closed them. A small white atomic-shape mushroom rose from the spot on the pavement where the pot perm had been.

There and then, as I tell Max about this, we take ourselves well away from Meyer Mansions with our bag of red oxide and aluminium powder and our little pestle and mortar for grinding things, and pick up some glycerine for rough skin and pot perm for athlete's foot, from a pharmacy along the way to Skoenmakers Kop south of west down the coast from Port Elizabeth.

There the Port Jackson willows impenetrably cover some square miles inland from the dunes of the beach, a place inhabited by its own unique fauna of tenth-generation donkeys gone feral because their owners could never find them in such dense growth. They must have turned browsers in one of those outbursts of accelerated evolution. Also small reddish tortoises, and dikdik buck just over a foot high, and one-armed monkeys whose foster mothers had snatched them away from the natural ones in infancy, leaving only an arm behind, and all because there was something wrong with the sperm count of local males, according to biologists in PE, and not enough pregnancies. Local jokers pointed out that we fellow-primates drank the same water.

There were also people in there, gone feral in much the same way as the bongols, totally indefinable by any bureaucrat on any Population Registration Board; who spoke a language unknown to anybody on such a board, I dare say, and certainly unknown to Max and me, and living off the local wild animals and roots and things. Hunter-gatherers they'd become, grovelling in vile ignorance, on their way back to Plumbin's pulmonate fishes. No upward spiral to the green lawns and Tchaikovsky around here.

The ceiling of this habitat is about four feet above the carpet of beach sand and the thick integument of fallen willow leaves. It is browsed to that height by goats gone wild, there being families of these in here too, each with its alpha billy. All is very intimate and cosy underneath, and I must confess, as we sit down there and plan a testing-site for our operation, that it occurs to me I wouldn't mind just disappearing from the known world for a bit and setting up here with this feral community. A small ownerless yellow bush dog sits and smiles at us, and waves its curly tail.

Forget all that sentimental twak! I might as well dream of Gauguin's innocents on Tahiti, syphilis-stricken and hopeless, however compelling the colours of his paint and the monumental forms and the existential message.

We push well into the willows, half a mile, leaving behind us a Boy Scout trail of small bits of torn newspaper because we've chosen an area where there aren't any paths, and clear a little place in there of all dry leaves, because you never know, some nosey person might just look in if there were smoke coming from the bush. We mix up about a half cup of thermite in a tin, mix it well for total particle contact, then make an indentation on the surface so that there will be good contact with the pot perm, and we pour some of that in and make a little crater on top, and drip in glycerine, all exactly as the sangoma did, and we look away. It splutters a bit, as indeed the old man's had done, then the little white-hot puff appears, but it isn't momentary this time, so when we look back we see the paint-store thermite is blazing away just so inexorably, man, hissing and white-hot and radiant to injure the eyes, and turning the beach sand to glass.

We've got it! So soon! Not that we're up to any schedule. In fact there can't be a schedule because we have no idea what in all we have to do. The only way is to go flat-out and rather end up early than have too much pressure at the end. The big day will be 16 December, Dingane's Day, who had nothing to celebrate, believe me, by the end of that day in 1838; the Day of the Vow, an insulting day which suggests that Jehovah did a deal with the Natal Voortrekkers and gave them victory at Blood River because they had promised him a free church built at their own expense in Pietermaritzburg if he helped them bugger up the Zulus. Never mind insulting to Africans, such a celebration of such injury, it's also a bit insulting to God, it's blasphemy, like he can't afford a church because he's got such an overdraft at Volkskas, and he can't any more go Pouf! just like that with his pot perm and stuff, and make a Gothic cathedral appear wherever he chooses, even in Maritzburg.

On our way out of the willows we take off with us the last stretch of the Boy Scout paper trail, and pick out waypoints and landmarks that will cut us across the remaining trail when we come back again.

We decide the next step is obvious: we intended to develop a timer, and the way the glycerine arrives in the pot perm is going to give us just that. We're straight into the Meyer kitchen/lab when we're back, not that we're going to construct anything, it's just that this seems to have become our thinking-place, and our pub too, sort of, where we relax best and get the few ideas we've had so far. We have a congratulatory shot of slaan-my-dood dop and moon about in this kitchen with long gaps in the conversation. We're way beyond the social formalities of obligatory chat: apart from the world of song, most of our communication is pretty abbreviated, and usually about some technicality these days.

Max announces What we need is a syphon. He looks amazed that he had the idea. He doesn't need to explain the relevance of it, for we know the problem of timing is on both our minds, to bring all the glycerine into contact with the pot perm at the same time. A device on the principle of an egg-timer would be no good, because the first drop will start the chemical reaction on some insufficient scale.

Ja. I agree. I nod my head, but it's no good. By the standards of the men who will use whatever apparatus we produce, Max and I are a pair of scholars who have access to all kinds of skills and abstractions and technology and physics way up there, and they're not going to be able to make this device themselves with any reliable success, and reliability is our first priority.

What we least of all need is a device to be found intact somewhere, complete with fingerprints and identifiable incriminating stuff, so we bring the explosive back to number one in the queue, but keep the timer up there along with it, keep it just a little bit at the back of our minds for now.

Six

IT BECAME CLEAR TO US AT ABOUT this point that Plumbin had been shooting his mouth off about the prowess of Max and myself in Die Baai. Why else would he tell us that Yoshke Slovo was anxious about the poor pace of invention in Joburg and wanted to see personally what we had in PE? By our reckoning we had bloody little anyway: a bit of old-fashioned thermite and a pavement shrink's trick was nothing to brag of. We felt unease which was never there in the newspaper days. Security was entirely in our own hands then; I don't think even Plumbin had known what we were about, and why should he have?

Well, he says he's off out of town on big business, and perhaps to speed up a good pyrotechnic display for Yoshke we should consider moving, both of us plus Jess, into his flat where we can cerebrate just that little bit harder if together both day and night. We agree this may indeed be true, but to be candid, which I can afford to be these forty years later, the first thing that sprang to my imagination was the bottles of Cherry Heering and the like goodies in his cupboard there, and no Chateau brake fluid. This was the reason for Max's immediate agreement too, I suspect, though such cynicism pains me to this day.

But good booze is darem one of the blessed bounties of this earth, the more blessed when taken with individually-wrapped little Dutch chocolates after supper, and we soon find out that Plumbin has got it dead right this time, and this place of his is indeed conducive to brilliant thought.

The brilliant thought we have after about a week of chocolates and lovely Lithuanian grub out of the fridge and various foreign tin cans, is that we can simplify the explosives routine by leaving out the detonator we had in mind, and seeing if the timer itself can ignite the ammonal direct. This would simplify the routine and again mean fewer chances of failure for the inexperienced operator. We had assumed that it would take heat as extreme as that of burning thermite to ignite our ammonal, but if the sangoma device was hot enough to ignite the thermite, why not just leave the thermite out altogether?

After another dainty glass or so of the cherry liqueur Max says to me Come on, let's do it!, and I say What? You mean now?, and he does indeed mean that and I say Shit Max, you don't mean we're going to shlep twenty bloody miles out of the Baai in the Oldsmobile and half a mile on foot through those bloody willows at ten o'clock pee em to poop off tests at the site, you must be mad, man! And haven't you noticed that we haven't ever yet made any ammonal, and now we're going to make our first lot ever by torchlight?

No, he replies, I know we made a rule after the thermite in Meyer Mansions, but we'll try just a teeny little bit of ammonal here in Plumbin's sink. Jesus, Max, you're fucken daft man, I say, what if we burn a hole through Plumbin's sink this time?

No, just a tee – eeeeeee – EEEEEEEny bit, says Max.

So. We empty our little liqueur glasses and go down and fetch from the Oldsmobile our khaki rucksack with the saboteurs' gear in it, and haul out the laboratory-grade ammonal ingredients we've just got that very morning from the laboratory-supply chemist. We mix up at the stainless steel kitchen sink under the shelves with all the jars of jam and bottles of Bovril and butter and stuff this infinitesimal minute wee tiny quantity of ammonium nitrate with about a snuff pinch of aluminium powder on the end of one of Plumbin's little sharpish-ended Lithuanian silver coffee-spoons, and balance it near the plughole in the sink. We're deft at grinding up the pot perm by now, and Max has a little bit done all nice and fine, in a trice.

It's messy stuff, and makes ugly brown stains on almost anything, even stainless steel, and it seems a pity to me that this nicely proportioned rectangular shiny hygienic sink is going to get so wantonly grubbied up.

Max is a very meticulous person, as one would expect of a photographer, I suppose, who knows how much salt to put on a fried egg, and now from a little foil funnel he's made he meticulously drops a dinky little Vesuvius cone of pot perm onto the minimal ammonal, and makes a dinky little crater at the top with his ballpoint pen. From another of the dainty silver coffee-spoons he drips a couple of drops of glycerine into the dinky little hollow and steps back and nothing happens. For five minutes or so nothing continues to happen.

We give it another five, and Max says I think I'll just poke it a little bit with this ballpoint, and he hauls his cheapo from his pocket and makes for the ammonal. I reach quickly to grab his arm, and blurt out For Chrissake Max! just open the ta. . . . .

BAAAAAAAAAAAAAANG!!!

I look at Max as we stand there under the stalactites of jam and the marmites of Bovril dripping from the ceiling. The wooden shelves are no more, and butter and mustard are all over the walls, thin, and horseradish sauce and anchovy spread, thick. I know Max is talking because I see his mouth at work, but I hear nothing and know that I'm now deaf like a post and from now on it's lip-reading for me. My eardrums have met in the middle of my head. I see he's pointing at the pen, which is still entire, and I realise he's telling me he was lucky it hadn't got as far as the coffee-spoon when the lot went up. I look past him and see that the windows are wide open, and that's our second bit of luck in disaster, for glass raining from the fifth floor in this refined neighbourhood on some rich indignant soul taking her curly Maltese poodle for a walk and weewee down there would have meant big big trouble in a criminal court.

But now the Big One hits me: Oh My Life! what the hell are we going to say when the police arrive? Such a violent explosion is serious stuff, boet: Plumbin's shiny neat rectangular kitchen sink is now a hemisphere, and sticky black. The stainless-steel draining-boards on either side are now at an angle of thirty degrees, and the sink touches the floor.

Just for a moment I contemplate running, forever, stopping only now and then to scream. We shakily sit down and shakily pour out a tumbler of Cherry Heering each, and wait. This is going to be the last drink we get for a long time, where we're going. We might as well have a good whack while we wait for the sirens. But the sirens don't sound, and the law doesn't come, and after half an hour or so it continues not to come.

After another hour and another tumbler Max says to me What's the date? and I look him straight in the eyes with disbelief as I answer The fifth of November. . . . I think. . . . .

Please to remember the fifth of November;
Gunpowder, treason and plot.
I see no reason why gunpowder treason
Should ever be forgot.

Next morning we found the stump of the Lithuanian coffee-spoon, the handle. The front part was vaporised.

On our way to the bombing range that next morning we were pretty silent. I knew though that Max was doing what I was doing, that is, working out whether we'd used up all our bad luck or all our good luck, as motorcyclists do after surviving a meaningful prang. So he wasn't surprised when I said to him after an hour or so: Max, never again. He had only to nod his head, that's all he had to do, because he knew what was going on inside mine. With Max one didn't have to quarrel and nag, nor were accusations necessary.

Our brush with disaster had made us really cunning, so I suppose one might put it down as a plus if one needed to rationalise our indiscipline. We'd become like a pair of wily old carp under a mulberry tree on the bank: never taste the fallen fruit inside your mouth, but blow a lot of water at it and jig it about, and sniff up the surrounding aromas, and if there's some dummy up there who's put a hook in it, let's see if we can get him to strike prematurely.

At least we'd learned the violence of the stuff with just a little bit of it, so now that we're going to do the full performance with a two-pound jam tin we know that we must retire immediately after pouring in the glycerine, which is to say nobody would think us bangbroeke if we ran like bloody hell. On further thought it occurred to us that whereas it might take two of us to assemble this infernal machine, it needed only one to do the final priming, and why waste the lives of two Peoples' Heroes when we could spare one to carry forward the Peoples' Heroic Struggle? So the new rule is that the bloke who sets the

59

apparatus is the one who is responsible for it thereafter: any failure, and he's got to decide what to do about it, and do it solo.

Okay, so this time we're into the willows along a track parallel to the bits of newspaper; it doesn't take a lot of hiking to make a path, and some inquisitive explorer to follow it. Within ten minutes or so of arrival we've got all prepared: the jam tin with the ammonal and the pot perm all ready and Max cool like a cucumber with the glycerine bottle in his hand. He's volunteered for it because he still feels a bit faulty about the Guy Fawkes debacle. He pours it in like this vegetable and takes off at full gallop; at the fifty-yard mark I join him and he makes it to a hundred in ten point five seconds flat, point five only in excess of the then world record.

He needn't have bothered, of course, because the stuff takes as long to react on the big scale as it did in Plumbin's kitchen, about the smallest scale, but even though we know what to expect, and lie down in a little hollow we've dug there, with our hands over our ears and eyes pressed to the sand, we are quite seriously shaky when we go to look at the site after the explosion. Thirty paces across it looks like a war painting of Delville Wood or a photograph of Eniwetok Atoll. There is no living leaf on a tree, nor any dead leaf upon the ground; it is swept clean. We sit down and smoke fags. Are we really going to give this to Plumbin?

We two old cigarette-smoking carp ask ourselves and each other even more insubordinate questions: are we really going to give this to Yoshke, the Pope? He is not renowned for scruple or conscience, duplicity is his boast in the Class Struggle, in which the rulers tell only lies, and why shouldn't we tell one? Indeed if we don't thus cheat the Ruling Class will have the edge on us.

Must we put our lives and perhaps random public lives in his dubious hands, and what with his coming grand tour of our testing site and examination of our programme, moreover, will he be all that good at security?

Well, we can't let such moral quandaries hamper our revolutionary progress. We weren't appointed as philosophers. What's more, we have only six weeks to the great day.

Thus we sit and scheme in amongst Plumbin's fancy food our immediate priority and conclude it is once again a timer, for whatever we're going to do about Yoshke we're going to need this timer for whatsoever apparatus we employ. And this time it is my turn for genius; almost as we decide this thing it occurs to me that gravity will work as well through a filter as through a syphon, as long as the fluid can come through with some sort of rush, and the two of us start there and then on mentally assembling the device. Before the evening is out we have it; a two-inch length of large-diameter garden hosepipe, a piece of broomstick that fits exactly inside that and some nylon gauze will do the trick. With contact adhesive we will stick one gauze diaphragm halfway up the pipe, using the stick to push it in, and one at the bottom. Between the two will be our thermite and pot perm. Above that will be a teaspoonful of ordinary PE beach sand; nothing more available than that! Nice and coarse, too, so the glycerine will come through as a flood. We will fill to the top of the pipe with glycerine, and time the filtration.

Max and I pull in at the OK Bazaars in the morning, early, and buy a broomstick in the houskeeping department and take it over to the gardening department. We're so bloody touchy these days we make sure nobody sees us shoving the broomstick up the end of a roll of plastic hosepipe to see if it fits. It does, for specifications of most things go for fairly predictable fractions of the inch. We buy a good length of the pipe, and on our way out of the OK we notice in the D.I.Y. handyman's department certain plastic jerrycans, for turps or the like, I suppose. Max directs a hooded carp-glance at me and I hood up my own eyeballs and give him one back. I look around to see nobody's looking and Max tries the hosepipe for fit in the nozzle of the jerrycan. It fits, precisely. We buy six.

What we had simultaneously in mind was another double experiment. If we're going to test a timing filter that fits exactly into the throat of a jerrycan, well, we might as well fill the jerrycan with petrol and see what happens to that. What a stroke of fortune if everything matches up! It was by the purest of coincidences that we happened to go to the OK and spot the jerrycans.

I think it took us longer to go to the beach for the sea sand than to make the hosepipe timer. We'd got some nylon gauze from a silk-screening place. A piece of this separating beach sand and pot perm, then pot perm and thermite. That's it. All we had to do in situ was shove in the timer, the teaspoonful of sand, our chosen measure, slosh glycerine in above that, roughly an inch deep, and depart post-haste.

I'd never have believed anything could work so predictably, first shot. We have the jerrycan with the petrol ready in it, three-quarters full to allow for nervous operators; we don't want the timer to get saturated with petrol before the chemistry starts. We dump it on the ground, neatly slide in the hosepipe and empty the glycerine down its throat and walk away noting the time in seconds. At precisely seven and a half minutes we get the satisfying whump. When all has burned and cooled off we go over to our charred patch in the middle of the Port Jacksons and sit down and light a fag to contemplate our success rate and decide on improved techniques. Well, there is no room for improvement, if I may sound so smug. We've foreseen everything. We've even got an uncalculated bonus: at the end of the entire process of combustion there remains only a teaspoonful of PE sea sand. Nothing else. Not even a dribble of molten plastic. The petrol has incinerated the lot.

We repeat it four more times. We get about seven and a half minutes each shot. We save one jerrycan for Yoshke. We are now ready for the big demo. We will take the Top Brass entourage to our private bombing range and burn for them this bucket of petrol so they can piss off back to Joburg and let us get on with our inventions in time for Dingane's Day. Then we will abandon the site as a security risk and look north of PE for something similar.

But you know how one gets a bit astrant and vokjouish, and Max says to me Come on Jock, my man, let's give him a right bloody shot and see what happens. Let's give him a secret shot of ammonal. And I grin at Max, because I have been having similar bad-security thoughts myself, and I say, Okay Max, my man, let's put ammonal in the tube along with the pot perm, a Mickey Finn, and see what a gallon's worth of atomised petrol looks like when it lights up.

But we have developed this experiential habit of suspicion about our own enthusiasms, and get up off the couch where we sit cogitating, and go to that cupboard in the stricken kitchen where the sealed corrugated cardboard case of Cherry Heering is secreted, and it's undamaged blast, so we unseal it and get out a bottle and back to the couch and our self-suspicion.

And it occurs to us after half a bottle or so, between us, that we have been thinking of petrol as if it were water, a natural extinguisher of fire that should not come in contact with other ingredients, and wet them, but in fact there's no reason why we should be so touchy, because petrol is an enhancer of fire, who would believe it?

In fact, as I express this thought another comes to the mind of Max: why are we using petrol anyway? Diesel fuel is a much better source of energy, ask any farmer.

After another half hour, Max points out something a bit chilling: we're not going to have an incendiary device here at all, with liquid fuel furiously burning. All the diesel will be instantaneously vaporised, and we're going to have a simultaneous double explosion: the high-velocity powder ingredient one inside a gas explosion. The compounded blast will be unimaginable.

So we rig up this special extra-long piece of hosepipe, full of H.E. ammonal below the pot perm and inner diaphragm, going right to the bottom of the jerrycan, but the sea sand filter and triggering ingredients still dry up top of the diaphragm of course, to start it all where there's some airspace. Sure, if there had been time we'd have gone and done another test of our new device, and designed a better construction, but what the hell about this demo, it's a big status thing for Plumbin anyway, let's use it as the test. A failure might take him down a peg, and do him good, and as for us, we know that if it doesn't work it won't be dangerous to dismantle beause the fault can only be that ammonium nitrate and diesel together don't ignite at all, ever.

We think about our good old site. It's a pity to waste it, and anyway Plumbin will undoubtedly insist on his presence at the show if he's back from his important business travels, and he can't walk half a mile through the willows to get there, we're sure, because of these things called palpitations which he gets with excitement or exercise, and he's going to get both. Yoshke seems no fitter. Max estimates the only exercise these two get is around the jaws, from the mouthing of ideological platitudes and the eating of LM prawns.

Next morning we're off down the beaches to look for a better but safe demo site. I use the plural here because there are many beaches. First, of course, there's the European beach, near to all the nice restaurants and clean toilets, then comes the Coloured beach with pie carts and dirty toilets, then the Asian beach, subdivided because it includes both Indians and Chinese, and we all know how ethnic communities everywhere suspect each other and hatred and violence well up. These don't have much by way of toilets at all, because ethnically they all defecate in the bushes anyway and don't need restaurants because they eat out of their own biryani pots and woks, traditionally, they prefer it. Then there's a beach for Octoroons and one for Mulattos and a last but one for Eskimos in transit, and ultimately of course there is a beach for Natives, now known as Bantus, which has nothing at all but the signpost, and by the time you've got to the end of all these signposts proclaiming all these beaches there is scarce anything you'd recognise as a road and you're twenty miles south of PE, i.e. as far away as our bombing-range, except it's on the beach.

Beyond all this we find an abandoned bog. If there'd been enough South Samoans they could have had a beach of their own there, and the use of this galvanised iron ghost latrine, but it's abandoned now for want of populations in terms of the Population Registration Act. From the rough dirt track there's a sort of traceable path leading to it some few hundred paces down the hill through some dense, heathery growth, so we know that if we make this our demo target Plumbin and Yoshke can drive up for a grandstand observation, and merely step out of the aircraft carrier, and not strain anything in their revolutionary constitutions, while we other ranks nip down the hill and set up our petard.

Max and I do a bit of stagecraft beforehand and go along in the Olds just before dark, and rig everything up expertly so that all we have to do is pour glycerine into the thing and tell Yoshke to give us seven and a half on his Rolex. We've packed it all around with sandbags to give a lekker upward blast. Nobody ever goes there, but I hang about for the hour or so to the arrival of the brass, because there's always the slim chance that some kids may come along, even though it's now night-time and really pitch-dark. Max goes off to fetch the intellectuals.

The Oldsmobile caravanserai arrives without Plumbin, who's still elsewhere seeking capital for expansion of his business, but Yoshke has brought with him a few thinking people we've read about in *New Age*, whose names I now forget. So it's a full house. And an increasingly insecure one, you will have noticed.

We say to all When we raise a fist in the torchlight down there you must start timing seven and a half minutes, and they find all this terribly thrilling in a revolutionary sort of way, and we go down and slosh in the glycerine and wave our revolutionary fists with our left fingers over the glass of the torch so as not to make a beam, and walk ewe gerus oh so confidently up the hill to the Olds. At seven minutes Yoshke starts some interminable ideological comment on what's going on, but its probable thirty minutes duration are interrupted at seven and a half exactly by a low-resonance stunning thud and a sphere of white fire the size of a smallish city hall, and in the middle of it a toilet seat spinning like crazy over the Indian Ocean.

Yoshke grips my left arm and cries POWER, COMRADE! and Max on my right grips the arm on that side and declares Comrade, if we're going to conquer all South Africa one shithouse at a time we'll all be in the grave before liberation, only he says this sort of sotto voce-ish to me, because, after all, Yoshke is the Main Ou in the Actual Party.

But enough of highjinks and facetious demonstration, I say! There also has to be got going an operational system as efficient as the *Izwe Lomze* one, but that's not for us to devise.

It turns out to be the job of Plumbin, by decision of the District Committee, because he is local minister of transport, as it were, and we're going to need a lot of that, and right soon. There's not only the Olds for this job, for Plumbin has a couple of leaden sons, as if one of him were not enough, and one has a snappy Peugeot and the other has a stylish Chev, and the only reason these two specialists, an anaesthetist and a gynaecologist, have not revealed their revolutionary proclivities thus far is because they have such a profound sense of security. They have been saving themvirginselves for the great and first and only and decisive moment of revolutionary orgasm.

The scheme is as follows: Max and I are going to withdraw further into our conspiratorial chrysalis, we are going back to the newspaper mode. We will be known to only one man, the drop-out man, the Mountain man, whose job it will be to meet Max and me at one new place per meeting, and get our latest, and go off to instruct the operators in the making of the explosives themselves, whatever these may be in the years, maybe, of struggle, and the assembling of apparatus and devices. Max and I will be inventors, and nothing else.

Strictly.

We smile a fairly ironic smile at this notion of getting us back into the womb, as it were, when Plumbin and Yoshke and assorted subscribers to *New Age* already know about us, and some perhaps adulate us, and adulators are great talkers, and competitive about the objects of their adulation. But you never know, maybe the Security Boere are as dumb as the triumphal propaganda says they are, and we can go back to facelessness.

Well, they were as dumb as that. We were not the only ones who had a hell of a lot to learn.

Anyway, the scheme was that the operators, the saboteurs, the troops would be delivered in certain motor cars, falsely numbered and driven by nameless and faceless persons at night to certain unidentifiable places, where they would meet this nonperson who would teach them the construction of bombsk. Thenceforth they would be delivered by certain other unmarked vehiclesk and drivers who were medici with pantihosesk pulled over their physiognomysk to other unpersons who would direct them to assigned sabotage sitesk.

Great.

We decommissioned the Fiat and Max's Rustmobile, which had in any case floundered to a halt and become terminal, a static exhibit outside his house and a bedroom to Footsack, who kipped in the cab lest neighbours by night fly off the wheels and wipers and detachable things as spares. Also the Fiat now came to sleep in a garage, a treat seldom experienced, I suppose, if ever.

Not that we got the garage just for the Fiat; we had realised with the increasing tempo of things that we had to have a workshop with a workbench and storage racks and the like, and a month before Day One we had scanned the newspaper and found there in the classified ads this garage of one Mr Levitan, a radio ham and amateur constructor of the primitive electronic devices of those years. Mr Levitan was some sort of loony, to be sure, because the garage was full to the doors with strange tangles of soldered wires, solenoids, valves, primitive transistors and radio dishes of incomprehensible construction. We asked him where the hell we were supposed to keep our motor car and he agreed there was a problem there and shoved all his goeters to the back of the garage, up to the roof, and gave us the front part half-price.

In fact he apologised because he couldn't find room at the back for a table with a vice attached, and we did him the favour of allowing it to stand in our half as long as we could have the use of it. Here we assembled our first operational bomb.

I think this was a good bomb. It was simplicity itself. The diesel bomb was far too sloshy and clumsy, whatever its advantages by way of blast. It was a thing to use on buildings, if you had plenty of time for placement. The case of this straight H.E. ammonal bomb was a cylindrical aluminium spaghetti container from the OK, with a screw-top. Good stuff, aluminium, where explosions are going on, for all will contribute to the blast and nothing will remain. This case would hold about two pounds of ammonal. The operator should cut a hole in the soft metal screw-top with a sharp pointed kitchen knife, to take the standard hosepipe timer/detonator. Pour in glycerine and catch the first bus going in any direction and cock an ear at seven and a half.

It is my turn for assembly, and I do it with efficiency and promptitude. I take a spaghetti tube from our stock and start cutting the untidy hole. I slip in the detonator. Then at this point I realise the pot perm is giving us problems enough to scuttle the whole enterprise. I first heard of the stuff as a small boy, when people used it for snakebite and athlete's foot, and all thought it pretty benign, but Max and I have realised just how malign potassium permanganate actually is, because our vision is affected and we're nauseous after grinding it, and that's most of the time, and we have no sense of smell at any time. The insides of our noses feel as if they've been sandpapered.

But apart from that, there is nothing that could possibly go wrong.

At nine or ten pm when the traffic has thinned out we're off to a pylon we've reconnoitred earlier. It is at a bend of the main supply lines to the PE industrial district, and carries fifteen lines, so there's a hell of an inward pull at the corner here, and the pylon is braced against that. It is one of the bracing girders that we are aiming for: break that and the huge inward drag of the fifteen wires will pull the whole pylon over.

It's about eleven by the time we've got the Olds suitably parked and make our way over to the pylon a mile or so off, with our sinister apparatus in the khaki bag and trying to look as much like a pair of multiracial hobos as possible. There's some sort of township here for black folk. The power lines take this angle to go round these houses. We can't arrive amongst a humble community like this in a half-acre Oldsmobile, f'r chrissake.

We know what we have to do and we do it promptly. We don't have to keep watch and glance about anxiously; if any police saw us skulking about or running off it would only make them the more suspicious, so in less than five minutes we have everything strapped in position with soft wire and Max shoves off because it's my job to prime the thing with glycerine, since I assembled it. This I do confidently, because I know what's inside the works and nothing premature can possibly happen. I walk away easily, and Max takes the time as I start walking.

We are so used to the thing going off at seven and a half that at eight we start getting anxious, and at half an hour we know we have a problem.

We lie in the grass for a further hour, trying to debate what the hell could have gone wrong, but not knowing what on Earth to debate: all our components and ingredients were simple and tried and tested, and now they're all in there, waiting, waiting. Max is smoking like blazes, and there's nothing in the world like a fag when you're in real trouble, man; you don't have to wait for the effect to arrive, it goes straight in the top of your head as through a funnel. But I can't smoke, because smoking makes the hands shake, and I have a nasty notion of what's about to happen since, as I say, I have assembled this bomb.

At about an hour I say Max, I'm going to have a look and see what's happened, and I grab the pliers and make for this bloody apparatus, and Max follows me asking What the hell are you going to look at, man?

By this time we're actually at the sodding thing, and I realise there is in fact nothing to look at, but at least I can dismantle it and pour the contents out on the ground, and take a chance with all the ingredients perhaps only a molecule or and atom apart in there. I tell Max to bug off, but he's having an attack of loyalty. I don't understand the logic of it, but it is comforting in some animal way. He takes the hand I'm extending to the binding wires and says Man, I remember the decision about all the folks who'll be coming past here from these houses on their way to work in an hour or two, but how the hell is it going to help to monkey about with the bloody thing in the hope that all may just come right with a little bit of good luck, while with another different little bit of luck, bad this time, you'll be dead?

I'll tell you what, he says, I'll go over to the houses there and get a bucket of water while you undo most of the wires here and we'll just drown it.

I agree to this and the poor bugger sets off at a run, it's so scary even to be near the thing. I undo all wires except one, with little success trying to think of Aristotle: Where I am Death is not, where Death is I am not, so why not stay cool and just untwist these wires, eh? But this deep reflection is interrupted by a hell of a hullabaloo from the houses, and Max comes breathlessly thudding back explaining he's just been bitten by one dog and there's another one right behind him which doesn't intend to bite him, just to swallow him whole, and there is to be sure such a Baskerville-type beast in his wake which we drive off with curses and cries of footsack and a shower of rocks in traditional style.

Irrelevantly I remember being in England where dogs don't understand proper dog language like footsack and don't fuck off when they see your fingers making for the ground; they think you're going to tie your shoelace and your throat is that bit closer to their canines. England isn't covered in rocks.

Well it wasn't Max's bum that was bitten but his broeks. I'll tell you what I'll do, he says, I'll nip back to the Olds and then to the garage and bring back a jerrycan of water and that paint drum from Mr Levitan's junk. Just stay put and don't smoke. So I retreat from the pylon and lie on the ground back there with my eyes shut and spend an hour non-smoking, until Max reappears in the Olds itself with its great sixty-watt headlights wildly shafting their white beams all over the cosmos and the earth, bounding on its plush freeway suspension over the veld of shrivelled grass and rocks and the accumulated rubbish that passes for landscape around these poverty-stricken townships. He slams to a halt next to me in a great billow of dust, and switches off.

Just think of the Revolution, he says, and we'll bound over to the fucking thing and undo the last wire and chuck it in this here bucket and drink this here half-bottle of Cherry Heering which I happen to have about my person, actually it's almost full, and smoke fags and have a good laugh and we'll piss off from this miserable place and catch a good kip and I'll see you tomorrow about midday, when I wake up.

He does stay at the car this time, though, as a matter of discipline, and I march determinedly over to the spaghetti bomb without thinking at all, determinedly excluding everything from my mind but the physical act of walking and placing the drum under the bomb and emptying the jerrycan of water into it, then the mechanical act of untwisting the last wire, and lowering the bomb into the drum. Whilst doing this last untwist I hold the bomb steady, steady against the pylon, no shaking, and the lowering into the water is slow, slow.

I pant to a stop at the Olds and Max hands me the bottle of booze and the cigarette all ready and alight, and I flop down and giggle, as predicted. There's one last thing to do, but it doesn't need steady hands. I go back to the drum and unscrew underwater the top of the spaghetti tube itself, and really flood every part of the container and all ingredients.

We'd made a point of never buying twice from any one place. Well, we'd gone twice to the industrial chemist for lab supplies, that's true, but we'd each had a turn, and bought in bulk enough to keep us in stock for the full time of our inventions. Going over our materials we could think of nothing that hadn't been used successfully before from this stock, except the glycerine, ordinary everyday glycerine, which I'd replenished just before the failed test with a small quantity from a little pharmacy at the other end of town, just to see us through the test. It looked like any other glycerine, but to be methodical I went back to this little place, and asked again for a bottle of glycerine. There you are, said the lass with a smile.

Is this pure pure glycerine? I ask. Oh yes, she replies, pure, pure, with rosewater of course, for chapped hands.

Stupid bloody cow, I think, where the bloody hell would I get chapped hands in November? From bottles of lager out of the fridge? I should have asked for the pharmacist at this chemist shop. But I smile a saccharine smile of boundless hypocrisy. Of course, say I. Yes, you can smell the roses, can't you? says she, smiling to show her innocent pretty teeth. She is generally pretty, I note absently, and a hundred percent innocent, though I still want to kill her. Yes one can, can't one, I retort, but it's not this one that can, think I, because this one's nose is all cauterised inside from breathing the pot perm.

Seven

BUT IT'S AN ILL WIND AND ALL THAT wise stuff, and the crisis of the night before finally makes up our uncertain minds about giving our H.E. to Plumbin and his unidentified comrades and, most importantly, to Yoshke. If it's as easy as that to make a vokop, for a pair as experienced as Max and I are in dumb disaster, how easy for a total illiterate, and wouldn't he just leave it standing if it didn't go off, maybe, and kill people? What about his prints? Would he have been furtive enough, and when the S.B. had traced it back to him and kicked his teeth in often enough, wouldn't he grass and direct them to Yoshke, and would he in his turn stand up to interrogation for a couple of days so his comrades could disappear? We doubt that. This is not a man of tough body. This is a man of tough unbending scriptural ideology, faith, megalomania, which offers no protection to the teeth. This is a man of posture and propaganda.

But it's the killing we're most importantly doubtful about. We've heard these revolutionary dudes talking often enough of The People having mass but no personal substance, and certainly no private soul, and we feel just so uneasy about their view of expendability. So long as they're not going to get personally expended expendability's just fine, because they are here to do the thinking on behalf of this mindless mound of muscle and bone, and you must suffer casualties in the struggle, so what's a few trashed here and there from the Millionmassen der Arbeit? So what if passers-by get ripped to meat by a terrorist blast, so long as we're getting advertisement for ourselves, and I don't mean just our party, I mean our personal selves within it.

One doesn't want to be too chi-chi about death. Death is an important experience in Life, maybe the most important of all. Ask an AIDS sufferer, but ask her soon. Good idea to use it for advertisement then: you must do as those Buddhist monks did in Vietnam, and don your saffron robes and buy a can of petrol at the filling station and sit down cross-legged in the village square and pour this petrol over yourself and flick your Bic. That will make people think about peace and love all right, and the preciousness of life.

It's the phoney altruism, though, the sanctimonious verbiage that goes with their cynical view, the actual conversational presence of these personalities, that finally tips the scales. They don't inspire trust, we feel insecure with them around, and we decide the very evening after the spaghetti-bomb debacle that we will withold this thing, and not let it get anywhere near the hands of Yoshke Slovo.

We foresee grievous punishment if we weaken and release it, and I don't mean just the sentences the courts will lay on us if we're caught. I mean amongst our own revolutionary selves there will be grievous harm, apart, that is, from the bodily harm of blowing ourselves up by mistake.

As some comrades hive off when the random killing starts and compassion disappears, they will get classified as poor theorists, deviationists, sellouts, mutineers, liberals, neo-liberalists, right-wingers, spies even, and revenge and arbitrary disciplining will become the revolutionary mode.

There will be no voice for these apostates. There will be ostracism and menace internally and punishment camps beyond the borders, remote gulags where there is no snow but desiccated yellow grass to the forty-five degree Celsius drought-stricken infinite distance where normal people are said to have their being, if there are any normal ones left, that is, where a terrorist mystique has struck its roots.

There will be punitive secrecy and ideological exorcism and condescending rehabilitation, and gradual unseen retribution to death, death, death for the recalcitrant.

We will have no moral case to make against the brutal régime we are trying to overthrow.

Maybe these are the intuitions of Mandela too, when on behalf of the High Command he says Umkhonto is to perform sabotage only, and strict instructions are given to its members right from the start, that on no account are they to injure or kill people in planning or carrying out operations. Four modes of struggle are available, he says; sabotage, guerrilla warfare, terrorism and open revolution. We have opted for the first because it costs no lives and offers the best hope for future race relations.

Neat thoughts, ou Nelson, Madiba, but don't you recognise a Leninist pseud when you see one? Not long at all after you personally and your Command are safely tucked away offshore it will start, and I personally will see the supermarket that was blown up on Christmas Eve, and the beachfront bar where the car bomb killed the young women, and the meat of the young Azapo guy and his missus stuck all over the trees on the Esplanade with the smell of shit and the polythene-looking bags of bursten bowels; and other people in other places will see their things, while our luckier dreamers who have taken their asses to healthier climes will fill the air with triumphal declamation and righteous platitude, and put in their leaden newspaper obituaries for the lads sitting in their death cell in Pretoria, and little spears on each side of the obituary, signifying our solidarity since, shame, we cannot be with you, physically. Comrades.

It's decided, then. That's a relief! It's only the fire bomb now. It's dependable and foolproof, and can do quite enough industrial damage, ou swaer, even though it's not so spectacular. Max and I were never after spectacle anyway; this is not a bloody circus. So we can now get on with the logistics of our enterprise in the three weeks left to us before Dingane's Day. Where everything is as secretive as this the simplest organisation takes one hell of a long time. For example, who is going to drive to distant places wherever in whatever vehicle to buy ingredients and parts, and elsewhere who is going to store these things, and who is going to supervise safe distribution with a drop-out man, and reconnoitre one-off training sites? And, and, and... The logistical list is endless if we're going to have any safety at all, even for this very unspectacular naive stand we're making.

Not that Max and I want to know these details, we just want to know that they are being taken care of, or have been done, so that we can be ready and lock into the system and establish our first rendezvous with the training intermediary.

There's one thing Max and I are good at, have made ourselves good at, and that's patience. But there's a difference between the patience required for letting a chemical or mechanical process take its course, or for the effective construction of some simple apparatus to take as long as it needs for reliability, a difference between that patience and the patience required for a dithering poep to pull his finger out and do what he's been appointed to do. Out of twenty-one precious days remaining, we spend seven kicking our heels, but nobody comes to us, and we can't use the phone.

At two weeks before D-day, that is Dingane's Day, we are still waiting all set at Mr Levitan's garage. It is the first time since forever that we have had nothing to do. We go for another health-giving hike around St George's Park, the cricket ground, but when we get back there is still nobody about. We don't need half a dozen such healthy hikes a day, mensch, waiting for action; there is not the time. This will be our eighth day lost.

At an impulse, I'm off furtively to Govan after our lunchtime sandwiches, and creep up the fire escape of the building next door and across the common wall to his, the *New Age* building, and down from the roof to the *New Age* office when nobody's looking. I know I'm breaking my purdah, but with reason, by my reckoning. I am prepared to face Govan's wrath.

But there's no wrath. Govan smiles at me with relief. Jock, he says, as I sit here I have been wondering how to get hold of you without using the phone! And suddenly you appear! They didn't see you coming in, I hope? No, I come down the chimbley, like Father Christmas. What? The fire escape, man! Aah, can you leave that way? Of course.

What Govan needs me for is a trip to Durbs. At this late stage, forsooth, I am to go to Durban, where they have been trying to make or steal dynamite or whatever absurdity, I can't remember, but sure as hell have got nothing going, at all. My breach of security is condoned for the greater good. I am winkled out of the womb and deviously transported first to the Levitan garage for bits and pieces, and thence to the airport, where stands a creaking old S.A. Airways DC6 Skymaster flailing its props about and filling the air with a sound as of people swatting flies with rolled-up newspapers.

From the Durban airport I phone Jess to say I won't be home for supper, and I'm whisked off to a flat with furniture in bad taste, where lies on a Queen Anne divan an exceeding hirsute youth of much pudge; hairy, that is, from crotch to eyebrow. Buttock to occiput, I dare say, though this is but conjecture, since he is lying on those parts.

He has a piepie point three two pistol in his hands, which he cocks and uncocks repeatedly whilst reciting the gospel according to Saint Fidel interspersed with pithy aphorisms from the collected wise thoughts of Che Guevara. He is Ronnie, codenamed Slim, on account of the agility of his mind. He wears only football shorts, this being coastal Natal in December, and lies with his legs crossed. He points the cocked pistol at the big toe of his right foot and dry fires it.

One day you'll have a round in there and shoot your fucking foot off, I observe by way of introduction, that's why so many policemen are cripples. Comrade Castro says power comes from the barrel of a gun, that's why I'm cleaning this one, he replies pithily, lifting from the black tangle around his navel a yellow duster, and briefly shining up yet again the exterior of the weapon. From his supine position he extends a comradely hand, with which he has been practising firm handshakes on doorknobs.

I declare my revolutionary mission and display the meagre artefacts we have devised in Die Baai. I have the timer with PE beach sand and a little bottle of glycerine, and explain that he must time his own thing with Durban sand. He nods his head in a sweat of conspiracy. I have thermite ingredients in separate bottles. You don't carry ready-mixed stuff in the air. I have the top part cut from a PE OK Bazaars jerrycan, just so the blokes here will know what size mouth to look for at the Durban OK, where they'll have the same in stock. I tell him how to be careful when placing the thing; don't slosh petrol on the timer, put the filled can in position first, then put in the timer/igniter. That's all I came here for. It took me ten minutes. I'm ready to go back home to a late supper, but the next flight is in the morning.

But no; we creep behind a hedge and enter a falsely numbered vehicle fraudulently borrowed from Tom Sharpe, with doors open and engine running. We drive about Durbs and two further revolutionists leap out from other hedges into open doors, and after half an hour or so we find ourselves at a grassed-over urban reservoir three or four blocks, maybe five, from the flat with furniture in bad taste. I'd rather have walked there with Max, and would have if he'd come along, we'd have given each other a smile or two, and we'd have had time for a smoke.

Slim produces a map from under his paratrooper's jacket and places it upon the floor of the vehicle, where, by the light of one of those little torches that you fix on your keyring so you can find the keyhole after a good dronkop, we scrutinise the approaches to this reservoir. This map has many arrows in many colours, and many times marked, GMT. We synchronise our watches.

We emerge from this vehicle all doubled up, and in pairs, and advance upon this reservoir from opposite sides, according to the map. I am with Slim. There are blocks of flats all round. Of course there are; it is where their water comes from. We are waiting for one minute nineteen seconds so comrades elsewhere on the perimeter can get in position to advance synchronously on a predetermined ventilator on this here reservoir.

What the fuck are we doing? I ask Slim.

We are testing this device under combat conditions, says Slim. Bollocks, man, you don't test chemistry under combat conditions, and in any case I've tested it, I say. Take it to the beach in the morning and see if it works, if you don't accept my test. You can try it in your garage, without the petrol.

Keep down! exclaims Slim, thrusting at my pate.

Oh chicken shit! I get up and walk off to my father's room in Moore Road not too far off, where the shopping centre is today. He's a late sleeper and an insomniac. Howzit? I say at eleven or after. Do you want tea? he asks. Ja, that's what I'm here for. Are you going to stay? Ja, I just came for the tea and a hullo; I'm off at six, wake me at five if you're up.

Och aye!

The Scots are dinkum dour; it's not just a caricature. It runs in the blood like a wooden leg, says my father.

The topic of conversation between Max and myself is increasingly and obsessively security and the H.E. The gods will punish you, I tell Max, if you weaken under pressure and hand it over.

I tell him what Athena did to Hector when he gave her uphill: she got his corpse dragged around the walls of Troy behind the chariot of Achilles, her relative and favourite laaitie. Max says ja, he'll remember that, make no mistake, it's so lurid, and if I give him a bit of time he'll think of a suitable Xhosa mutilation for my carcass if I behave like a bloody fool.

We have time to contemplate these horrid Homeric and Nguni retributions, even after my excursion to Durbs, for nothing even yet has happened back here at the arsenal.

We start getting a bit indignant, and then asking each other what the bloody hell people like these professional communists are doing in a revolution anyway? We look at our watches. These tell us that if we break discipline and march into town we will catch Govan at the *New Age* office, or to be accurate the office of the paper which came after *New Age* when that was banned. I can't remember its name any more. *Spark*, I think. *Iskra*. There were so many over the years.

At that time of day maybe the Security Branch would have got a bit bored and started thinking it was beer time.

So we get lucky, and as we arrive at the bus stop so does a bus, and we make it at the last closing moment all unconcealed and desperate to get to this new *New Age* office, and there standing on the pavement outside is Govan himself, but he doesn't greet us with a gentle fatherly smile as is his wont. In fact he hardly looks at us at all, his attention is so rivetted on what's going on in the traffic. We follow his gaze, and there in steep perspective we see disappearing through this traffic our Oldsmobile, followed like a mother duck by a snappy Peugeot and a stylish Chev. Where's Annie going? Max asks. Surely the three cars aren't supposed to be seen together? I remark.

Annie has been having trouble with his palpitations, explains Govan, which have come on again because of something he saw in his kitchen when he came back from his business trip with new investors. Something about Marmite and jam and paper flowers, though I didn't quite follow it, he was too distraught. Something about no cherries and things for his guests. I don't know.

His first stop will be Tel Aviv and his second Swiss Cottage, London, says Govan. Fuck, say I, he's not going to drive to Tel Afuckingviv in our fucking Olds, is he, and why don't they all go in one car, the Peugeot preferably, if they really need to go?

Govan looks at me in benign puzzlement. Govan, I say, we're down the plug 'ole, matey, we're on our way to boep, you realise that? Yes, Jock, he says, I know. What's it about, Govan, man? I ask.

Class, Jock, says Govan.

By this time all the wheels had been stolen off Max's bak, and the wipers too and all other detachable bits, also Footsack himself, who turned out to be the only retrieveable item, for he walked home after three days, because the food was too bad in the township, Max explained, whereas he, Max, didn't eat chicken skin and the like for reasons of health and embonpoint, and Footsack scored these and other tidbits along with his nosh at home. Also there was affection at home, he explained, though as he spoke he wondered why, the way this bloody animal craved nothing else, all the time, and lacked all killing instinct.

Anyway, the bakkie is probably still there, fused back into the geomorphological mother-body of Gondwanaland, like those skeletal fishing-boat wrecks on the Skeleton Coast, returned to Gaia.

So it's the Fiat then. We recommission this modest stalwart and shove up her wheels to circular trim with left-over copies of radical literature, and wash her down. We're not after any shine here of course, she's painted by brush with housepainter's enamel, quite a pretty blue, but it's nice to see her clean, and it's a sort of farewell congratulatory gesture, a valediction like rubbing down a gladiator with olive oil before the great oaken doors open and he bitterly bravely strides out into the Colosseum arena and takes on the lions with his pitiful net and trident, repeating the while a passionate plea to Minerva, alias Athena, she who done the dirt on Hector, to give him a break.

Ave Caesar, morituri te salutamus!

I'm not sure because I was in boep without watch or calendar, and so far on I find it difficult to remember so far back, but within a year or so Yoshke has blown too, against specific Central Committee decision and directive, leaving the modest David Kitson, another gutsy gladiator or Fiat, you might say, to carry the ramshackle responsibilities of the Communist Party into the unpredictable chaotic unMarxist future, and get bust doing it, and push twenty years while Yoshke, a right piteous victim of the system, goes off to Marxist majesty at Hampstead Heath, there to bemoan the loss of his rightful real estate at Sea Point, Cape Town, which is getting to be a bit like owning rightful real estate in central Tokyo, and to flood the world with righteous revolutionary claptrap, finance provided by Cold War slush funds.

But never to worry, he got his own back on Kitson later after these twenty years, for Kitson took himself off to his missus in the land of UK on release, bad mistake, and Yoshke got him there, and nailed such stigmata on him because he wouldn't denounce his missus for deviating from modes of anti-apartheid demo prescribed by himself, Yoshke, that no single exile soul of the Party in UK, no leftist of UK, no trade unionist of UK, nor any normal citizen of decent sensibility in UK would take a cup of tea with him, or her. Lucky for Kitson it wasn't East Germany.

Well.

Here were all these vibrant youths in overalls and berets supplied via the Greek grocery a/c and full of fire, but who the hell was going to supply them with substance for their furious expectations but Govan and Max and myself? I mean there may have been others behind Govan, most certainly were, I'm sure, but we didn't enquire; the more ignorant we were just now the fewer people would go down the plughole with him. He, then, would organise these groups and hand them over to us, and we would demonstrate incendiary bomb construction and materials and techniques. There would not be time for us to designate targets, as had been intended after the emigration of the Plumbins. The best we could do was to suggest certain categories: Bantu Administration buildings, pass offices and the like, also industrial sabotage targets, but no private property nor personal attacks, no personal vengeance and NO killing.

NO random murder.

Govan enquires what number of these enthusiasts Max and I can handle at a shot, and the number is four, decided by how many people can sit on each others' laps in this our automotive miniature, which is a two-seater, and wee tiny seats too. That's why it's called a Fiat Cub. With me aboard it's like students crushing into a telephone booth for a Guinness record. We work it out thus; that I will drop Max at the bombing range to get the demo ready while I pick up the four lap-sitters and squash the Five Hundred flat on its humble suspension and deliver them on her solid-state treadless wheelwork to our place in the Port Jacksons.

Comradeship is complete in the silence there. One is allowed to smoke in amongst this remote foliage, and that's what we do in the absence of conversation. There is to be no talk, no names, no chat, excepting enquiries about procedure. We are very close. Max and I are getting an awareness from all this, of people sticking to commitment in adversity and calamity, though for me there's an additional quite cynical perception, of the puffed-up posturing of our leadership, perhaps leadership anywhere. It occurs to me I might be a better existentialist than I am a Marxist.

I dropped these lads where I'd picked them up, and that was at the lights five blocks down from the *New Age* office. How they got home from there was tough, with black townships the hell out of town, but that was part of the story: they were not supposed to know where we came from, nor we where they came from.

Who were we kidding? One of these lads was called Siza, codenamed Julius by Max, nineteen years old and slight of build and come with nothing whatever but a bus ticket from Butterworth in the Transkei, really in the fourth world out there, and without food or access to a toilet or a tap he would hang about when we'd dropped him, for twelve hours, and then another five or six in transit back to the Transkei. We made a bed for him with assorted soft things and a blanket in the Levitan garage, and brought him a great coarse breakfast sandwich with three fried eggs in it, and plenty of pepper, and a mug of tea with plenty of sugar, and took him to the municipal loo for ten minutes with a bog roll and a cake of soap, and dropped him at the lights there with a busfare home, if he knew where to catch it.

We had no time for refinement and etiquette.

So the great night arrives, and the first explosion happens at an electricity sub-station, and Max and I seek to stave off the jitters by cleaning up our premises, trade and domestic. Everything seems to be covered with slithery silvery ammonal: the walls of Meyer Mansions, the junk of Mr Levitan's garage and the inside of the Fiat. We buy feather dusters and dust everything, but all it does is float about a bit and settle somewhere else, mostly inside our noses. Statistics tell me that the inner surface area of my lungs with all their ins and outs and convolutions is that of a football field. Our particular football fields are silver end to end with high velocity explosive. We respire the stuff, and wonder about smoking.

M'lud, the deceased expired not from an internal implosion consequent on an external explosion, but from an internal explosion consequent on an internal detonation consequent on an external ignition.

My home on Mr Meyer's premises is littered all over with silver newspapers. We'd even gone out and bought a dozen or so fresh and fragrant and absorbent straight off the presses, for wiping and soaking this abominated stuff off the entire surface of our habitat. Where the hell were we going to dump it all? That's tomorrow's problem; let's mop it all up first, and see if we can get a reasonable night's sleep before next morning, though of course by this time the sun is up and down again and it's the next next morning. Come on man, where can life be as controllable as all that?

We're nigh up to window level with silver newspapers when Max says Enough, man, I'm going to catch a good bath and fuck off homewards and the revolution can wait till I've had a good hot soak, and he's off to Mr Meyer's all-white-tiled bathroom and fills up the bath nice and deep and hot and sudsy and submerges himself in it. He's a very black sort of Black, and in the bath there he reminds me of the British working class who keep their coal in the bath as soon as you give them half a chance to be civilized, and his teeth are of the same glaze as the surrounding tiles and the basin and the lavatory cistern.

These teeth he displays as he parts his lips and launches forth with O Saw ye not My Lady? in his luscious baritone, and he really lathers up his body and face with Lux toilet soap as used by female film stars so that most of these Pre-Raphaelite words come only as a sort of gurgle through the foam.

Thanks for the towel, he calls, as he chucks it towards the laundry basket, I'll see you when I've caught a good kip, and he's off! I quite like the personal silent privacy which follows, and decide to have the day off myself, for God's sake Max and I deserve it, and I run myself a bath as full and sudsy and smug as that of Max and strip off all my threads and stick my big toe into this lot to see if it's hot and soothing enough, and as I do this thing I hear a dreadful violent hammering and shouting out loud at the locked front door of Mr Meyer's mansions, and I withdraw my big toe from the bath and nip all naked over to the window and peer out, and there I see a trio of really ugly men who will become my closest associates in the nearest future.

If I'd had that bath it would have been my last for many a year, but I didn't have it. I didn't even dry my foot, but flung on once again my filthy reeking sweaty silver shirt and shorts and off barefoot to the back door and the gate of the back yard, which I slinkily unlatch and start to slink out.

O my Here, daar staan die Law! A heavy man with blond hair and blinking eyes is standing there, and he fixes the muzzle of a great nine millimetre Browning FN Parabellum pistol to the end of my nose and ostentatiously releases the safety catch, and pushes me back by the nose the way I've just come, saying Make one move and I'll blow your bliksems face off.

Oh I'm not moving, I reply.

His two colleagues come pounding round the corner, one of them Erasmus van Vuurwapen, the smoking police chauffeur, the other an anthropomorph of the species Agricola robustus in a safari suit, name of Jordaan van den Gruweldaad, who has strapped to his gluteus medius dexter a firearm in compliance with regulations, but scarce needs it because he has in his hands a Kung Fu device of hardwood batons and connecting chain, which apparatus is just coming into fashion amongst men of enormous muscle and small cock.

Eight

SO SIZA ALIAS JULIUS HAD GONE straight and eager back to the Butterworth General Dealer for a plastic jerrycan and a piece of pipe, and got all the apparatus dead right because he was an intelligent youth, and went straight to the only chemist shop in Butterworth and bought his necessary ingredients there okay, but there's no beach sand at Butterworth, so he used coarse sugar instead, then went to the only filling station in Butterworth and filled the jerrycan to the brim and submerged the timer, sugar and all, in the petrol and climbed through a window which he'd forced open at the magistrate's court in Butterworth, leaving plenty of fingerprints all over, and parked this thing under a clerk's table where he'd been insulted a month before, and that's where they found it in the morning.

The Tontons Macoutes of the Transkei were known as the White Sheets, an image as sinister, any day, as that of the black felt hats and black suits and the steel-rimmed black shades of the Haitians.

Never in Sunny South Africa nor in Smiley Transkei nor Happy Ol' Haiti did one need all that corny verbiage about You have the Right to Remain Silent, as in the L.A. Police Department movies, themselves thought too brutal for our youth to see. These ghostly gents took off Siza forthwith and roped him up spreadeagle to the enormous wheel of a roadworking vehicle, and tied the steering of that vehicle on full lock with another rope, and started her up and released the clutch and left her running round and round on her own track on a football field, with Siza attached, while they went off to tea.

I don't suppose one should be too delicate about this; after all, they were only giving him what Hector got, but using available technology. I mean there weren't any chariots around.

Mind you, Hector had been dead.

After tea they gave him a free lift back to the Bay and Major Op't Boud, the person with the white hair and blinking eyes. Major Op't Boud also had a loud voice and a habit of shouting at people. SHOUTING VERY LOUDLY, that is. VERY.

The trouble with Major Op't Boud's eyes was that they didn't blink synchronously. If you waited a bit you would catch a point at which they both blinked together; then you could try to work out a cycle at which they would once again coincide, but it was mathematically very advanced, because in between there would be left blink right blink, left left right left, right right left right, and then the whole statistical system would fall apart because they would suddenly go random like three blinks of the left eye to one of the right, or vice versa, or anything, before suddenly going systematic again and coinciding.

The left side of his brain wasn't connected to the right. The artistic faculties necessary for his rôle in the Security Branch were disconnected from his rational mind, and each side had its eye.

Or something.

It needed concentration.

Well were they? asks Major Op't Boud. Hmmm? I reply, and as true as God I'm not being evasive, I've just been watching his eyes, that's all. Nee, slaan my dronk, he yells to Warrant Officer Rassie van Vuurwapen, hierdie bliksem is mos bliksems mal, man! CAN'T YOU BLIKSEMS HEAR ME, MAN?, shouting like an Englishman asking his way to Thomas Cook's in Paris of a frog-eating foreign fiend who can't understand normal language. Ja, I say, would you just repeat the question, perhaps?

Vuurwapen and Gruweldaad have both of them the coarse bone-smashing hands of assaulters, heavy and calloused, and I notice that Rassie's right is abraded around the knuckles, with some fresh scabs forming there, like he's been about his employment recently, and it occurs to me I'd better start concentrating on the Major's words and leave his eyes alone if I don't want to get what's left over from Rassie's last guest. Maybe Siza.

It wouldn't be a bad idea, though, to leave alone and undisturbed also the notion that I am mentally disadvantaged, which could come in handy if I need a moment or two to think of explanations for things in the foreseeable future.

Well, anyway, the White Sheets hadn't tried at all to get any recorded and signed confession from Siza, because they were in the main too dumb to know what to ask for, but also because much of his blood was deposited in a neat circle on the sand of the soccer field and he was now unconscious, incidentally not dead because the veins and arteries to the hand run through the carpal tunnel at the wrist, there by evolution performing the vital function of maintaining circulation even though the bones of the wrist are exposed by the slashing of predators' teeth or tying to rubber tyres with polypropylene rope. His ankles were somewhat protected by canvas ankle tekkies and the denim cotton of his jeans.

But they'd pulped and softened him up enough, as one did with an orange as a kid by chucking it against a wall for a while, and it would be easy for the South African SB to squeeze the juice out of him now.

Also, of course, it was a bit urgent to get him to some sort of hospital if he was going to be useful as a state witness, before sepsis and gangrene set in from cowshit and stuff falling into the wounds from the tread of the great tyres of the road grader, and the natural goggas found on dirty ropes, and killed him before he could come to court.

I don't mean that his conscious moments in hospital were all that lucid, and if they were a little bit lucid from time to time they certainly were not happy in their expectation of improved health. Part of Rassie's job was the assessment of lucidity. If he deemed Siza lucid enough it was Rassie's job, nay moral duty, to ask him for certain names and addresses and intentions, and if they didn't come now, now, to smash him back into unconsciousness in his hospital bed with this great bone of a fist, and come back tomorrow. Thus the scabs.

Rassie was not a handsome man. He was very tall and rangy, with a very large red and ginger face featuring a nose upon which his dentist appeared to have placed his foot for leverage while pulling Rassie's teeth out, assuming of course it was a dentist who had done the repair job in there, which was seriously doubtful, for Rassie spent his every moment, except when actually eating, or sleeping I suppose, clicking and clanking between his gums a great pair of dentures, to get them into some tolerable placement, so that he could concentrate better on his duties, like wondering if Siza would be awake for supper this evening or would perhaps like just to continue with his peaceful sleep.

This constant motion of the mandible gave an appearance of his chewing the cud whilst thinking, except of course the brittle rattling sound was not in keeping with the calm of rumination.

Sepsis and unconsciousness are two separate medical conditions. You can be unconscious and your body still healing up. Ready for court. So maybe Rassie was ruminating about that.

Well of course the first names Siza had given him were ours: Govan's, Max's and mine, and bloody stupid not to. If your ideologically-tactically advanced-genius political leaders haven't taken into account your desire to continue living they've read their scriptures all wrong, or maybe they should dump their present scriptures and get some new ones or get back to the old ones they started with. It might do a few I can think of a bit of good next time to have a crack at the practical side, and a turn at being victim.

Slim, maybe.

At his second return to consciousness Siza managed to remember another place, but it was difficult to be precise in his present confused mental state so, Rassie being a man of understanding in these things, Siza was allowed to fall asleep in the biological way just for a change, and produce whatever, whatsoever, useful information about anything whatsoever the next day, and when the transcription typiste had got it all neat and fair on a sheet of foolscap, to sign it.

Of course he didn't know the address of Mr Levitan's garage. I never knew it myself. I dare say Mr Levitan didn't either. Rassie was sensitive to human nature and human memory, of course, and there's no point in being inhumane. Not to allow one to summon up remembrance of things past to the sessions of sweet silent thought is only to kak on one's own ondersoek, and Siza had thus an entire hour at least to be driven about Die Baai, smoking free fags, until certain triggering clues were there and voila! Mr Levitan's garage!

So it was that Siza scored a second night of biological sleep.

The koevoet is a great invention: a cow's foot, a split hoof there at the end of its shaft of steel. Also it's a cobra reared up with its double tongue, a crowbar, one of the road tools of every police vehicle. Chopchop they had the garage open, for evidence of Siza's having slept there, I mean blankets and the like, but when they saw Mr Levitan's electronics they took Siza straight back to his hospital bed and put an armed guard on it and one on the garage too, while they assembled a panel of police technologists and top theoretical physicists, to sift through this stuff.

You must remember, this was only four years after Sputnik, which deflated in one day all Western arrogance, especially that of NASA, and extra-especially the CIA and their sub rosa chums in the South African intelligence system.

Thus it was that Siza scored a third night of biological sleep.

I can't say I myself scored many nights of any sort of sleep in the next week or two before being moved to Die Rooi Hel, though not because of the attentions of Rassie or Jorrie. I was lodged in a police cell with a certain convocation of politic Marxist bedbugs, who quickly arranged between themselves and myself a redistribution of blood cells, so that by the end of that time my body mass had halved and theirs had doubled. Your bedbug is your only emperor for diet: they were e'en at Mr Levitan, down the row at the PE police cells here.

I had read of techniques used by the Portuguese security police for the extraction of evidence which were very subtle compared to those of our jollie kêrels hierso, who saw it as essentially the same thing as the extraction of teeth. These PIDEs would stick one in a cell with great fluorescent lights, regularly spaced about, and all walls, plus floor and ceiling, painted in complementary colours of exactly the same tone – yellow/mauve, red/green or blue/orange, and all in squares of exactly the same size, so that the open eye could settle nowhere; then they'd divide the day up into three exact periods of eight hours and feed you then, punctually, with identical meals. No starvation, because you can steel yourself to that; this thing was in the head. With the big lights going all the time one might have calculated after a month that it was midnight, and be deep in sleep, the deepest, when the door would open and one would be off to interrogation out of doors, and it would be the midday, in broad Portuguese sunlight. All had been in silence, hey? Not now during the interrogation, naturally, where you made plenty of noise by way of talking, after you'd finished weeping, of course.

The traditional technique of our lads here, was just progressively to smash up your bones until you concluded you'd better talk fairly soon while you still had a few whole ones left.

But if any of you up-and-coming young party enthusiasts in our new future find yourselves in the latter-day VOPOs, the new Volkspolizei, which God forbid, and you want to get stuff soonest out of Peoples' Traitors, lock 'em up with a team of specially hungered bedbugs. A week would just about see you right, if you're not in a hurry. That bit about redskins or was it Arabs smearing you all over with honey and pegging you out in the desert so the ants could come and eat you alive while you stared about at the sky all crazy hoping death would come soon, that's for the comic books, man.

Well Op't Boud wasn't in too much of a hurry, because all explosions had stopped, and Siza had to get healed up a bit, and maybe even fattened up a bit with some porridge, before his appearance in court, and mainly of course in the Levitan garage over there the really heavy cold-war rooi-gevaar technology behind our attempted putsch had to be analysed and understood, and built into the fundament of an important impending trial, perhaps international.

If it weren't for the fact that the Security Police have been disbanded since those days, and the Soviet spy system collapsed, I should honestly believe our kêrels were still at it, there was so much of it, up to the roof as I've described, and curiously assorted, and not a single clue to any rational use of any single item. Mr Levitan didn't even understand the questions. He thought Op't Boud was mad. Op't Boud thought I was mad, and I thought Mr Levitan was mad.

Anyway, one thing everybody understood: they found the Fiat in the garage, and Mr Levitan personally understood one thing eagerly enough after a few nights with his own squad of cranked-up bedbugs, as I say, a few cells down the corridor, and agreed forthwith to give state's evidence, and to say whatever the police wanted him to say, after a bit of rehearsal. I mean they didn't have to give him any orange treatment and hurl him against the wall. So within a few days he was back in the sunshine wondering at the strange random nature of the universe, explained in physics these days as Chaos Systems, and what in Heaven's Name had made him put that innocent classified advertisement in the *Eastern Province Herald?*

So the next week or two they spent on sort of probing about and establishing that system one reads of, where another specially cranked-up team, this time not of bugs but of boere, really give you hell and harrass you, mainly mentally, without particularly asking for confession, until the Good Cop appears and gives you cups of tea and fags when you've been without, and chides the brutes for the insensitivity of their behaviour.

Op't Boud thus sits and bawls inartistically, but can't resist during the spells in between whilst he's drinking a cup of coffee without offering me any but stuff him anyway, to tell me that he's related to Queen Wilhelmina of the Netherlands, and his name is noble even if in all modesty he must stress that the relationship is remote, and I'd better bear in mind whom I'm talking to here, and I ask in my lunatic way what that means if Holland is a social democracy and would get along just fine without a queen, and at this he gets so bloody enraged he has to go off for a pee, bellowing that if I try that sort of insolence again he'll invite v.d. Gruweldaad to hit me in the face when he Op't Boud gets back from the lav.

From the caves beneath the thick, dense skin of his brow like the sole of a ricksha puller's foot, with hairs on it, ou Jorrie looks out at the world as one looks at the TV cosmetics ads of ladies taking a shower behind arctic glass; puzzled, and a bit curious like, about the detail and the intricacy of it all. Though, to be fair, maybe he just needs specs but can't wear such poofter stuff because it doesn't really go with the Kung Fu ninja artefacts he carries about his person; little shaving-sharp steel stars for hurling at folks, that sort of thing, you know. I do get anxious, then, I must confess, lest he just perhaps construe his senior's threat as an order. But I'm saved by ou Rassie, who says while Op't Boud is in the bog that all that Queen Wilhelmina stuff's boggerol, man, and kak; he, Rassie, is descended from Desiderius himself, otherwise why the hell is he called Erasmus? Jorrie says he can break bricks in half with his hands.

There's a lot of competition going on within this band of brothers.

I'm not going to give you any phoney chutzpah at this point, dear reader, of how I was able to exploit this competition. I wasn't able to, didn't even think of trying to. I was poep-scared man, with no idea of where I might end up. If I became anything, apart from imbecile, it was obsequious. Hey Mr van Vuurwapen, I say, I wasn't trying to be astrant, honest, I just want to know how it all works with the Dutch, that is, sorry, the Netherlanders.

Op't Boud's problem was that he already had the accused he wanted. Certainly the details had to be filled in, to get maximum sentence at trial, and other accused might crop up, which would be a bonus, but no need to rush anything with the supporting circumstantial evidence he had, and the signed statement coming from Siza and a few others who would fall into the net, never worry.

So we go through the softening-up harrassment programme anyway, but I don't let on I'm not suffering really from the deprivation of fags, though one would be nice just now. I gave them up when I was at school, with all the related agony, and now know from that experience a sort of mental technique, a trick, of defining myself as a non-smoker.

Also I've dodged the bedbugs by sleeping on a narrow wooden bench bolted to the wall of the cell opposite the bed; one shoulder hangs over the edge, but I turn end-to-end in the night and give the off-side shoulder a turn.

I can't honestly say, though, why they didn't thump up Govan and Max and myself. They'd done it to plenty of people just to find out about organisations of protest. Just for the sport of it, at times. Looking back, I think this thing was just too monstrously improbable to be guessed at. As I said, they were as dumb as we were. Whatever those reasons, for my part I played silly artist. Maybe that's what I am, and that's why I found the act so easy. I don't know what the other two did, I didn't see them at all before we went for trial, but we all three managed to remain silent until outside pressure was such that they had to allow us access to lawyers, who told us to shut up, and this was official, from officers of the court, attorneys.

This was before the days of the Internal Security Act, of course, which allowed no access to anybody at all, ever, not even God if you were dying and in need of a priest, for as long as they chose. One had the choice of silence back in the time I'm talking of here; well, theoretically and legally, anyway, though in practice increasingly unlikely. Ask Siza, maybe he's around somewhere.

But we go through the daily grind anyway in this miserable grey gloss-enamel-painted police office, with Vuurwapen and Gruweldaad balancing on the hind legs of their varnished meranti government chairs against the wall, and cracking their knuckles, and Op't Boud hammering and yelling away at wide-open directionless questions, until suddenly in the middle of it all one day they all fall silent and jump to attention, excepting Op't Boud, that is, who gets up slowly and at ease because he's staff rank, and stands only as a matter of etiquette. I notice though that his voice is now quiet; the good cop has entered the room, about time too, and he's a full colonel, a Kolonel.

He sits down wearily and sighs and looks at his feet. There is total silence as he sighs, and the two warrant officers look embarrassed because big rank is sighing. After a bit he raises his sorrowful eyes and asks Have you got everything you need? and smiles sadly at me. Cigarettes? No? WHAT! He's in such haste his hand trembles as he takes ou Rassie's personal packet and hands it to me, bestowing an outraged fix-you-later-my-boy scowl on that former owner. Keep them! he exclaims, as if that's just the first taste of punishment for Rassie.

I wouldn't mind a can of insecticide for the bugs, I observe, reluctantly leaving off breathing on the fag to pronounce these words. There and then he sends off Jorrie for an aerosol of Doom, with money from his own personal Kolonelial pocket.

He has come a long way, and fast, through the police ranks of the Security Branch. Because he was of mature age, and earning a good salary in Bantu Administration, and had a degree in something, he started his career here straight away but six years ago as Warrant Officer Gribinis. This he tells me on a later visit when we're all alone, just the two of us in our new private and nice personal one-to-one companionship, that's how I know. It's intimate one-graduate-to-another stuff that he's established, and he confides many a confidence with me, about the poor intellect of your average Boer.

He hasn't had time to do background stuff, poor fellow, such are the pressures of the revolutionary moment, stuff which might have revealed to him the fact that I myself am a Boer, via my Oupa Van, and those bits left over from being a Boer are straight first generation Scots, and that's a good combination for the recognition of tyranny when you see it.

I wondered about something indefinable at the time, and couldn't quite put my finger on it, but was able to many years later when I saw a nail-biting movie about the Boston Strangler who was Rod Steiger and George Segal who was the detective, and George Segal's generally anxious old mama, who's just so particularly anxious about her boy, wrings her hands as he sets out with his revolver to trap this ogre, and asks Who ever heard of a Jewish cop?

I suppose one gets in the habit of seeing Jewish history as persecution.

So what's this suave spiv doing in the SA Geheimestaatspolizei?

Okay, I admit it; I've enjoyed being sarcastic about this worthless bastard, and showing myself a wee bit full of confidence and in control of the situation. But the fact of the matter is that he wasn't stupid, and maybe he had all those refined Jewish sensibilities agoing, however vile his personal life, or something, for the fact is, he scored a bullseye on my soft spot as cunningly as anybody ever has, before or since, and beautifully timed too. In the middle of all the bollocks about cigarettes and cups of tea and smiles all round he turns to the door and stands up like a gentleman and says Oh yes, do come in, and in comes Jess with my nice new baby but six days old, and Kolonel Gribinis smiles like he can't help smiling at babies and says to Jess: Do sit down, Jess, and to me: wouldn't you like to hold your daughter? He knew it was a daughter before I did.

I mean, FUUUCK!

I mean this guy has it all worked out. I take this child in my arms and ask What did you decide to call her, eventually? Susan, replies Kol Gribinis, and I know at that point what he's about in his game of ascendancy, because he's made this clumsy mistake.

Susan is all redolent of mother's milk and Johnson's Baby Powder and the natural aromas that come off small creatures: puppy dogs and kittens and little chickens. She's done up in shawls and all the usual baby wrappings, but I dump most of them and take her in my arms naked and plump and delicate beyond belief and floppy and helpless, but don't believe the helpless bit too much, the way those primate eyes are moving about, learning by the minute. I can't believe anything can be so cuddly, and yet so smart, and I give myself a minute, roughly, to wonder at all this, and love it all, and then say to Jess: Smells a bit, doesn't it? I hand Susie back to her and look at Von Gribinis and ask him if he has a match for this stompie, and maybe further fags, since mine from Van Vuurwapen have now run out. He turns to call for fags and I give Jess a quick sign with the head to leave.

Gribinis is a bit confused at her sudden departure, perhaps he had further manipulations in mind, but if her lift is waiting there can be no dissuasion, it would be ungentlemanly of the Good Cop.

Van Vuurwapen and v.d. Gruweldaad come back in and sway on their meranti chairs again, and crack their knuckles. We're all sitting in silence round the table, except for the creaking of bony hands and furniture, and the stirring flamenco rhythms of ou Rassie's castanets.

I get out a fag and Gribinis makes haste with a match, leaning forward to light it, nice timing again, for in the middle of this friendly smiling gesture he looks straight into my eyes and says We know about Annie.

Who? I respond reflexively.

We know you been having candlestine meetings with him, interjects ou Rassie. Hell, I say, with a name like that he must be a Jew. Ja! blurts out ou Jorrie, they all bloody Jews! Gribinis droops his eyelids about forty per cent and slowly turns his head towards ou Jorrie and puts the ice on him straight. Jorrie slowly gets all four legs of his government chair on the floor and goes pink. I mean this bugger's a Russian, he says, jammer Kolonel, I just got the wrong word there, my English isn't so good.

It wouldn't have done any harm to say I knew Plumbin. It also hadn't done any not to, of course, because at some future time they'd argue on the precedent of having talked once why shouldn't I talk again, and it must be for some guilty reason that I'm not talking again. Colonel Gribinis, I say, very politely, because I have this feeling he just might turn his dogs here loose on me, or rather get Op't Boud to do it, who isn't the nice cop, Colonel Gribinis, you will appreciate, I'm sure, that one must obey one's attorney when about to face trial, and mine, Mr Silber, has told me strictly to answer NO question, whatsoever. But sorry to appear so uncooperative. No no no, he says, I wasn't asking a question, I was just telling you I know.

Mazeltov, I say, with an unctuous smile.

Nine

I'M OFF TO DIE ROOI HEL AT this point, Port Elizabeth Prison, called the redhell because in his search for total regularity, and with so much free labour about, some aesthete on the staff there at some time got every singlebrick inside the place individually painted an identical earth red; a lurid burnt sienna like the planet Mars. Later another anal artist got all the mortar between the bricks separately painted white. It's a big boep, three storeys high, and the visual effect is beyond description.

Let me then describe instead my enlistment and accommodation here. In the reception office a sneering youth of proportion suitable to such occupation holds by his ankles a small inverted man, a boesman, who turned out four years later to be one Jafta Fortuin. The reason he turned out to be such at that point of time was that it was then I wrote in a newspaper about this and other jollities of Die Rooi Hel, and got eighteen months for it, and it transpired at the trial that this Jafta Fortuin boesman had escaped from a working party, and was now being welcomed home.

Anyway, the interesting part of this welcome is that Jafta Fortuin is stark naked in an icy winter draught with his head in a bucket of brown water that a bantoe prisoner there is using for cleaning the office floor. Not that the condition of the water is of any interest to Jafta Fortuin, whose immediate problem is that he's drowning upside-down and vomiting at the same time, since this bantoe prisoner belonging to Warder Botha holding the ankles there has just slammed him in the guts whilst upside-down, with a great Jorrie-type fist, and is now supervising the management of his underwater head, to see that he doesn't instinctively jerk it out of the bucket for a quick illicit breath.

Slammed him a few times, that is, of course.

The bantoe retrieves his mop and stands there with it in his hand. He doesn't look appalled or guilty or anything, he doesn't give a damn, because he's just straight criminal himself and in most of his life has been about mindless violence anyway.

Warder Botha has a more entertaining notion. He lifts his boesman from the bucket and deposits him upon the floor. He takes from the cleaner the mop, delivers the boesman a kick around the kidneys to get him up and about, and places the mop in his hands, because we are now going to have parade-ground drill. Jafta Fortuin must now march up and down bollocks-naked with the mop over his shoulder to the commands of Warder Botha, you know; leeft turn, riiight turn, all that side-splitting stuff from our merry militarist culture of countless Kaffir Wars, two civil wars, two world wars and a border war. Also Korea. Add what you will to this miserable military mix. Later you can include Vietnam too, vicariously via TV, if you so choose.

Why does a prison warder have to look like a soldier? Why indeed does a bus driver in certain countries? No prize for the answer here. Worldwide you'd think they were at war with the populace. Why don't they wear blue jeans? Blue is peace. Okay, make them black jeans, but get the Schweinerei out of their military caps and shiny leather boots and badges of rank.

Samblief, my baas, pleads Jafta Fortuin, samblief. Please, please sir, my master. He's finished.

Vat hom raak! says Warder Botha to the floor cleaner, touch him. The cleaner moves in and takes aim and lands the boesman a forehand klap to the side of his wet head that turns him clean over and slams him against the wall amidst a great spray of dirty water from his hair and face. There is the dull Doef! of bone against concrete. This is a small boesman and a big Xhosa.

Jafta Fortuin marches about naked with blood at his nose, and it's a fucking joke every time he gets the Afrikaans military order wrong and Warder Botha says Vat hom raak!, touch him, and the bantoe cleaner dances in with his hands up and gets the adrenalin going as he lands him a blow from his personal repertoire that Cassius Clay as he was then would have been proud of, for he'd now know how to stun a man with a flat hand, so as to leave no bruise on the living body or corpse.

I don't know whether he lived or died. Four years later when the matter came up in a Durban court his name and the matter of his escape and recapture were there in Prisons Department archives, but no record of his release from prison. I don't think the Department was being secretive, there was no way they could be with all the media publicity focussed on them. They really just didn't know. He had disappeared, maybe he had been disappeared.

Maybe he'd escaped again, alweer gedros?

Who will ever know?

But what the hell. I move into my new premises, a cell five feet wide and eight and a half feet long, work that out metrically on your calculator, with a felt mat a centimetre i.e. half an inch thick and and an army blanket, for sleeping, and a small cylindrical galvanised iron pot the size of a paint can for defecation. Also there's a galvanised lid for this pot. Oh ja, also a big tin mug full of water. That's it. No outside window. The one on the corridor is seven feet up and has half-inch steel mesh attached to the bars. I do have a forty-watt electric bulb for light during the day, though. As Spike Milligan said, when you switched it on the cell got darker. I didn't, couldn't, switch it on or off of course; the switch was in the corridor. Allow a prisoner a switch, and he'll use it to his advantage. Maybe he'll find a way to light tobacco with it, maybe he'll kill himself, who knows which is the worse?

In the morning before porridge time at six I come out to walk round and round a little courtyard ten paces square for some twenty or so minutes, and look at the sky and hope a nice cloud will come over and catch the early light. I empty the shit pot and fill the water mug and catch a cold winter shower.

I sit on the felt mat for four and a half months, solo; sometimes I sleep on it. Sometimes I stand up. No bugs here; the surface of everything inside the cell is misty white with DDT, whilst outside in the little exercise yard and shouse everything is sloshed all over once a week with bucketfuls of Jeyes Fluid.

Sometimes I am taken off to court, and I really get to look forward to this, because I know I'm down the drain anyway, and it's interesting to see how the drama develops, and what sort of show our defence team can put on. Max and Govan are accused numbers two and three. Our defence team are Harold Halton QC, Advocate Arthur Allbright and Solly Silber, Attorney. We are as yet busy with a preparatory examination, conducted by a magistrate whose name I forget.

At night the slams and groans of assault give way to the screams of rape, but you get used to it, it's like living next to the railway in London, which I once did; a train would come clanking and hammering into Waterloo every few minutes, but I heard none of it, day or night, after a bit. These were just the sounds of urban nature.

Supper was at four in Die Rooi Hel, and one supper-time at the end of these four-and-a-half months when my belly is getting a bit rumbly for my piece of badly shaved boiled pig with hot fat from the boiling poured over a mound of boiled cabbage, suddenly I hear irregularities to the second-by-second predictability of the day, and my door opens and there stands a foreign screw from another section. I get very insecure at such gross novelty, and when he says Trek aan jou baadjie, kom, I'm really afraid I'm going to miss my delicacies, and I say to him, Nee, man, wat van my aandete? Never maaind, he says, you'll get food, and I go out full of wonder, because nobody except the staff ever leaves a prison at this time of day, late afternoon, almost early evening you might say. It seems unnatural, and naughty, and adventurous.

There in Reception stand our cheery trio, all strapped about with weaponry. Ja ou Djok, says Op't Boud, we are teiking you to Durban to traai you for Riotous Assembly. Your warf too.

Make a change, I think cynically to myself. What pissy extra bit of extra sentence can that add to what I've got coming? The journey will be a holiday. We will be travelling at night because nobody would expect that, I calculate, and there would be no rescue roadblocks. By what hysterical fantasy did they think there ever could be, with our organisation?

It is the same risible inline Chev that pursued me in vain along the Uitenhage road. Erasmus is driving and smoking again, and the Major sits in front with him. Ou Jorrie puts me in the back and takes the belt from his broek and straps it about the doorpost on this port side so the door can't be desperately flung open for baling out. I sit and wonder how the hell he pictured my doing this with handcuffs and leg-irons, which allow you a pace of ten inches. He moves around to starboard and climbs in holding up his trousers. He wears his howitzer in a shoulder-holster, but doesn't cover it with a jacket. It makes him look real sinister, American-style. I mean he would look sinister if he didn't have to hold up his trousers.

Hell it's nice to see a world that isn't painted with grey enamel or made of varnished meranti, and to see it in perspective again, in depth. It's nice to smell things other than sheep-dip. Christ help the poor bloody insect that settles on me. I am powdered all over with DDT like the wig of Louis XIV with talcum.

After a bit I say to Jorrie: Nee man, I say, in boep graze is at four o'clock, and I see on your watch there it's now five, and I'm fucken hungry. Hel no, says Jorrie, you can't have supper at five o'clock, man, nobody does, and don't swear like that, man, the major belongs to the Full Gospel Church of God. Why can't I have supper at five? I ask, I have it at four every day, and I want to say fuck the major and fuck his church and fuck you too, chuck it all in, in a general curse and eschatological blasphemy, Italian-style, a basta per Dio, down with God, the sort of words a renegade modern Roman would paint two metres high on the embankment of the Tiber.

But I don't, because I'm going to enjoy this holiday, and don't want to ruin it with confrontations.

The major says Let him eat, and hands over from the front seat this big square biscuit tin of padkos packed by Mejuffrou Op't Boud, and Jorrie opens it and hands it to me. It's full of boeries and skaap tjops and buttered white rolls and a little tub of Colman's mustard, and I get into this lot with no table manners whatsoever. I eat half of the contents, and as I do so I observe ou Jorrie getting noticeably anxious, and looking like he might make a grab to get the tin back, because this is padkos for four, and by process of long division which he learned at the Voortrekkerskool vir Seuns he is now able to work out that three of them will have to share the remaining half, which means each of them will get one sixth of the padkos instead of a quarter, on account of my gluttony.

I move the blik round to this my port side by the window and lift it up near my mouth, and hunch up my shoulder to protect it until I am finished. I am prepared to bite any hand that comes within range. They will have to blast me with their sidearms to get back this grub.

Anything else? I ask, and there's a terrible uncompanionable silence, because there is indeed something else, and if I can work such depredations on the boerewors, what unimaginable inroads will I make on these koeksusters?

Any coffee? I ask, as I lick from my fingers the syrup from the last of these, all four.

The friendship, as I say, had got a bit diluted, so I found it in order to catch a sound post-prandial kip on this gutful of ware boerekos, lolling back on the Chevy vynide upholstery there in my assorted manacles.

You wouldn't believe it, but there was more to come.

Sort of eight o'clockish, at a guess, we're low in petrol, as estimated, and we're near Kokstad, as calculated, and it is now time to pull in here at the police station, as arranged and appointed, and tank up this vehicle and sign for it all and move on to Durbs, where I will be purposefully locked up solo once again, and the dangerous interim of transit will be safely over.

But there at the police petrol pump stands the Sergeant Station Commander, Kokstad, who himself and his missus have got themselves in a right old tizz of expectation because police brass, plus a newspaper headline political prisoner who is also an artist, are hauling in here for petrol. His right arm is near lame from saluting, because the Security Branch are an élite in the force, hey, and the SB trio are near shooting him from irritation, but I myself am in no hurry to go anywhere as he explains that his wife has tea ready and we must be in need of refreshment after such a long journey.

It is true Afrikaner hospitality, and however odious this our trio here may be, they are deeply embedded in this culture, and they can't say no to its hospitality. Besides, however urgent it may be to get to Durbs and get me shut up again, they've had only one small piece of sausage each, with one roll, for their supper, and they're all three big strong men in need of big nutrition, and maybe there'll be a little cake or two with this tea spread.

Me, I'm all smiles, I'm in no hurry, time is what I've got plenty of, and it's just lovely to be out at night.

Alle wêreld! Such a cake I see again in the furious fantasy of the mind's eye, and salivate as I write these words: a coffee cake, iced around with coffee icing and frillies at the rim in a lighter tone of coffee brown, then the top spread over in white whipped cream and studded all about with glacé cherries and pecan nuts. It stands on a silver pedestal, as indeed it should, and this pedestal is surrounded by plates of small sausage rolls and home-baked biscuits with chocolate topping and walnuts, and a great plate of replacement koeksusters such as Madame O'Bum never got right, koeksusters like hers I wouldn't throw at a dog, and I have regret like the emperor Caligula satiated at a Roman orgy that he consumed so much at the beginning of the feast while better things are now appearing, for me now especially these new koeksusters, so beautiful and golden and crispy and oozing syrup all over and odorous as heaven itself. But maybe they'll cheer up my companions.

I am so busy drooling over these miracles that I fail to notice two small kids standing in their pyjamas and dressing-gowns at the door, a little boy and a girl just a bit bigger.

Afrikaans kids are very polite, as kids should be, and their pappie and mammie are good examples of politeness, and Pappie, because he's so polite, never mind the matter of rank, doesn't want to tell the major, but does with fumbling words, that he doesn't like his innocent kids seeing a friendly polite man like myself all chained up by the legs and hands, nor ugly guns suspended from peoples' bodies, at the table. There's an interesting couple of moments, with eight pairs of eyes darting about and picking up all the nuances of the situation. I know what O'Bum is thinking, because he does sort of telegraph his punches, you know, and what he's thinking is this prisoner's an athlete who knows how to run, but then on the other hand he's an athlete who has had no exercise for five months, so maybe he won't be able to run as fast as a bullet from W/O van Vuurwapen's Walther. In any case, he schemes, all that makes no difference to the problem of these two kids' presence, and even though I am senior in rank to their father, according to family cultural protocol he has ascendancy here, and what about the mother, in God se naam?

I didn't think I could ever see one of these bullyboys helpless nor, especially, embarrassed. Op't Boud is both now, and looks appealingly at me. I cross my heart with my manacled hands and he gestures to Vuurwapen to unlock me, though he clearly hates it.

It occurs to me it may just for now spoil his love of life, even love for these beauteous sisters of cakehood.

We take our seats at the table, and the kids fetch a couple of high stools from the kitchen. They don't speak, because they haven't been spoken to; night-time is grown-ups' time, and they've been allowed to stay up late after their bath for a treat because of the importance of the occasion, and the cake, of course, which has been an afternoon's hushed ceremonial creation.

It seems to me that tea would be out of place with this cake, and anyway if this woman can make a cake like this with coffee, what sort of coffee will she make with it? My mind turns on these things, also the notion that I'd better do something about table manners and not behave as I did in the risible Chev, and I've decided to concentrate only on the cake for optimum pleasure, but politely. So I've had my second sociable slice, when I feel something warm at my right elbow, and a small touch there.

I look down and round, and there stands the little girl. We smile. Pappie thê oom ith 'n kunthtenaar? she declares. Ja, dis waar, I say. Thal oom vir my 'n kwagga teken? she asks. Am I an artist, and will I draw her a zebra? Nothing else on the entire earth could make me so happy, I reply. Make a change from eating pigs, or even coffee cakes, I think. Her slippers are a pair of pink rabbits, and she puffs off in these to fetch her autograph book. She puffs back presently, and pages through her trophies: there's a birthday greeting from her headmistress and a Bugs Bunny cartoon copy from the man at the pet shop who is also captain of the Kokstad cricket team. That sort of thing.

I feel, no actually I smell, a soapily perfumed warm presence at my left elbow, and there stands her kleinboet in his wee tiny dressing-gown, his shampooed hair all smartly combed, with a nice straight parting, and already smiling as I turn to look at him, because he knows something nice is about to happen. Without further ado he starts climbing up on my knee, sort of clambering, as you would to get up a tree or on a camel.

V.d. Gruweldaad here doesn't know what the hell to do; am I going to run yelling out of the house that I've got two kids hostage? He reaches reflexively for his pistol, but that's been dumped along with my personal ironmongery on the sideboard: as I say, you don't wear your weapons to the table any more than you do your hat. What the fuck would he do anyway, shoot me in the middle of a tea-party, or maybe Kleinboet here, to stop his mountaineering? I reach down and get an arm round Kleinboet and heave him up on my knee.

Kleinboet hasn't reached the age of shedding teeth, he's just finished growing his pearly new ones, so he doesn't lisp. As Oom klaar is met die kwagga sal Oom vir my 'n errie teken?

This autograph book has a good-sized page, good paper too, and I think Buggered if I'm going to hurry this one, what with the SB crew caught in their cultural trap. I ask for a sharp knife to sharpen the pencil, and the Sergeant unclips his jack-knife from his belt and hands it to me without thinking I'm going to slit his childrens' throats, and I notice the whole thing has become something of a ritual foreign to present company except the kids, and there's no conversation going, and that's okay, it's time I had a bit of power, and I take as much of that time as I need, and draw for this sussie hierso a galloping zebra which might be the best drawing I've ever done in the whole wide world, ever. I know equine anatomy, for I once had a horse; a sort of one, that is. Apart from the kwagga there's a jagluiperd in the background, and I've caught it in full stride, unbelievable in its elegance, like a Hawker Hunter, and the little girl says to her boet Kyk net die cheetah, né?

Man, if ever you want to try true hypnosis, just sit close and quiet by a kid when she's drawing: the concentration of it, the unblinking closely focussed eyes and the breathing suspended to the last moment because these functions might distract, the total removal from this world, and they do something similar when they're watching you do the drawing, so long as you know how to latch them in. It doesn't depend on skill. It's intentness, dedication to the moment. It's really like having someone run fingers through your hair or scratch your back.

Kleinboet hasn't got an autograph book yet, he's too small, so I say to him I'll tell you what, I'll turn Sussie's book upside down so her last page can be your first, and she agrees to this because possession of paper is less important to her just now than the miraculous hypnotic process of a real live kwagga appearing from nowhere, and a jagluiperd too, leaping along in its five-metre strides.

The errie I draw for Kleinboet is a Spitfire Mark IX, probably the most devastatingly brave and beautiful of its line, possibly any line anywhere, and it's in the middle of a victory roll over Tangmere. I write this name on a hangar roof, and though there's an anachronism here because at the time of the Battle of Britain and Tangmere they'd got only as far as Mk V, never mind, Kleinboet wouldn't care, and nor do I, so long as the spirit and the courage are there.

Hoekom vlieg hierdie oom onderstebo? Why does this uncle fly upside-down? Because that's what you do to show people that you're the best.

Ek wil dit ook doen.

Nou ja, dan SAL jy dit mos een dag doen, né?, as jy werklik waar WIL.

Maybe the Spit was better than the zebra or the cheetah. It's hard to say, because the techniques were so different. But I wish I could draw like that all the time.

I don't know why the Major was in such a bloody hurry to get to Durban, nor why he was so bloody irritated by waiting two hours at Kokstad for the eating of cakes and fidgetting about with kids' autograph books. He could have done his arithmetic better. We arrive in Durbs a full hour before Durban Central opened, it is still dark, man, and where to go? Well it isn't exactly still night-time, but about that time when you've got your tackle all set out on the beach and the reel on your rod and you're just putting on that first sardine bait with a feeling of expectation by the paraffin lamp on the sand there, while the surf you know is just right. This you can tell from its subdued thumping though you can't see it. The waves are just the right shape for shad.

We sit in the car. Where must I go, Majoor? asks Rassie.

Go to the Blue Lagoon, I say, enticingly, though neither the Umgeni River mouth nor the Danube was ever blue, but a suspicious toxic brown. O'Bum shrugs.

Here we get a glimpse of the shad sammies about their skills, a moment of great smiles to know that there still exist dedications in the world other than people dedicatedly persecuting each other to death in prisons and police places in the name of righteousness.

I don't mean this holiday was like a week in Paris, nor even like a modest weekend back in the old flat with the new Susie kicking and grasping about and learning the use of limbs and fingers there on the bed while I scratch my legs with my toenails. Enough for me just now, though!

At the Big House, Pretoria Central, if ever you have further charges in Durbs you can get a six-months' supply of tobacco from many an A-group bandiet there with tobacco privilege if you declare him to be a witness, even though you may never have seen him ever in your natural life before. You get him sent at taxpayers' expense to loll about for two weeks amongst the cockroaches and slothful screws here at humid Durban Central, down the bottom end of Pine Street.

You don't actually call him as a witness in court, of course, because you've changed the tactics of your defence by then, and don't need him after all. But it's your legal right, and it's his free holiday, in winter the best.

The cells were big, and so were the cockroaches, and there was sunshine. I was able to see Jess in court, accused number two, and hold her hand in the dock.

So. The court rises, the magistrate nods, the court settles. People take oaths. We get into the matter of our assembly two years ago at this very Durbs Local where I presently reside, and examine the degree of riotousness of our behaviour there.

The prosecutor seeks to establish our rôle as leaders of the band of angry men marching from Cato Manor to bang their Zulu carrying-sticks on the big teak doors of this prison. No, we explain, we weren't leaders, we came out of a painting class at the Durban Tech and saw all these people waving and chanting on their way somewhere and we went along to see, and when a police captain at the prison told all us white spectators to move because there was going to be shooting, we moved in front of the crowd because we thought the presence of a couple of whites might just prevent it.

We'd thought that catharsis might have been reached by the time the remaining hundreds reached the prison. We'd thought the police might just let the thing burn itself out. Maybe that's what happened. But it had been uncomfortable all right.

Yes, but you knew there was a revolutionary situation in the country, did you not, and that you were by your very action presenting yourself as leaders?

No, we weren't, we presented ourselves in defiance of a racist government put in power without due electoral process, and that is not revolutionary. Revolutionary is when you change the class structure of society and seize power in parliament.

Ah! (pouncing) so you're Marxists then! Communists! says the prosecutor. What else would an honest person be in this country? I reply.

I know I'm safe here, because the Suppression of Communism Act doesn't disallow one to be a communist, only the promotion of communism.

We had spoken to nobody, we explained. We'd made no gestures, kept our hands folded. We'd stayed put until the stick-banging had stopped and the wielders had dispersed, then done so ourselves. A wheedling gatkruip sycophant in the provincial government, a dude called Douglas Mitchell, had got his pic in the papers by crying out for our arrest after he'd recognised my marathon blazer in a photograph. If you look at this photograph you will see we have our arms folded, we explain.

So the examination grinds on, and one is so inured to guilt, so used to assuming one is guilty, that we can regard all this as time off, for hand-holding.

The big smile, though, was that we were both acquitted on grounds of an interesting sophistry, which established that whereas we had moved our feet neither inch nor centimetre when ordered by the police to disperse at this riotous assembly, since everybody else had hastened off when the guns came out, and left us alone there, we had dispersed because we had become dispersed. Also, of course, the magie thought we were a bit loony.

Howzat?

No LBW, the ball came from the wrong direction to hit the unbudging leg. The hand with the fatal finger is stuck in the pocket of the white coat.

Many a zealot has told me since then that we had fascism in South Africa, and Yoshke wrote a book called The Fourth Reich, designed, I suspect, to substantiate his megalomaniac belief that he was about to achieve revenge for the third one. Also, I suspect, to justify his taking off when the pace got too hot, though the two don't really seem to go together, in my opinion. But he had a power base over there in the Soviet Union, so he could propound whatever system of political morality, and present whatever phoney bullshit construction he chose, so long it was red and approved by the KGB, like Henry Ford and his black model Ts.

Well, you don't get away with court acrobatics like these in a fascist country. Even a decade or two later, when we had the really heavy stuff in the book, like that Internal Security Act I mentioned a bit back there, even when Biko and Goniwe and Griffiths and Victoria Mxenge were murdered by the régime and the liberal press was in outrage, even then we still didn't have fascism. Fascism isn't about an independent press and judiciary. Fascism isn't about bad laws, fascism is about no laws.

Well not political ones anyway.

Fascism is about Führer decrees, Nacht und Nebel decrees, night and mist, fog, secret murk, so if you went to the corner for a litre of milk and the secret state police, the Geheime Staatspolizei, the Gestapo, didn't like you, you would vanish into this fog unseen, forever, and it was lawful. Most of your mortal remains would go up a chimney at a place where you would become free, since Arbeit Macht Frei, after the gold had been taken from your teeth for spectacle frames, perhaps for Heinrich Himmler eh? and the fat from your body used to make soap for Russian prisoners of war. Of course it would be blended with many other peoples' fat, like inferior blended whisky or vin ordinaire, so nobody could ever protest Hey, wait a minute! That cake of soap you're handing to Ivan over there is made of my Onkel August.

That's the Bittere Gelächte. That's gallows humour. It's either that or weeping. That's fascism. What we had here was a police state.

Uncle Joe was better. He had his own source of gold, and didn't need your teeth. It was also a bit cold for showering in Siberia, so you didn't need his soap.

He just buried your deceased self intact by bulldozer with the rest, in the tundra, the permafrost, deep-frozen so the liberal press maybe one day will see to it that you get dug up with your deep-frozen fingertips so fresh they can take prints off them and identify you and attest that the gold wasn't unlawfully taken from your teeth.

The problem for these scoundrels in government in South Africa was to get round the courts and the capitalists. They never did.

They never got round the trades unions either, nor the press.

Not even Helen Suzman or Dezzie the Toot. What a combination.

Ten

THE BAAI JUDGE TOO THOUGHT I was a bit dippy. He was Mr Justice Zelftevreden. Max also, he thought, but not so much, because he was an ordinary bantu and one expects ordinary bantus to be stupid anyway and easily misled by unscrupulous white maladjusts and black quasi-intellectuals like Govan who'd been a teacher and now ran this deplorable cheap rabble rag.

During the evidence of assorted witnesses of Govan's ken, whom I'd never seen before, and more so during that of Mr Levitan, this judge sat picking his nose in puzzlement, and rolling something up in little balls and dropping them into some container down there, I supposed, for he glanced down with each dropping as if to take aim, then mopping off with his hanky the stray bits left on his moustache. His gaze he shifted back and forth between Govan and Max and me; but it was when Major Op't Boud began his evidence that he started that strange thing that dogs do, that intense staring at O'Bum's face, and tipping and turning his head from this side to that, and cocking alternate ears, trying to get some sense out of the sounds he was hearing.

Maybe it was the O'Bum eyes that made it all difficult. Maybe it was his tendency to shout when he didn't like certain questions put to him.

We all went out to the court lock-up garage to look at the Fiat. Van Vuurwapen's evidence on the use of this vehicle was the most puzzling of all, about our starting a revolution with this old powered pram, which was going to take on the South African Defence Force eventually, after the police. Being thorough in their work, they'd examined everything on the car, as do the diamond detectives of the IDB squad, Illicit Diamond Buying. Exhaust pipes, upholstery, fuel tanks, inner tubes; these are the favourite places. Nothing in the first three, but the last, the tyres!

They'd spent five months arranging the leftist literature first chronologically, then according to political content, then by cryptological cross-reference. Other ways too. Even invisible writing done with onion juice they'd tested for.

Nothing!

That amount of slippery silver stuff had no rational explanation either, for ou Rassie and tjommies hadn't so far read Robert Graves, and nobody thought of testing for explosives. Indeed, to be fair to them, I dare say you won't find one single person of your entire acquaintance who has to this day ever heard of ammonal; it's not even on the Internet. You have to be as desperate as an officer corps on the brink of defeat in a world war to dream up something as agricultural as this. I mean that's how they do it on the farm, man, with nitrate fertiliser.

So then why in the name of reason, if we had needed aluminium powder for the thermite Siza had told them about, should I have it all over the inside of my car, and for that matter all the premises I occupied too? Why not just pour it straight with the iron oxide into the thermite bomb?

Nobody doubted our daft intentions, nor our guilt; there was the silver stuff in the Levitan garage, there it was at the sub-station, and there it was in my flat, stuff nobody had ever seen or heard of before, nor read of in German military histories or that fateful novel.

Nobody doubted these things; it was just that we were so weird.

Well, we three weren't embarrassed by all this, not a bit, not any more, for we'd been through it all with a magistrate in a Preparatory Examination, which was practice in those days, to sort and sift the evidence to be produced in the main trial and save the court's time by leaving out irrelevancies. The only thing we hadn't come to in this the main trial was the evidence of Siza, and he'd been thoroughly cowed and had given exactly the evidence the prosecution wanted in the preparatory examination, following closely the sworn statement he'd made to the Security Branch. As far as we three were concerned, the only trouble with his evidence was that it was all true, only too true.

Here we were then, all three sitting sweating in this stuffy courtroom and trying unobtrusively to loosen our ties a little bit without appearing too much as a trio of ducktails. The time of looking forward to court as a break from prison was long gone; what we wanted now was to get sentenced and have a bit of progress in our lives, however horrid that progress may soon turn out to be. In prison parlance it is called Getting Settled.

Govan has been brought a copy of New Age, and I am idly paging through this down there on my lap where the judge can't see it, wondering whom they've found for a cartoonist now that I'm out of circulation, and bored to stupefaction as the same old evidence drones on and on, a repetition of the prep, when suddenly Max here on my left stiffens. I feel the static coming off him, and turn to look. Jesus! he exclaims, and I follow his eyes to Siza, and start listening to what he's saying. I too say Jesus soon enough when I hear Siza's words, because it's evident that he has been giving some serious and desperate thought to his situation in the dark lonely night hours of solitary confinement.

I suppose it's possible to over-threaten a witness. He may just realise he has something in his possession which is critically, decisively, precious to you, otherwise why are you getting so agitated? The more precious it is to you the better the bargain he can strike. Sure, if he betrays you he'll get what you're menacing him with, maybe his life even, and his life is his choice, but what is the bargain? The bargain is that, if he's pivotal, the kingpin, he can wreck your entire case if he cocks up his evidence, whatever other lesser witnesses may declare. He doesn't have to prove that what he's now saying in contradiction of a sworn statement or preparatory evidence is true. All he has to prove to the judge is that he could be lying now under oath in court, which means by the same token he could equally have been lying in the sworn statement or previously in court in the prep; one or the other must be a lie, and he is a liar.

He has made himself an unreliable witness, and of course any element of doubt must always go to the benefit of the accused. Any attempt by the prosecution to rescue something from his evidence could now only further confuse the issue and make him the more unreliable; even if he goes back and swears now under oath that what he originally swore to was true. It shows how he can chop and change.

I swore to that statement because they beat me! cries Siza in horror at what he's doing. I gave that evidence in the preparatory examination because my memory was bad after the beating, they hit me in the hospital; I don't remember the accused at all!

Mr Justice Zelftevreden believes the police.

Mr Justice Zelftevreden believes IN the police. Siza has neither bruise nor contusion nor scar. He is nicely fattened up with porridge, and his trousers are ironed. Ja, okay, the police say they didn't assault him, and the judge believes them, and Siza knows he will believe them, but that means Siza is a crafty perjurer who can swear to whatever is to his advantage on whatever occasion. Siza gives an alternative version of every single incriminating thing he said in the prep and in his sworn statement to the police.

Evidence in the prep cannot be on the court record as evidence in this trial, of course. Also, as I say, there is now no concealing from the defence what was in the sworn statement, because it all came out in the prep.

Maybe this is why they gave up preparatory examinations shortly thereafter. The prosecution in future would be able to try different tactics with a hostile witness in the main trial if the defence didn't know the contents of a sworn statement.

I don't think Siza was a practical sort of person, so I wasn't just being sarcastic back there when I said Siza was an intelligent young man when he'd ballsed-up at Butterworth. He was that, and shrewd too, and a few other stomach things that some of our bombastic Party orators never came near to being, whatever the content of their personal propaganda. Well, no, not orators actually. They never could distinguish between oratory and declamation.

See that this witness is charged with perjury, instructs the judge to whomever is responsible for charging people with perjury. He makes a note of it in a book.

Accused numbers two and three are acquitted, he states coldly. Max and Govan look at each other in utter disbelief, then leap to their feet in the box and literally run to the door; strange, purely instinctive behaviour.

He turns his eyes on Siza. Get out of my court, he hisses, OUT! GET OUT!

It's not only perjury that Siza is going to be charged with, believe me. But he's got that bargain, though: two for the price of one, and one of the two a top leader in the struggle. Pity it couldn't be three, but my being the lessee of the Levitan garage and the Meyer flat and the owner of the Fiat put that out of reach.

That, for me, is comradeship. Applied comradeship, guts, that is; no verbiage, no posturing, no bullshit.

Siza turns in the witness box and starts for the door in some confusion, because he knows for sure he's not just going to stroll out of here. Gruweldaad ups from his seat amongst the prosecution and strides across and at the door plucks Siza up by his lapels and carries him out thus with his toes just touching the ground, into the corridor, whence we hear a cry of anguish and dread as he sets off for the next phase of his personal ordeal.

Starters.

If I'd researched this thing properly I'd have been able to tell you what happened to Siza. Well, I'm slapgat by nature, and my excuse is that I'm not an historian. I have heard from one source that he got eighteen months for perjury, that's likely, and from another that he was settled for six years on the precedent of the sentence which I shortly picked up, and both are probably true. One thing I do know is that he was reinstated in the ANC, probably a wiser not-so-young man any more, and that's enough research for me.

Ja. Govan and Max came back shortly and made their way to the public gallery, looking at me a bit sheepishly, because they hadn't shaken my hand in farewell, I suppose, nor said Good Luck. Never to worry. We'll say Hulloes soon enough when the struggle's won. What do we need Farewells and Good Lucks for? I wink an eye at them.

I suppose they were a hundred metres away when Siza came out of court to start his jolly journey home to his security police accommodation. I reckon Govan would have done something if he'd been around and seen Jorrie at work on Siza. But what?

I am charged under the Explosives Act, not political legislation, but the best available at present for the prosecution. It carries a maximun penalty of twelve years, and I can see no reason why I should not get this, since I am at least a hundred per cent guilty. Zelftevreden takes out his hanky again and mops up the sweat of his brow with it this time, then breathes on his specs and polishes them with this hanky. I wonder how he can see anything at all through those lenses, what with the new sweat and the old snot smeared all over. Harrumph, he says, and launches into a long diatribe first against the political left, then against the irresponsibilities of the inhabitants of the Art World, wherever that may be. He blathers on for ten minutes, stops, riffles papers, and says Now we come to the accused. That's me, and my heart just sinks, because I inhabit both these reprehensible places, and serve me right whatever stretch I get.

I am going to make an example of the accused, he declares, I am going to demonstrate to romantic artists that they cannot just take the law into their own hands. Just so lucky I didn't give evidence; he'd have found something other than Romanticism about. Well, he babbles on about a lot of other moral stuff besides, but that's the gist of it, and enough too; if my heart was sinking before it is now hit below the water-line and on its way down. It's goodbye, adieu, adios amigo, go with God ou pellie ekse, and next time I see my daughter she will be twelve years old with little titties.

I sentence the accused to six years' imprisonment, he states, and I start to smile on the inside of my face because this must be Christmastime in May, and as I'm busy controlling this smile for fear of irritating the judge, I realise that he's saying even more astounding things, such as Half of which I suspend for five years after the release of the accused from prison. I can really smile on the outside now, because sentence is passed, and I do. Thanks, pal, you old pampoen, I think. Thank you, M'lud, I say.

All stand, he leaves the court, and Op't Boud stomps enraged and red-faced to the door followed by Rassie. Out in the passage we can hear him storming and cursing for a full five minutes.

So I'm down to the Grille now, as it is known to the criminal population, that holding cage beneath the court from which accused without bail rise into their box, so that they never have to walk about corridors and places, and can't make desperate bids for escape amongst the public. As this grille slams and echoes shut and keys clink and clatter about I see there, on one of the benches bolted to the wall, a certain Elston Greenbough, King of the Ducktails, Port Elizabeth. I've been in the grille with him before.

Howzit Elston? I ask, have you been settled? Ja, he says, and you? Ja, what'd you get, man? Twenty, says Elston, and you? No, I got lucky, I picked up only six, man, and half of it suspended, the judge was a doos. Shit, says Elston, I had bad luck, my fucker was fucken waais, man. Jis 't was my betlak dag vandag!

It's just the two of us in there so far, we're the first from the courts. His was a straight case and his judge had given himself a weekend to think about sentence in amongst his golf and stuff, and all he had had to do today was say the words. My case was shorter than expected, of course, thanks to Siza, so I'm out early. I'm busy trying to find a bit of sincere consolation for ou Elston without being too smug myself when everything clangs open and shut again and a bloke in a wrinkled suit and loose tie enters and sits down next to me and wrings his hands and sighs.

Woe, oh woe! Woe woe woe is me! he sighs, my future is but a meaningless mockery, my life in shreds, a mere fiasco! What can I say to my wife when she comes to pay my fine? Furthermore, what am I going to do about the board meeting at head office? This being Monday, I am supposed to be there at nine, and it's now twelve, and I've slept in my suit and by the time I have got home and showered and shaved and dabbed camomile on the places where the bedbugs have fed on me it will be Tuesday, O tragic fool and worthless trash that I have turned out to be! Woe is me!

What was the charge? I ask this criminal. O disaster, he replies, woe! I ran through this red light and as Fortune would have it, who appears to hate me, a police vehicle was behind me at the robot, on its way to a road-block, and when they stopped me other side of the lights they decided I was intoxicated and put me in a cell, all night, with no pyjamas, and my car is now impounded and my wife must come and fetch me in her own car and pay my fine for the red light and O what on earth can I say to her, she who has always held me in such regard, and high esteem?

Yes, I take your point, I answer.

Steek her up lekker, says Elston, and she'll be okay.

Ah-h-h-h, woe, he sighs, after a longish silence during which he stares at his wrung knuckles. He pushes a tousled lock back from his brow: Have you been sentenced? he asks. Yup! I say. What for? he asks, because he needs empathy in this bitter world. Conspiring to cause explosions in a public place, I reply. EEK! he says, and backs away from me down the bench until his reversing backside touches the hip of Elston Greenbough. He turns around; Sorry, he says, what are you sentenced for? Murder, says Elston.

How do they spell it in the comics again? AAAAAUGH! I think. Anyway, that's what he says, and takes himself off to the bench bolted to the opposite wall.

Cannibalism too, says Elston. I et a ou. Wrinkled Suit slides his clenched hands along the government meranti bench until his bowed forehead touches the wood.

So what happened? I ask Elston. No, I taught this bastard a lesson not to fuck my wife, says he. For Chrissake, Elston, how has he learned a lesson if he's dead? Ja, replies Elston, that's what the judge said, God hy was waais daai ou! W.S. shudders there until his missus arrives and pays his fine. We can see her way over there between the government office furniture. Jis! I smaak to fuck her myself, says Elston, illogically enough.

Wrinkled Suit groans.

Illogically enough I'm not put back into solitary at the Rooi Hel. I was too dangerous a political presence to live with corruptible criminals before sentence, but now I'm settled I share a cell with eleven assorted convicts. All sorts. At this end of the scale of guilt is Elston. At the other is Len Patton who sleeps on my left here and is pushing six months for making love with his sweetheart, who has a Touch of the Tar Brush and presently inhabits another part of Die Rooi Hel with the Bantoe females. He should first have applied to Population Registration to be reclassified as Coloured. She can't be classified White, of course, to get to the marzipan and icing sugar and cherries on top; there's a ratchet built in here, downwards.

On his mat on my right lies Tokkie Waters, in for grievous bodily harm, GBH, and he's pushing five to eight. Tokkie too sleeps with a coloured woman, in the coloured township of PE, but gets away with it, because he has kroes hare and looks a touch Hotnottish himself and has no class except criminal, and nobody gives a shit about him, whereas Len is a schoolteacher – was – and noticeable in the community. In fact Tokkie has two children by his woman, and a permanent relationship. I find it interesting. I ask him Tokkie, what does your lady call you? She calls me Master Darling, says Tokkie.

We are allowed to put our mats down during the day because there's no furniture in this cell, except a lavatory pan without a seat and a small stand with a canister of water on it and a metal mug.

Boef Biljon has been longest in the cell so he occupies the prime spot other side of Tokkie in the corner where the sewage pipe comes through from the cell upstairs and down through the floor and provides some extra warmth. Boef makes a living by mugging old-age pensioners at post offices at the end of the month. He should be good at it, for he's a great big bugger, make no mistake. Boef of course is also GBH, and he's waiting to be off to Pretoria Central when they've got a batch of eight long-termers collected, to fill a railway compartment.

He is a bloubaadjie, he's pushing an indeterminate sentence, so habitual is his GBH. In a way he's quite looking forward to Central, for he will see his dad there. Dad is a double bloubaadjie, presently doing his second indeterminate of nine to fifteen years, which makes eighteen to thirty out of one's natural, also for violent assault. Add to that lot the twenty of youth, and one wonders how he found time out of jail to produce Bertrand i.e. Boef, never mind cuddle him a bit and take him camping.

We do bugger-all in this cell, all day. Elston and I make an illicit set of dominoes from the thicker back page of the Bible which an ancient toppie called Calthorpe who was an accountant but is no more has requested for praying purposes. He's allowed only the New Testament, because he will use the Old Testament for purposes of onanism, hy sal dit vir draadtrekdoeleindes gebruik. Jews can have the old one, but who cares if they abuse themselves to death anyway; Hitler could have saved himself a lot of Zyklon B.

If we are found to have made dominoes out of the back leaves of this Bible we will cease to eat for three days. Smoking the actual text of the Bible, however, will earn you six days without food. Trouble is, it's good smoking paper, the best, when your snout is illicit and you can't get Rizla rolling papers. Newspaper is bad news for the lungs. Not that we get newspapers either, but sheets of it are put on the dishing-up table at graze time, to soak up spillage.

We think of snout all the time. Some think of boom also, and rush to the window to press their cheekbones to the bars and inhale every time an awaiting-trial prisoner downstairs lights up his pot on return from court.

If we all seem to be in deep depression because of our hung heads in the exercise yard it is because we are examining every square centimetre of this yard for a single shred of tobacco dropped by the screw who smokes a pipe. One or another bandiet may be seen every half-hour or so to lick a surreptitious thumb and press it to the ground and transfer whatever may have stuck there to his pocket. Every three or four days there are enough shreds jointly to make a skyf about two millimetres thick, comprising two shreds or so of snout throughout its length.

The ritual here is as important as the addiction. The going-through of pocket linings could take an hour. Hours we have plenty of. It takes two men and a boy, called Laaitie because he's only eighteen and pushing small time for shoplifting, about another hour to assemble this skyf and prepare for fire.

Man, let nobody bore you with all that stuff about the intellect of early Homo erectus that got him up off the ground to free the forelimbs for the use of tools, nor let anybody bore you about the tool-making hands freeing the mind of Homo habilis for abstract thought.

The first thing ever, forget all that fancy twak, was to Make a Skyf, as soon as the protohuman eye fell upon snout or boom; whether the head or the hand got it going first is academic, it was dogged addictability that made it happen. Fire-making skills, the beginning of technology, came in consequence of this, after the initial eating of such flora. You will never stop a roker from making fire, somehow.

So the trick for the dope-ape Australopithecus fulminator is to smuggle away after shaving time a razor blade, or even a half-blade, and use this as his flint, for the making of sparks, as the name of his species indicates.

At the end of World War Two the Prisons Department bought from the Department of Defence one million toothbrushes made of a substance called bone camphor, for those were days before petrochemical plastics. In a cellful of bandiete there is always at least one from the gutter, who has no personal cash in his account down there in Reception for soap and stuff, called Toilets, and who has been issued with such a toothbrush and a tube of paste called Euthymol, which tastes like an intensive care ward and has been sold, the entire accumulation of it, lock, stock, barrel and voetstoets, in addition to the original million brushes, to the Prisons Department on the collapse and liquidation of the antisocial enterprise which produced this repulsive emulsion.

Section cleaners know the beamptes use it for polishing the brass components of their uniform insignia, and themselves use it on electric light switches in their sections, though that's about all the brass there is in boep; other than those just about all metal is steel.

Anyway.

To Light Skyf without Matches:

With contraband razor blade or half thereof scrape fine twirls from bone camphor toothbrush. Make small cone (kardoos) from The Gospel According to St Matthew and drop twirls loosely into this. Put to one side.

With razor blade or 1/2 such remove suitable arc of black floor polish from cell floor. This will expose concrete. Put polish scrapings to one side.

Station one member of skyf consortium at end of arc with kardoos positioned to catch sparks.

Stand another member by with skyf at inhaling position.

Strike blade along arc of concrete to make sparks and catch same in bone camphor. Fifteen minutes should give at least one ignition. Member #1 should immediately blow on this, whilst member #2 should insert skyf and suck.

All other members should be on standby and waste no burning time. If such consortium has nine members each will receive one draw.

Replace floor polish on exposed arc of concrete and stomp down with heel.

Well one day another old toppie called Oom Piet Joubert who was short term, one year for stealing copper from the railway, Oom Piet I say was doing his snout harvesting with hung head when he spied there upon the ground a dried blade of conventional grass which, though not tobacco, might alleviate the pangs a bit by at least catching fire, so he stuck it to his thumb and placed it in his pocket. Attached thereto by a short stem was a small seed. This he took from his pocket, back in the cell, because there wasn't much else to do in there after lock-up, and he might as well spend some of his time while the lights were still on looking at this his grass seed.

Oom Piet has a big frame and big bulbous nose with big open pores to match. Next time we go to shave and shower he plants this seed in one of the enlarged pores at the front of this nose, to see what might happen.

I believe the young of some Australian mammals are little bigger than this when they make their way from the insides of the mother to the marsupial pouch and there attach themselves to a teat, and Oom Piet now has the same aura of motherhood about him as such a marsupial mum would have, I suppose.

He consults me as the brains of this cell community about matters of germination. I tell him I once read of a child who stuck a bean in her ear and had to undergo surgery to get the root out before it got right inside to the drum. Could of entered her brain and changed her personality, like? says Oom Piet. Ja, I say.

Blood-flow to the nose is good in mammals, and so is the moisture content of the pores, because this organ, probably, was used for sniffing out prey originally, or sniffing predators which might want to eat one. So this seed has a good warm and moist incubation environment and sure enough puts forth after a couple of days a small small sprout, a millimetre or so in length.

Oom Piet takes care not to slosh his face when washing, but to wipe all around with his hand, avoiding this sprout. Nights are getting cold, but he doesn't pull his blanket over his head. He lies on his back and pulls it up under his chin and around his ears. The sprout grows to almost a centimetre in length, but etiolated, pale greenish yellow, because of its indoor existence.

On Saturday the section warder Lyons brings to our cell a bandiet with a pair of scissors and a stool and we all get haircuts that make us look like Frenchwomen found guilty by the Resistance of fornicating with German officers during the occupation.

We all shower and shave and get clean clothing for the big arrival of the officer commanding on his Sunday morning inspection. The reason why we have to shower et cetera the day before is that it wouldn't do to have water all over a shower place on the occasion of a ceremony of such pomp as this inspection; all must be dry as hay in there according to that curious suspicion of anything flowing and free and sensuous and sinful, like hair and water. Water is dirty.

Lyons gets all thirty or so occupants of the White Section into its little upstairs exercise yard. Stand in a straight stripe! he cries. We all get arranged accordingly, holding each one his prison card under his chin. The Super walks down the rank and stops at Oom Piet. Wat is dit op jou neus? he asks, with an expression of dismay on his face. Nee, Meneer, dis 'n soort van 'n groeisel. He comes right up close and subjects this thing to profound perscrutation through his bifocals. Is dit seer? Ja, meneer, dis vreeslik seer. The Super knows he's also about the right age for The Big C to bust out on his body too, somewhere, anywhere, the shnoz maybe, and backs off appalled. He tells Lyons to take Oom Piet to the district surgeon on his visit tomorrow and get this growth removed.

He comes forward again to examine the next man, one Landman, a pallid bandiet of frail constitution, with pale grey eyes, so pale he appears to have no irises at all, just the contracted black pinhole pupils in the brilliant white light of the exercise yard.

He is illuminated within too, by brilliant intelligence. Landman is short and generally shrunken. He has an imbecile grin and left leg and right arm partly shrivelled by polio. He has got the barber bandiet to snip off all his eyelashes when Lyons wasn't looking, then shaved off his eyebrows too, at shower time, plus his residuum of hair, and put his false teeth in his pocket. He has exchanged jackets with Boef, and the sleeves hang down to his knees.

The Super bends down to look at him, and Landman raises his face to look at the Super. As the Super's bifocals bring the staring pinpoint pupils into focus Landman lays the toothless idiot grin on him. The Super gives a startled backward jump and a sort of gasp and says to Landman What's wrong with you man? It's my religion, says Landman, I'm a Christian Scientist.

So that's why he asked me the other day about daft religions. I had thought long about lying starkers but for a cotton turban on a bed of nails at the top of Annapurna.

Well, everything worked out satisfactorily: Landman lost three meals for insolence, so did Boef, you can imagine what he looked like in Landman's jacket, and it all made a nice break from the dreadful boredom. I suppose Oom Piet's growth is still in some government oncological path lab somewhere, in formaldehyde.

We line up with stainless steel crockery and spoon for our pig and cabbage and a piece of bread and a mug of coffee made of a bean unknown to botany. We take all this surgical tableware into just another cell grandiosely called the Dining Hall because it's got two wooden tables in it, and long benches, and will accomodate thirty bandiete sitting instead of twelve lying down. Hasie Saunders stands at the head of one of the tables. He's called Hasie because he's a sodomite, and he's at the head of the table because he's a bloubaadjie, fraud, sent down from Pretoria to do the records of the Reception Section for the duration of his nine to fifteen.

Saunders, say your vokken prayers! cries Lyons.

We all bow our heads and close the eyes nearest him. If you close them both somebody will fly off your bread.

Dank die Here
Vir kos en klere,
says Hasie.

We're engaged in sport one afternoon, trying to see who can stick a ball of plasticine bread closest to a target on the wall across the cell when the door rattles to its keys and slams open and the steel grille clangs open, and a big Scandinavian seaman is thrust amongst us who has been sentenced for fighting and assault down at a dockside hotel. Same old GBH I suppose, only with things all over the vowels: Gråvøus Bødily Härm.

That makes thirteen in our cell. All the places around the walls are taken, so the Swede dumps his mat in the middle of the floor and stares around at everybody and offers to all about him his opinions of the country and its police and prisons personnel, which we scarce need since we already have each of us personally a fairly inflexible opinion of these institutions and the staff who run them. But he's a loud sort of man, and aggressive, and goes on and on all afternoon and after graze too until the lights are out and we all fall asleep. He has a vocabulary of about five words, two of them Fuck and its present participle. He has an American accent.

It's scarce light when he's off again, and after the porridge and coffee too. Quite suddenly Elston says to him If you say Fuck again I'll fuck you up, man, this is Sunday! Where the fuck do you think you are, man, says the Swede, do you think this is a fucken church?, and Elston leaps from his mat and slugs this fucker on his way upright. Elston's normal mode of street fighting is to butt his opponent's face, but this bugger is big, big, and Elston comes only up to his neck, sort of, but he does his best in this cell, slamming and grunting away and the Swede yielding nothing. The other eleven of us dodge and duck as best we can. The cell is a bit smaller than a boxing ring, and it's hard to get out of the way, so every now and then there's a great pile of wriggling bodies on the floor.

But the Swede concentrates on Elston, though he's been hurt a few times from being hurled against the lavatory pan and the bars of the door, and just at the right moment he gets him off balance and lands a heavy ungloved right hook to the temple and drops Elston where he stands. He rearranges his mat and sits down and restarts his loud harangue about the Prisons Department. One would suppose we all loved this department the way he goes on.

He gets up for a pee. He doesn't stop his crass cursing even when he's having a good piss, one of few pleasures in jail. He goes back to his mat but before he can sit down Boef gets up and steps over to him and lands him one moer se vokken vuisslag to the neck, right on the thyroid cartilage, the Adam's apple, so brutal the Swede looks like he forgot to buckle up this morning and went through the windscreen. He makes it to his mat and a squatting posture instead of falling down, and sits there trying to sort out his whiplash. He finds he can't turn his head to the left, so if he wants to look at anything over there he must turn his entire self either 90° that way or 270° the long way round. This I am able to construe from his body language, for his voice has disappeared, I'm not surprised, and a good thing too, though it's sad about the whiplash.

Boef has resumed his discussion with Tokkie about the virtues of dagga from coastal Transkei.

Eleven

BOREDOM IS WHAT YOU GET WHEN you're with other people and there's nothing to do and too much distraction from them to let you get on with your own inner thoughts and memories and fantasies. Well, that's my theory anyway, and I would soon enough get a chance to prove it. One afternoon after graze as we stood about waiting for Lyons to lock us up Hasie sidled over to me and said here's a little farewell present, and slipped into my pocket a cigarette, a quarter of a split matchstick and a small piece of slatch from a matchbox, all stolen from the Reception boer. You mean we're off? I asked. Tomorrow, he said.

I don't know why he gave me this fag. It's not the sort of thing that people do in prison. Maybe he had some feeling for the political left. The strangest people do.

Inside there I stand in the middle of the cell on the Swede's mat and say OK, all in favour of an after-dinner smoke stand up. Nobody even smiles, it's such a stupid joke. I take the fag from my pocket and hold her aloft. All nine smokers rise in awe, slowly, wide eyes staring, as if at a vision of the Holy Mother of Christ. Come on Elston, you're top stretch, light it, and I produce the quarter match and piece of slatch. In the close silent standing group each ou gets his puffs, even the Swede, whom the others have got used to since he's lost his voice.

Sure enough, next afternoon there is Lyons to collect the long timers for Pretoria Central, the Big House. We four from this cell move over to the door when we hear him getting the next-door batch into the corridor. He lets out Tokkie, Boef and Elston, but when I come forward he shoves me back with his fingers. Not you, he says. What, I think, am I going to push my full time here? I've quite got to look forward to Central, though it's a grim, disciplined place, I've heard.

The other three who've been there before tell me I'll be A-group, privileged, in a few weeks and have a job in an office because I have matric. Also everybody has his own cell in Central, you're one-out, as they say, and the relatives of the bandiete there have been allowed to buy some sort of hi-fi or low-fow so they play records for an hour before lights-out with a speaker in each section. The katkop, the bread, is nice, I hear. But maybe I'll be A-group here, and maybe I'll be put to office work here. I think of Warder Botha in Reception and my heart sinks.

I'm just getting nicely settled down after a half hour or so with the remaining ouens in the cell, and note that the Swede has moved into Boef's place at the shitpipe, like he's now alpha bull, when the door once again opens and Lyons says to me Trek aan jou baadjie, kom.

Down in Reception stand the Marx Brothers. I note that ou Rassie has a short length of rope in his hand, and I calculate I'm in for a trip to Pretoria with this mirthful trio and ou Jorrie won't have to go about holding up his pants this time.

We take a strange route out of Die Baai, though. Sometimes it seems to me that we've passed the same place twice, but what the hell, you cease to wonder about life too much in this company, and if they want to get to Pretoria by dirt road and the long way round the Earth, well let them, I'll just enjoy the scenery.

They look often at their watches, and plan things accordingly. We turn off the dirt road on to a track with a middelmannetjie, and after a bit we stop at a railway siding with no platform, no name, you know the sort of rural thing for picking up milk cans in those old days, no buildings nor trees nor people nor anything in sight, just a sign there for the engine driver to stop if he sees these cans to be collected for a dairy combine somewhere.

I climb out of the risible Chev with all my chains and things clanking about me like an ancestral ghost. I've got something extra now: a chain that connects the leg-irons to the handcuffs, so as to stop my lifting my hands more than waist high. Rassie hauls out of the boot a rolled-up blanket with the ends tied together with string. He undoes the string because my hands are cuffed, and places the roll over my head and one shoulder, then ties it all together again. He hangs upon the string a tin mug. He places upon my head a wide felt hat of brown, and in my cuffed hands he places a wad of pig sandwiches sewn up in a piece of sacking. They have plastic bags all right in the Prisons Department, but regulations for prisoners in transit haven't caught up with today's technology quite yet, and nobody in the system wants to stick his neck out and try something revolutionary like a can of spaghetti with cheese, or baked beans in tomato sauce, perhaps. Maybe some desperado would cut his wrists with an edge.

I turn for a pee on the yellow grass. At least I have no problem with that operation. WHAT ARE YOU DOING, MAN? yells ou Jorrie, you can't just relieve yourself in a public place, man!

Where's this public you're talking about? I ask, there's nobody here but our team. No, WE are the public, explains Jorrie, and the Major is a religious man, you know that, and you should show respect for a man's religion. Oh I do, I do, I say, piddling away, he can keep his legs crossed all the way back to Port Elizabeth and piss in his church toilet there.

Jorrie is bloody sour now: first I eat all the koeksusters, then I get away with only three years and now I'm facetious about pissing in public, but what's he going to do, shoot my cock off? Then suddenly, in genuine anguish, OH NO! HURRY, PLEASE! THE TRAIN'S COMING!

It's true, a train is coming around a curve about a mile away. Hmmm? I ask, and turn around to see this train, still with the old man hanging out. Jorrie is distraught, passengers with binoculars may see this thing, and he moves in front of me and spreads out his hands. I give it a good shake, and stow it.

Strewth, such a loco! In the dinosaur movie we see these two kids eating raspberry jelly in the kitchen, and this jelly starts a series of regular quivers, and they stop eating it in horror, because they know these are the dread seismic vibrations from the footfall of Some Great Jurassic Predatory Beast whose intention it is to eat them, and it's not far off.

This loco, closer by the moment, does the same thing now; I feel her under the feet and in my jelly, and it gives me the creeps, man, the chicken skin. Her urgent DJOEF!DJOEF! DJOEF!DJOEF! up the long incline slows to long sustained hisses as she makes straight for me here next to the line, at walking pace, almost hidden amid the monstrous cumuli of her own winter condensation and smoke. She means to swallow me, and does.

The great black thirty-metre megalosaur goes gasping and bellowing past us as high as a house in her huge blasting ball of steam, to the grind of steel wheel on steel rail and the hellish roaring of her firebox.

The Satanic fireman is clinkering her out as the mechanical stoker feeds her insatiable appetite for coal like deviant souls relentlessly thrust kicking and frying over the brimstone brink, and showers of red-hot stuff smash down and sparkle beneath her metal belly. The driver sits at the nerve nexus of this 4-8-2 Seismosaurus and leans on his elbow at the window there, nonchalantly lifting a hand in greeting as he trundles his train past us until the right one of twelve or so coaches is more or less opposite.

Every window has heads sticking out, and faces curious about their stopping in the sticks. Prison regulations say that prisoners in transit should never ever be put in an embarrassing situation amongst the public, not in any way, ever. Balls, and what the hell, I'm way beyond embarrassment, and anyway I can see a situation coming up for my kêrels hierso which is going to provide these curious faces with something to smile at.

I have to make my way, I can scarce call it walking since my pace is twenty centimetres, about a coach length to where I see a whole lot of bandiet heads sticking out of a compartment's windows amid huge billows of tobacco smoke. I remember the tradition I've been told of whereby escorting boere buy much Boxer snout to keep the ouens cheerful and compliant.

Eventually I'm at the steps of their coach, and I look up at them and shout Make a skyf, man! Elston gets a lungful of Boxer and purses up his lips in kissing position and blows a long plume of smoke at the winter landscape. Get in, jong, he shouts back, it's just like home, man!

Have you ever tried to get aboard a train without use of a platform or ladder or chair or something? The first step is a full metre above the ground, man. My maximum leg-reach, as I say, is twenty centimetres. Furthermore, though there are two hand-rails there to grip on one's way up, I can't lift my hands above my waist. The Security Branch stand with all these weapons strapped to their torsos and arses and ponder this problem while the whole bloody train waits for them and gets off schedule.

It's easier you just shoot the fucker! calls Boef to ou Jorrie. Ja, skiet die bliksem! yells the criminal chorus. After a bit of a conference there the SB comes to the conclusion that willy-nilly they will have to take off the leg-irons, or drive to another place where there's a platform.

But the engine driver has already blown one hoarse howl on his whistle, and there's the old protocol thing again, for the Security Police have asked the schedule man of the SA Railways, PE, to ask the driver of this express train to stop at this depopulated place in the gamadoelas, and this driver is the man in control around here, and wants to get on to Bloemfontein with his metal monster.

O'Bum purses up his mouth in a wise sort of way and gives a sage nod towards the leg-irons. Jorrie unlocks these and Rassie draws his Walther.

Skiet hom! yells Boef. Run! yells Tokkie. I reach up and grab one of the hand-rails and place a foot upon the first step, a bit more than waist-high. I give a good heave; hell, I could have jumped up there when I was fit, but I'm not now, and in any case I have both cuffed hands on the right hand-rail and I'm off balance, and as I give a heave there I swing away to the right and my foot comes off the step and I'm back on the ground.

Hoera! yell all, and it's not just the bandiete now. O'Bum is really unwilling to take the cuffs off though. However, since they still have the chain on them which had attached them to the leg-irons, ou Jorrie puts his best brains to it and climbs up the steps and stands in the coach doorway with the other end of this chain and says Reg! Nou! Stoot!, and I have a foot on the first step while Vuurwapen and O'Bum push at my buttocks and Gruweldaad pulls at my manacled hands. But I don't really put my heart into it, you know. I just sort of hang there, man; I'm not being paid to do this work. Ou Jorrie reaches down for a better grip at the moment that the other two tire of pushing my backside, and he loses his balance and comes dondering out of the train and lands on all fours on the gravel by the rails. HOERA!! cry the passengers. Even old varicosed ladies have hauled themselves over to the windows for the circus.

O'Bum finds it sort of indecent to take the cuffs off, it's like not wearing underpants to the Full Gospel Church of God. But the driver has now given a long, long blast of impatience, and O'Bum gives the nod and draws his FN Browning and Rassie still has his Walther out while ou Jorrie unlocks and removes the cuffs and produces his Colt Forty-five and they all three step back and cover me from three quarters, and O'Bum says GET IN!

RUN! RUN! shouts Elston. SKIET HOM! yells Tokkie. GO UNDER THE TRAIN! cries Boef, and Jorrie dives in amongst the wheels down there just in case.

HOERA!! chorus all passengers. Jorrie is so peeved with Boef by now that he starts to point his artillery-piece at him, grave indiscipline, and he knows it, and O'Bum hollers at him and he sticks it in his belt and Boef shouts Hey poeliesman, you stick that thing in there you will blow your bloody balls off man!, and all laugh at this seething poeliesman. HOERA!! cries the chorus.

They've forgotten my pigburgers. As the train moves off ou Jorrie tries a sort of forward rugby throw at the window, but misses. The pigburgers bounce off into the veld.

HOERA!! cries the chorus.

You wondered how all those long-term convicts were able to lean out of a train window and shout things, did you, and nobody bothering that they might just leap out and run, according to their own advice, desperadoes that they are? Well it's easy: inside the train they are chained together by the ankles, and though the boere who provided the snout are merry enough in the matter of tobacco, they have made it clear enough that these firearms they have here are not cigarette lighters. Small bottle of big poison, this, says our boer, Tokkie's and mine, shortly, patting his thirty-eight special, the one specially designed for the New York police for indoor use, accurate at no more than ten paces, but which will smash your entire thorax in with a bullet that size and the charge that this round carries. The round is nearly the length of the barrel.

Tokkie has been chained to this screw, at the ankle, who now unlocks him and chains him to me instead. I can scarce see the ouens on the seat opposite, such is the density of Boxer smoke in here. We're getting suffocated and choked by the bloody stuff, but never mind, these are old inhabitants of Central, and they know they're going to go through Madhouse first, which is solitary with nothing consoling for six weeks, not even unrewarding work, and after that they'll be C-Group, still no tobacco, no reward, no any bloody thing, for some years, maybe, with just a bit of bad luck.

Night falls, and the problem of sleeping both of us on one bunk is left to our own discretion and decision. Tokkie has done it before. The bunk is too narrow by far for lepel lê, side by side; the only alternative is end-to-end, with our manacled right legs doubled back or stuck up straight, but there's not much room for that because there's a bunk just above our noses. As I sit here I try to remember how we spent the night, but I can't. I think we slept on our guts, prone, with my right leg and Tokkie's left hung over the edge of the bunk. Maybe Sigmund Freud won't let me remember it, but never mind; next evening seven o'clockish we arrive in Pretoria full of varkburgers and water, and cured in smoke like ham in a German peasant chimney, or snoek on the Cape Peninsula.

Each Siamese pair is got off the train with great skill, it's all been done so often before without disconnecting the twins, and here we all stand in a straight stripe on the platform in our cuffs and irons waiting for transport to Central. In our khaki prison gear and our big brown felt hats and our rolled-up army blankets over neck and shoulder with the tin mug tied on with string down there we look like some frontier platoon in the Redskin wars. Passengers gape at us unashamedly, you don't have to be ashamed with criminals.

A little boy holding his mum's hand comes by. We all fancy this mum something sinful; Hey, check these tits, mutters Elston. The lad pulls at his mum's hand; Hey Mum, he says, look at the cowboys! Come along Johnny, says Mum, those aren't cowboys, those are crooks.

A teenage girl was singing about her lonely heart in this lonely world, and wanting to be wanted, when we pulled in at Central. Beyond the six gates, the main one of metal-studded oak, the rest of metal-clad hardwood or simple one-inch steel prison bars, but big, an entire wall of steel bars with a gate in it, beyond these the main hall glittered in black and silver and earth red, vacant, sterile, ominous, huge and square: black floor polish, polished steel bars and brick walls a metre thick. An imperious sign opposite the main entrance said SILENCE, and silent it was, except for the teenager's sad song and a lonesome trumpet now in support.

Lonesome, lonely, my God what a lonely place. Here dwelt a thousand men, each sealed for the night in his peter, his rock, in this nightly catacomb. The mortar of the masonry is one part cement to two of sand; it's like granite. Silent, silent. Not even an insect moved here; there was no point, no reward, no sugar, no left-over table scraps, never mind no blood because of the DDT on bodies and blankets.

The trumpet and girl came to the end of their sad song and a shrill electric bell announced the beginning of sleep. The only sound now was the echoing thumps of boots as the duty beampte went round and round, nine floors of three sections, three arms of a great Greek cross about the vast nave, switching off a thousand lights. It was like a fuse burning to its end. The silence was now so complete we could hear each other breathing outside Reception.

Maloney is the bloubaadjie running it. I don't mean he's in charge; he makes it work. He sits there in his cotton boep pyjamas and crude sweet-potato shoes and writes us new latecomers into the system. Standing outside we can hear his ballpoint at work, every sound amplified under the great corrugated iron dome on the wrought iron and girder pendentives of this huge punitive Basilica.

We take off our Baai threads and give them to the Baai beamptes. Mooi slaap, kêrels, they say, môre sal julle 'n lekker bord pap kry, and they're off to an evening of booze without their wives. We each get an assortment of Central corduroy clothing and a cotton kitchen cloth for drying the body, and we're away to our new habitat in the dead still of Lights-out.

There it is: a cell seven feet square, two metres, painted in grey enamel. When I stretch my arms across it either way I am thirty centimetres short. It has a small barred window way above my head, with the glass desperately smashed out for ventilation in summer, and a steel-meshed ventilator in the wall opposite. I sit in it for eleven months, solo, silent.

A1 Section, this, the Madhouse.

Die Bybel is 'n Glorie-Paradys, declared the cyclostyled sheet stuck on the wall. You could have that in the other official language too: The Bible is a Glory-Paradise. It is a Rose of Rare Fragrance. It is the Traveller's Staff. It is the Mariner's Compass. It is the Shepherd's Crook.

Some sceptic has written in pencil at this point It is the Crook's Shepherd.

It is the Jewel in the Crown of Life. It is the Lover's Heart, said this notice, whilst another cynic has written here with his pencil It is the Fucker's Condom. That should get them three days' ricewater each, him and the crook's shepherd, by my calculation and short experience of boep. The ricewater is the tablespoon of rice boiled in a litre of water which you have to consume daily when you've lost meals for three days or more, so your gut doesn't do the natural thing and stops asking for food and you don't feel hungry after the second day. Oh ja, I forgot; no salt.

It is the Cosmos.

Blimey, you can't get much bigger or better than that.

Come to it with Praying Hands and Open Heart, Bow before The Lord Jesus Christ, God is Watching Over You.

I had a nasty feeling that someone sure enough was watching over me. I would get this telepathic feeling now and then and turn round fairly suddenly and there at the spy-hole in the door would indeed be Somebody's iris and eyelid, which may have been God's, I agree, but I doubt it, because thereafter, whilst showering solo one day, I here beheld the Chief Psychologist, Luitenant van den Beestekraal, thus peering into somebody else's spy-hole, and not only that, but blowing cigar smoke through this spy-hole too, where some poor soul inside there was trying to make it through life without snout.

Just lucky I still had the glass in my spy-hole. My Judas.

Luitenant van den Beestekraal had gained a three-year Bachelor of Arts Degree with Criminology, Theology, Psychology and Things at the University of Potchefstroom. His psycho degree had secured for him the post in the Prisons Department, in charge of the mental well-being of South Africa's worst thousand white criminals.

None better than he, of course, since the other ingredients of his education gave him access both to Faith and modern Scientific Sociological Thought.

Situated as I was down his end of the passage I was soon able to construe what system of psychotherapy Beestekraal adhered to.

Kyk hierso, said he, fairly loudly and irritably to a patient apparently entering his office for treatment, Jy laaik my nie, en ek laaik jou not a vok.

Lt v.d. Beestekraal may have been a little understatured, shall we say, in the way that some unfortunates are said to be underprivileged, as if privilege were a normal condition. But let nobody lay either stigma or facile prejudice on him for that, myself especially, since I myself am a skinny weed who took to marathon running because it was clear I was never going to make it into Sumo wrestling.

Lt v.d. Beestekraal of course needs moments of respite from his continual concern for the spiritual condition of his wards, and these moments he often spends in recitation to his bandiet clerk and the three bandiet section cleaners of his success as a rally driver. Then too, since the spiritual human animal needs also a certain amount of physical exertion for his own good spiritual health, some other moments are spent in games of cricket with a tennis ball and plank bat sculpted by a bandiet under punishment, and in these games appear the selfsame clerk and section cleaning bandiete, in the long wide corridor between the double rows of cells of the Madhouse, whilst certain accurséd inmates of these premises are going off their heads for want of a bit of visual reassurance that a world still exists outside of their forty-nine square feet, four square metres, of grey enamel, and serve them right. Don't dice with Jesus, my friend.

When you've made Jesus your friend, maybe you will play cricket again, with him and Beestekraal and his tennis ball and the bat made in some madman's cell with Beestekraal's pen-knife.

The Madhouse, this head section cleaner called Blackbeard explains to me, is thus called not because you're mad when you go in, but because you're mad when you come out. Blackbeard is an authority on madness. Blackbeard is another bloubaadjie, he's pushing his indeterminate for stealing somebody's jacket in a nightclub. With his previous record of theft this sentence is mandatory. Nine minimum, twelve, fifteen years maybe of anybody's life is worth more than somebody else's tuxedo, he thinks, whatever has gone before. This, really, is mad thought, and if you want it explained Lt. v.d. Beestekraal is there and ready and waiting to earn his salary. God is there with him, of course, though also of course He needs neither wage nor salary, in spite of financial problems with Volkskas and the Church of the Vow in Pietermaritzburg.

When Blackbeard speaks it's fast speech, and whispered. A1 is a Silent Section.

When the metal-clad outer cell doors are opened and only the steel bars of the inner doors are locked Blackbeard collects dirty dishes from the last meal.

That's when I glean wisdom from him. He tells me in the ten seconds he has at my cell that I will be here six weeks and then do a big psychological test which Beestekraal has devised. Prison regulations say that every prisoner shall have a thorough physical and psychological examination on admission to determine what type of work is most suitable to his personality and health, and Beestekraal takes care of the personality bit.

The first step towards rehabilitation of an antisocial being who can't live decently with other people is to lock him up all alone with a New Testament Bible for six weeks. Staring Christ straight in the eyeballs for that long will fix him all right and give him a sense of guilt and make him truly moral and social from now on.

It seems to me a good start to a career in Satanism.

Anyway, I ask Blackbeard to get me an Old Testament because I'm a Jew. A nice bit of King James English wouldn't come amiss just now, all rounded and fleshy and nourishing and classical, the Bible can't be beat for that, except by Will Shakespeare of course. But that's day-dreaming, man, for what I get instead is neither James nor Will but an angry clattering of keys and my door flung open and there is the psycho's small scowling face glaring at me. My Port Elizabeth file tells him that I am not a Jew, not even by birth, and an atheist to boot, and if I'm capable of lying about religion I'll lie about anything, and he knew that about communists anyway, and my rehabilitation will start with three no-meals and no Bible at all.

Three no-meals. The Chief Warder, the Opper, is at his elbow to confirm things, he's the sentence man. Between graze at four today and breakfast at six a.m. day after tomorrow, no food. That's thirty-eight hours; so what, I've often been as long as that without food, running out of grub on a mountain slog in the Drakensberg, getting stuck for lifts while hitch-hiking as a student in the middle of Africa. In this cell I have a wooden stool, so I sit on this by day or lie on the floor by night for thirty-eight hours until the door opens and Blackbeard hands me a bowl of porridge and a New Testament, in Afrikaans.

Everybody should read the New Testament in Afrikaans; Pretoria Afrikaans, that is, Oxford Afrikaans as I once heard an old Namaqualander describe it in his Afrikaans. Here is only the dead hand of moralism, and genteel official language. There's no majestic measure here, no lovely prosody, no poetry in the psalm nor, on the other hand, any Capie Creole tang to divert the attention from the dreadful cruelty and pain and suffering and grief that it's all about. No Anglisismes, no foreign impurities, nothing that isn't straight out of the box, new, so one gets to wonder where the hell human speech ever came from. It's only marginally worse than the new Bible in English, true's God.

After some pages I realise the truth of what Sam Goldwyn said: Enough is Too Much. I've got enough sorrows of my own just now, but thanks anyway, and as I close the Good Book and put it to one side I think to myself What would much sooner restore my moral fibre just now, and make me a good citizen of this republic, is a good weekend in bed with a good friend and a bottle or two of the late harvest wine of this republic, and A Midsummer Night's Dream on the little bedside table there.

Further unrewarding silly fantasy.

Here I am allowed to have my personal shaving gear, and I split a razor blade to make a sharp little chisel, and sit for six weeks and carve the plastic handle of my shaving brush with some excellent Trajan lettering: Jess's full-length name well composed around the cylinder, a bit like Trajan's Column, I suppose. I go about it like some mediaeval Irish monk in his island monastery illuminating another sort of Bible. Time is no factor. The more, in fact, the better.

In addition to the wooden stool I have a tiny table and a bowl of water and a mug with a spoon and a kakbak with a lid, enamelled. That's beside the felt mat and army blankets. These two blankets and the mat are very mystical, I soon learn from Blackbeard, as the Section Boer Ferreira stands over him during five minutes of instruction on the rules of this section. On awaking at five o'clock one folds them in a certain ritualistic way, the one as a concertina, but with strict proportions per fold, and the other wrapped around about this first, in strictly relevant depth, so that the whole assemblage is strictly rectangular in every dimension, and the corners plumped by hand to make them as near a right angle as possible. This assemblage is called a Wireless. It is stood on top of the tightly rolled column of the felt sleeping mat. It is a totem pole.

This totem represents the progress not of a man's life, but of his day. This totem is immobile and sacred during this his day. It is not to be touched, for any reason short of death or illness certified by the District Surgeon. But after graze and tally and final shutdown of the Great Panopticon Mill there is the music of the great god Pan, the libidinous half-goat god, semicaper deus, and his pipes. The Saturnalia of the private night begins. That locked door with no handle on the inside does not keep you in, it keeps them out. Once it is locked no living being may open it who is not a judge or a government doctor or the Super, the officer commanding of this prison. You're safe!

Here the king of the day is killed. With no vengeance, but exquisite pleasure, the wireless is collapsed with but two fingers of each hand. Now I reign! I shall think of nothing but soup while I drink the soup, and nothing but bread while I eat the bread, and as I balance the tin mug of coffee on top of the mesh cage of the light-bulb on the wall, to keep it warm, I shall think of nothing but balance. Then the Great Slack Time will come, the bacchanalia, the Calypso Bacchanal.

This is winter, and we're on the highveld, five thousand feet plus, and bloody cold. There's no glass in the window and of course the wind whistles in there and out the ventilator opposite, and this cavity in the masonry is really just a cement cave. So what? I've spent many nights colder by far than this in other, limestone, caves in the Drakensberg at ten thousand feet plus, and for pleasure, nogal. At least I'm dry here. So after the soup and bread, as in the 'Berg I get every available fabric thing on my body, even the dishcloth bathing towel, and make a pillow of my two amadumbe tuber shoes toe against heel, and get as snug as one can without a down sleeping-bag, and I drink the coffee before getting my head down and wrapped up, thinking of nothing but coffee until the great moment arrives of having my own hours of free-ranging remembrance of things saved up during the day.

During the day one sits and looks at the grey enamel on the wall two metres distant. One doesn't have to look at this, of course, one can shut one's eyes. Also, of course, one can move one's bankie over to that side and look at the enamel on this side, presently behind one's back, or the wall at ninety degrees. Lest readers conclude this is a pointless way to spend a day from the precious few given in one's life, let me remind them of happy hours as a kid wrapped in a bath towel staring at burning coals in a grate, or lying on one's back staring at the changing shapes of clouds, as sentimental American art tells us we should do for reward.

Sure, those are moving, changing shapes there, and the game is wondering what they'll change to next, but you can get something as good here by re-interpreting random forms this way and that: here is a map of the Free State, or is it the profile of a man with a long straight nose looking westwards? Maybe this is the first with a long straight nose arriving in what was there before the Free State, somebody pushing into the land of Mantatisi, the land of the Mantatee Horde. Maybe there's a story here; work it out in the rough, perhaps, and remember that rough, but save the yarn for lights-out, your own personal story time.

Here is a Pleistocene bipedal lizard, possibly warm-blooded and gaudily feathered, and big as a bear, with a falcon beak and the forelimbs of a mantis with all those fearsome spikes, red maybe, along the inner edges; an impossible piece of morphology, but let's build a good SF yarn around it, lots of science and genetic engineering and no magic.

Here's a Junkers 52, a Tante Ju, coming out of a cloud. The cloud part is easy; most of the random shapes on the wall are clouds, but the Ju is distinct and singular. It is making its way into Stalingrad to fulfil the vainglorious boast of Reichsmarschall Göring that the besieged garrison will be supplied by air. In Stuttgart a fellow-student was a Stalingrad survivor, or was he an escapee, who'd been flown out of Stalingrad in an Auntie Junkers on its return flight, after he'd had his face rearranged by an anti-tank gun. He was a Jew, too, one of those ginger ones, who fairly near the bottom of the barrel had been pulled out of some sort of camp for Jews terminal by decree, and stuck into the

Wehrmacht where the Russians would kill him if he didn't kill them first, though his nose had been the wrong shape. No problem now, though, with his Aryanism, for he doesn't have a nose any more. We'll build him into the story for tonight. His name was Lanski.

Already I have three stories, and I need only two per night!

After the stories comes the sentimental bit. Here I arrange the furniture of our new house in Durbs, though I don't have any idea what on earth they look like, neither the house nor the furniture. I have one letter of five hundred words, written with a pencil on exercise-book lined paper, every six months, plus a return, also five hundred. I've had the first one, so I've got three months to do all this rearranging before Jess comes on her once every six months half-hour visit, spaced between the letters, and explains the layout of everything, so I can start all over again in the next three months. Maybe she will bring me a photograph. When Blackbeard fetches my dirty dinner dish I ask him about this.

No, no photographs here, at all.

Twelve

THE SECTION BOER FERREIRA IS predictably called Vatjougoed. Where Beestekraal looks after the spiritual side of life, he is in charge of the earthly side, you know, grub and clothing and getting everybody washed and keeping everything clean, all that goeters.

He is a living flesh-and-blood replica of Michelangelo's marble David, except his hair is cut all short; well, round the sides and neck it is. Maybe up top there it's all curly like the hair of that pouting sullen youth, but there's no telling, because he wears this great big oversize cap on his Michelangelo Saint Peter's Dome, resting on his big pink lugs which stick out at right angles to his skull, as a sort of cartilage fulcrum. He wears it always. If he starts walking forward too suddenly the plastic peak rises above his brows, and if he stops suddenly it slowly descends, like an eclipse of the sun, and he doesn't know what's going on in the world. Not that he's too sure what's going on there anyway.

If you were to cut off his ears the plastic peak would veer round towards the back of his head as he turned a corner.

Standard labour for those in segregation is repairing mailbags. The pitched twine used for such repairs makes a fine stockwhip. You start with a handy piece of wood – the mailbag bandiet starts, that is, but it's not his; the warder who is getting the stockwhip woven for him brings the materials and takes off the whip – then around one end you braid thirty or so strands of twine, and leave one out at regular intervals until there's but a single strand. This gives you a sweep of about twenty feet, six or seven metres. You get some of the pitch and work it into this lash like one of Cap'n Bligh's Jack Tars working the pitch into his pigtail. It comes to a fine point, and gives a good crack. Vatjougoed has such a stockwhip.

He is a busy lad, of course, with nothing near the leisure of the psycho, and there are no games of cricket for him. But now and then on a Saturday, when the pressure of work is not so intense and Beestekraal is not around to get tetchy and irritated, his sport is to pursue the nude and wet section cleaners from the showers round and round the two double aisles of the Madhouse with his whip, with many a shriek and cadenza of giggles, and hiding away, and lunging out from ambushes. Although this is winter, it's not so terribly cold in the afternoon, and the ouens need the exercise anyway; it keeps them warm.

But it's bloody cold for me at night, especially round the feet, for two weeks ago my socks didn't come back from the wash, and last week I got none back because I'd handed none in, and for two weeks I've been trying to get Vatjougoed to get me socks, for fuck sake.

I stand on my bankie at the ventilator, and wait for the cleaners to come guffawing and thwacking past on their bare feet on lap six or so, then as Vatjougoed's boots come galumphing by I yell MENEER! He stops, stumbling and surprised, at such din in an all-silent place. Wat is 't man? Meneer, asseblief, my kouse. Ek kry vreeslik koud in die nag.

You think only of yourself! he expostulates. I've only got two hands and two pairs of feet; what do you think I am? and the answer clearly is that I think he is a centaur, but I can't say this to him because eating is important in my life just now, and don't know the Afrikaans word for this creature anyway.

Ja, Meneer.

I've had only two months in this place and already I know the culture. My world is small: if I lie down I can touch the North Pole with my foot and the South Pole with my fingers, and that's with a bent arm, too. But I'll tell you what, it's comprehensible because of its minute size, and secure in consequence. If I were an old bok I might be anxious that my heart would stop in the middle of the night and there'd be no help, but I'm in full flower and rude health and robust and randy, and my only problem is space, but I know that by an act of will I can shrink the Galaxy into a few hundred grey-enamelled cubic feet. It's a small world indeed, with bitter min joy in it, but I understand it.

As head section cleaner, Blackbeard is in charge of laundry matters. When he comes with my soup I ask him Blackie, man, how can I get some socks, for fuck sake? My socks have disappeared from the system. Yiss! he says, I'll think about it tonight and see you soup-time tomorrow, it's difficult to fly off things in the Madhouse.

So he's an assiduous bloubaadjie, and by tomorrow he's found from the psycho's bandiet clerk, one Roux, predictably known as Kanga, what my history is, by furtive illicit scrutiny of my file in Beestekraal's office, and when next Blackie delivers my soup he has a deal worked out. He has found I'm an artist. He will get me a pair of stolen socks if I draw for him a naked goose i.e. bird i.e. chick i.e. woman, I mean girl. I wonder why he wants only one such drawing if Kanga has to be paid too for the file scrutiny. There's no possibility of sexual barter in this section, so the deal must be tobacco. Tobacco is a scarce commodity, but drawings come for free, from nowhere, you pull them out of the air, out of nothing. I realise there's a chance to save Blackie's snout by doing a drawing for the clerk too, but I don't suggest this economical thing just yet. One must not show all one's cards until the stakes are high enough.

Look, I say, this will be a good drawing, it's my profession, and I don't want kak old socks you've flown off from the rejects. I want new ones, and when I hand them in for washing I want a nice fluffy pair back. He thinks hard, but fast, because you always think fast in this place if you want to survive. OK, he whispers, I'll bring paper and goeters tomorrow and we'll see.

The paper he brings next day is a sheet of the exercise-book stuff with lines on it, and all folded up to fit in his pocket, and the pencil is an HB stub found in a wastepaper basket. However cold my feet, I realise it's worth a couple more nights of misery to hold out for a better deal, and while I'm about it to get a shirt that isn't made of steel wool and a pair of blankets that aren't stiff as fibreglass with ancient semen, if these things too are within Blackie's reach. He's the ou who can swop around socks and shirts and whatnot, and give the horrible inferior stuff to moegoes who have nothing to bargain with, and the best to me, but blankets would be difficult; he'd have to get them into the section deviously, they're too bulky to smuggle in the way you do snout and stuff.

Nee, ou Blekkie, I say, but fast, I can't draw on this bloody paper, man! There's plenty of typing paper in this prison, and tell your china Kanga to get me some Indian ink and a pen and I'll do him a drawing too, it'll save your snout. Blackie has a glass eye, and he fixes this on me with utter astonishment, for he realises he has here a currency hitherto unimagined in boep, and he can make himself king of this place if he organises the trade routes properly and taps the source intelligently.

Wait a bit, I think, as he gapes at me; Elston made me his apprentice, as he put it, in Die Rooi Hel, and the first rule always to remember, he said, was You come to boep alone and you push your time alone. Don't trust anybody, starting with me, Elston. Everybody here is a snide, no friends, and if you do a deal cover your tracks fast, and have no witnesses.

Well soon enough Kanga sort of casually suggests to Vatjougoed, just in passing, that his section would look lekker smart on Sunday inspections by the Super if every cell had a tidy little rectangle of typing paper above the door with the bandiet's name and number on it and the length of his stretch, all neatly done, and artistically, by one of the occupants who is an artist, and has nothing to do all day anyway.

The speech of Roux is most flink and Florentine, that's why he's here for fraud, and the mind of Ferreira most malleable and Mediaeval, his Renaissance visage notwithstanding, so within two twos, maybe three the most, Vatjougoed is off to the stationery stores for pen and black ink, and during that time Roux has suggested to the junior psychologist, name of Koornhof, that his office would look more classy and relaxed with a nice new blanket on the gloss varnished meranti table so the typewriter doesn't scratch it so, and if he likes the idea and will requisition for one, he might as well order a second one for his senior Beestekraal, who would appreciate it for sure.

It is Vatjougoed himself who brings me the stationery and ink and pen in the morning. The slick turn of the key in the lubricated lock always makes the heart sink if it's not at predictable times, for that means trouble. But there he stands, with a sheepish grin on his Michelangelic face, and a pair of nice new woolly socks under his arm and some sheets of paper in his free hand.

He explains the plan like he's just conceived it, and I nod my head assiduously and agreeably, but there's not enough paper here, for one makes many mistakes in lettering, and in any case we could do with something of better quality if it's available, why not have the best for one's section, eh?, and he goes off and comes back with a dozen sheets of stuff with the Prisons Department logo on it, such as is used in correspondence with the Minister. The best.

The metal doors are opened at six a.m., pap time, while the grilles remain closed. The tin plates of pap are slid one under each grille, and you hold your tin mug through the bars and a junior section cleaner sloshes in the soukol coffee. As Blackie arrives at my grille I thrust the drawing through the bars and he drops my pap on the floor. I have here a goozoo with a pubic bush as dense and extensive as the Knysna forest, there are wild elephants in there, man, plus a set of breasts you could ski off, given a bit of snow.

I tell him quickly this one is for Kanga, done in a hurry, but don't crumple it up under your shirt there, hey; yours will come tomorrow, with the reciprocal socks.

I mean this is highveld winter, you know, and what screw doing a personal body search is going to take off my amadumbe shoes and count the number of socks I've got on my goddam feet, hey? I shall need a bigger size shoe though.

If I can do this piece of porn in a hurry, what will a leisurely one look like? Blackie can only nod, he's so breathless.

Well, Blackie's is twice as good, at least. There are two goozies in this one, rather one and a chick, and they're doing rude things, and I make sure I have got my pap first, this time, so I don't end up with another upside-down breakfast on the floor.

I follow the sound business principle, and saturate the market whilst it's safe and profitable. I have ten drawings out there, available for trade, and I have also for my personal self a nice soft khaki shirt, a baadjie that fits, and a new jersey along with the four socks and clean blankets and things, also a neat pair of soft shoes to contain the multiple socks. Getting the blankets in was the difficult number, but Koornhof requisitioned them and signed for them at stores, and Beestekraal and Roux got the spunk-stiffened planks on their tables.

Koornhof is called Mielies because his head is made of phutu, pap, but he isn't so stupid, hey? Sure, as a beampte he has only to take these semenous blankets out and exchange them for other, further new ones, but he's intrigued about where the original new ones went, and finally finds from Roux what the deal has been. There's no menace, here, otherwise Kanga wouldn't have spoken; he's a crafty old veteran of more than one long term, and knows this psycho will want dirty pictures too. There's just professional wonder from Mielies Koornhof to start with: what on earth was going on, but Roux, cunning bastard and conman that he is, realises that if he can pull Mielies into the trade it will make things that much safer.

However, I decide there is to be no more trade, now that I've got what I want, and I shut down the production line. Almost, I mean. Mielies gets Vatjougoed to unlock my outer door on Monday, for psychological reasons, and such reasons they truly are, for he stands there looking as if he hasn't slept all weekend, nor shut his abraded eyelids in that time. He looks as if he's just walked through tearsmoke.

I know he's been looking at Blackie's fine art, and for reasons of power I let him fumble a bit, but I know what he's after and at the right moment I ask him if he would like a drawing like those I did for Roux and Blackbeard, but he can't bring himself to say yes, nor even nod his head, such is the guilt of it all. Okay, Sir, I say, tomorrow, same time, and I'm personally quite reassured, because if a prison officer is involved in this pornographic enterprise one can hardly charge the prisoners concerned without pulling him into the net too, and is such a charge worthwhile? Good staff are scarce.

For Mielies I do a drawing of such unspeakable indelicacy as to turn the stomach of the most shameless. This graphic has poultry in it like the Rainbow Chicken farm at Umlaas Road, and the permutations of sexual aberration are beyond belief. If Mielies' eyeballs looked sandpapered before, they now look like NASA maps of the planet Venus, hot enough to melt lead. I don't think he'll be able to blink them from this day forward, such is the realism of it all.

Not that this should really matter all that much anyway, since he will in all probability jerk his way to blindness soon enough.

Maybe even death.

Now recounting all these adventures of body and soul in the Madhouse may give the impression, dear reader, that the day was as full of events as this page is full of words. But that's not seg. In segregation you don't have any adventures of anything. My interesting conversations with Blackbeard lasted ten seconds, perhaps twenty if it was a long conversation, and that only if the boer was at the other end of the passage when the soup or pap was being delivered, and that meant only every now and then. Well, actually, they weren't conversations at all, but staccato communications.

So how do you describe eleven months of solitary, then? You write three hundred and thirty ditto marks on three hundred and thirty pages and request the reader to take one day to read each page. It's a great old skill.

What I'm trying to convey is that I'm caught in a trap here. If I were to describe the repetitious trifling details of each day's worth of trifling routine over such a stretch of time it would make but boring reading, whereas if I were to try to sustain a lively interest in this narrative from you, dear reader, you might just get the idea that this almost-year of nothing happening was lively and interesting.

Well, it wasn't. It was madness of the animal brain. Chain a dog to a peg in the ground without any sensory experience and see what it does to the first other animal that comes within range, including you, you arrogant ape. When you bring its food you'd better put it down on the ground at arm's reach. Chain's reach.

I still spent my day examining grey enamel and preparing for nocturnal fantasy, and trying to see that this fantasy didn't become silly and excitable, and assume the meaning that the word so often has, of being all magical and hysterical.

I'd been thinking of changing to a programme of construction rather than stories anyway; you know, go to a tool shop and buy the right tools, go to a timber or metal place and buy the right materials and spend a couple of months building something that works, getting all dimensions right so one can start the next night where one has left off.

My pondering this proposition is cut short, the decision is taken out of my hands, by a sudden flinging open of the cell door one morning and a cascade of filthy old canvas mailbags descending all about. Fifteen of them, huge bloody things, all ripped and rubbed and smelling of mice and cats. Vatjougoed gives me a short stout sail needle and a metal thing for the palm to push the needle through the canvas. He chucks a bundle of pitched twine on the floor and tells me if I don't get all bags done by graze time I'll get no food tomorrow, those are the rules.

So I go like all hell to start with, because I fear the hunger, but I have nimble fingers and I know how to use tools, so within a week or two I can get through the fifteen chop-chop and even have time for a ziz on them during the boer's lunch break, and wake like a dozing antelope at the slightest sound of his putting his key in the lock way down there at the end of the corridor. Even if he oh so craftily slides in the key, and removes his shoes so he can slink in and catch the ouens sleeping, I still hear the swish of his trouser-legs as he walks, and can even distinguish one screw from another by the different swishing.

My senses have become so acute month after month with so little sensory stimulus that I can gauge the minute-by-minute measure of everything in the boep by distant unrelated and mostly meaningless sounds. One sound is meaningful and normal, though also distant. At night in the total silence I can ever so faintly hear the sound of the Pretoria City Hall clock, how many miles away? But in the afternoon I gauge the passing of time differently; when that inexplicable wood-on-wood thumping happens, followed by certain formless shouts, I can expect to hear shortly a great metal thing clang about, and when that happens I know that if I don't get my exercise in the passage here within half an hour I won't get it at all and that's another day without leaving this cell, because the katkop trolley with the bread will shortly come trundling along its little tramline and the day will be over. So frustration will build up to rage in me, since often enough I have been three days or so without leaving these two-by-two-metre premises except to empty the balie, the prison shitpot, at first light. Rage is very bad for you in a place like this. You must pick up your feet and float.

So:

With the mailbags occupying so much of my day I haven't had time these days to examine my grey enamel, and have probably used up all its Rorschach images anyway. But I have another device. Get ready to work on the Tiger Moth. I can make this preparation during my sewing.

I don't mean actually start work on the Tiger before eight, but just to remember that I have the trestles under her at those points on the airframe where there's a little red arrow stencilled, and the words Support Here. I am going to go piecemeal over her entire structure, including the engine, and recondition it as new.

Where has she been kept, and has she been properly hangared? If she's been well cared for in the Transvaal the casein bonding adhesive of her wooden parts might be okay, but questionable if she's stood too long out of doors in Durban, at sea level. There were problems with wooden aircraft in damp hot tropical places of the Empire, and that's the era of this Tiger.

If you could smell dairy products when you climbed into your aeroplane at Mombasa, it was a good idea to climb out again, because the probability was that the casein glue holding all together was decomposing with the heat and humidity and bacteria, and your aircraft was now held together with cheese, which assorted insects were probably devouring at that very moment.

Well, what has to be replaced I'll replace, what has to be adjusted I'll adjust meticulously over the months. The new linen covering and paint job will take as long again. I can spread this work over my entire stretch, if necessary.

I have other advantages besides the Tiger, what with my new acute hearing. Before maintenance and restoration start at eight, I have an hour to listen hard, hard, to catch the words of distant music in remote other sections. There is one song which sounds like My Lips are Falling, and another sounds like Lead Trousers for a New Baby. From the whole remote repertoire I remember two from before boep: one is Sad Movies make me Cry, and the other is Adios Amigo, that kitschy sentimental western number about the end of the road we two cowhands have travelled.

The habit of association takes the place of reason in the Madhouse. Mind you that's true of the rest of all jails anywhere. You're never going to get a rational explanation for anything at all, so you do what dogs do, relate every sensory experience to your present physical circumstance, on the chance that it just may be the cause of this circumstance. If for example you see one of your pack die when there's a certain smell or sound in the air, that's enough! The adrenalin will flow when you smell or hear it again. Even if it happens not to be the cause of danger, you're conditioned to go into survival mode.

You can come to some odd conclusions this way. For a while I found myself believing that on those days that the Catholic Priest came we would get boiled brinjals for dinner. Why not? Were the ways of the Heavenly Father ever scrutable? Whenever Vatjougoed asked if we were Catholics, because the priest was here for communion, there were brinjals at graze time. It didn't have to be Sunday. Much later on this priest got me a pair of specs on Thursday, and we had brinjals.

He got me the specs from the kindness of his Christian heart, I reckon, but he sure as hell despised the Prisons Department; there was a touch of unChristian unforgiveness in it, hatred even, for unexplained reasons. Mainly, I thought, he disliked the Department because he was an otherwise Irishman. When he came to fit the specs and the Super himself stalked into the little cell set aside for religion, to find out what was going on between the two anti-Christs, a Red and a Roman, and Father MacGinnis had threatened to turn the she-wolf loose on the government of this country and the Super had withdrawn for the nonce, That'll fix that bastard, said the priest.

Well, inductive reasoning is better than none, and thus it is that after four months in the Madhouse I come to believe that when Adios Amigo is played at seven of an evening I can expect a clanging of cell doors down the passage when the City Hall clock remotely clangs at three-thirty in the morning, and not long after that, I believe, Adios Amigo also causes the pap and coffee to arrive when the sun is up and shiny, while normally breakfast is in the dark.

I give this some inquisitive thought after a certain late breakfast, and decide to wait in the next weeks for the cowboy song and see if this time I can predict the gates clanging with the clock chimes, and another late breakfast, but they play it so seldom, it must be unpopular.

I haven't had a chance to speak to Blackie for weeks now, but a relief boer called Spiers comes one Sunday, and leaves all the doors open as they do in other sections while waiting for the Super's inspection, and we all lean on our elbows at the locked grilles and smile at the ouens in the cells opposite, an arm's reach away, though talking is still a bit dodgy, and what have I got to say to this ou anyway, he's not worth losing meals for. I know he's going to ask if I've got tobacco, and how the hell am I supposed to have it if he hasn't, and if I had would I be so dumb as to give it to him?

But when Blackie comes idling by I buttonhole him briefly and he smiles expectantly and asks if I want to reopen the porn trade. No, Blackie, man, I was just standing here wondering why they don't play that nice old song Adios Amigo so often, is it out of fashion?

Hell no, says he, they don't like to play that thing, man, it's bad luck, it's what the condemned like to request.

And when the gates and doors slam at half past three, what's that?

No, those are the other condemned waiting their turn, next month maybe; they lock the white condemned up in the Madhouse, and take the kaffirs somewhere else I don't know. If they leave them in B2 they panic. What's B2? No, B2 is the condemned section, Death Row.

Shit, it fits. So that's what they're doing; they're hanging people.

That's bloody awful, hey Blackie?

Ja! You know, last time, day before hanging when we just bringing the aandete graze through the saal, they brought this woman through from the women's prison, and she tied up in a strait-jacket and strapped to a stretcher, and she crying, crying, loud, loud, man, and shouting also for God to help her, and they taking her to B2 to hang her in the morning, man. Jis, 't was vokken vreeslik, man. You know, when they hang a woman all her inside things fall out between her legs, man, and they got to wear special trousers to catch it, like. Jissis, nee, man, dis vokken swaar!

And why's the breakfast late today? No, they hang them at six o'clock, man, it takes a long time to get them ready, you know, with priests saying prayers, and injections, and all that goeters. Then afterwards they don't let the kitchen span out of their peters until they got all the other condemned back into B2, and they can't do that until the District Surgeon has examined the six dead ouens to see they really dead, and it all takes time. It's against regulations we can see the condemned, it's rude to stare at a ou who's going to die. Also, you know, when the kitchen span come out they don't work so lekker, man, they just want to sit down and make a skyf.

Balm of hurt minds, a skyf.

When another highveld hailstorm has hit Central and the great golf-ball stones have smashed up the glass roofs of the section corridors three storeys high, and the mirror-polished wax floors of the big passages are littered end to end with splintered glass and ice like it's Kristallnacht all over again, and the boere of all ranks are enraged and abusive because they want to get home and the Godvervloekte gevangenis has got no vokken roof any more, and what the hell next can go wrong in this vervloekte place, and the section cleaners must be to blame, what do the section cleaners say, especially since they are already at home?

When your missus writes to say she's met a real gentleman this time, with permanent employment in the Post Office, and consider yourself dumped this time, what do you say, especially since by equal probability she might have met a gentleman with permanent employment in the Prisons Department, this time?

Et cetera? Make a skyf, man!

Knits up the ravell'd sleeve of care, a skyf.

But I digress. I'm still with Spiers and the Sunday morning inspection, which duly happens, followed by the main meal at eleven and last graze, supper to be posh, at three, and all staff eager to get off to the braaivleis and just shut this fucking place up, it's Sunday.

Spiers is tall and lithe and the middleweight boxing champion of the Transvaal. He looks, most of the time, like a reared-up rinkhals. There is no fat whatever on his body, you can read his musculature as if it were an anatomy diagram. He is the beampte, the official, who delivers lashes. His body gestures, whether in walking or standing or boxing or lashing, all of his movements are balanced and elegant and a pleasure to the eye.

Lashes are what come beyond six days' ricewater. You can earn six lashes by assaulting a beampte, or threatening to assault him, or cursing at him. Lashes are given with a cane of specified dimensions. It is a Malacca cane, five feet long and half an inch in diameter. The front end, the lashing end, is whipped around with string, to absorb salt. This cane is stored in salt water, in a container like an old-time walking-stick stand. It stands in Reception, for some reason; I've seen it there. Perhaps I amongst others was supposed to see it there. They should have it on the departmental crest instead of all the corny symbols of rehabilitation and care: Two Malaccas Rampant and a Tochis Sinister, against a field of blood, Carmine.

I've also seen a bandiet getting his lashes, in Durban Central, by my balancing on a stool on a table and peeping through a window. There's this big mediaeval hinged stand like an artist's easel, quite artistically carpentered in oak, with mouldings around the structural members. There's a little platform for the naked prisoner to stand on, and a ring with a leather strap up top to which his wrists are buckled. The stand is opened a bit for the prisoner to climb aboard, his hands are strapped up and it's opened wide so his body is at about forty-five degrees, the optimum for delivery of the cuts. When I say cuts, that's what I mean. These are not those things called cuts one got at school. This thing doesn't just bruise, it cuts, as with a very blunt knife. A leather cushion is strapped over the prisoner's kidneys; if one of the lashes should land there they would rupture for sure and he would die for sure.

These are not canings from your schoolmaster. Your blood is running down your thighs when this master has finished his business.

This is heavy assault.

The District Surgeon is present to supervise. He has a wad of cotton wool and a bottle of iodine, which he sloshes onto the buttocks when the prisoner has finished writhing. Have you ever had iodine on an open wound? You've already had the salt, but iodine is something else; it's worse than the lashes. Well, they use it here because mercurochrome would stain the bum, tattoo it, and we wouldn't want that, would we?

A true bandiet, a real man bandiet, a bandiet in the Pretoria Central image and power game, a tough fucker, barters tobacco for some fingerprint ink, and goes back to his peter and rubs this into the wounds and fuck the fire of the iodine.

Such tattoos are as stripes of rank in the army. Around the prisons of the country, one may occasionally see the bums of these NCOs at shower time. Some are just varying tones of black, all over. They look like retreads. A rubber arse.

Anyway, Spiers is the beampte appointed to deliver lashes around here, and he should do it well, with the concentration of energy in the blow he has learned from boxing. He shakes his head as he tells of Johnny Scholtz, called King of the Bandiete at Central, and that's some claim, may I add, who got six lashes from Spiers for threatening to fuck up a warder who was persecuting his, Scholtz's, laaitie, his lover, a newcomer.

Love and loyalty take many forms.

Spiers is good at reading body language, hey, once again it's part of his craft, and he notes that Scholtz doesn't even clench his relaxed fingers as he gets his lot. Maybe Scholtz knows Spiers will look at his hands, that's what malehood's about. The District Surgeon comes to do his business with the iodine as Scholtz is released. Scholtz shoves the doctor out of the way and sits and rubs his naked and bleeding flesh on the concrete of the exercise yard where all this is happening, and marches up to Spiers and says Ja, and I'll fuck you up too when I'm finished with him, and fuck you anyway for what you've just done, jou vokken vark!

He can't get further lashes for six months, by regulation. I was told this story at a time much later when I often saw Mielies, and there were a few moments to ask questions. Did Spiers charge him? I asked. Nee, los 't man, Spiers had said, the ou was excited.

So here's Spiers then, efficiently getting through the Sunday routine of the section, amongst other stuff exercising the inhabitants in silence there in the little yard, but not me, because I must not have even visual contact with other criminals, and he doesn't find time during the routine to exercise me individually. He comes to me along the way, though, and says Look, you didn't get exercise this morning, and you haven't had it yet this afternoon, but I'll fit you in somewhere.

But what's wrong with you, man, you look like a bloody spook? Ja, I say, I am a bloody spook, because I don't go outside, I haven't been outside for six weeks. Balls, says Spiers, you get outside an hour a day, that's regulations, half an hour morning and afternoon. Where do you exercise if you don't go outside? I exercise here in the passage, where you stand, half an hour a day with luck. The passage is little wider than his shoulders. Bullshit! says Spiers, I don't need bullshit. He shuts the door and saunters off.

There's an extra-hasty rattling open and slamming shut of doors as dishes of soup get shoved into cells, mine too, at three; hasty because at half-past on Sunday every beampte is out of here and off to his sport and the place and its whole system shut down, switched off. But just as I'm settling down to my ritualistic evening the door opens again, and the grille too, of all things, and there is Spiers, and what the hell is he doing here, when all staff have taken tally and they're at the main gate ready to be off in half an hour, to the rugby and the family and the braai?

Eat your graze cold, says Spiers, come.

I walk out into the blazing red brick brilliance of the three o'clock sun in the exercise yard, and can't open my eyes it's so extreme. I do what I saw Nanook of the North do with a piece of flat whalebone and a narrow slit in it, and put my hands over my eyes with a little gap there between the fingers, and after ten minutes or so, such is the adaptability of the Caucasian eye, I'm blinking about and grinning and feeling like a beach-boy, and I've taken off my shirt, no shit, and I'm sunbathing. I run around this cramped exercise yard, though I'm not all that good at running these days, and I can't manage more than two laps, a hundred yards. But it's darem nog lekker, jong!

Back at the main gate the staff are off their heads with impatience. Three-thirty has come and gone. At the gate to A1 the Chief Warder is beside himself because he can get no response out of this place and Spiers has the key. DANKIE HEK! he yells, and rattles his bunch of keys against the steel bars, but Spiers goois him a doofie, as the saying goes, he cocks him a deaf ear, like Nelson seeing no signals with his blind eye, because this Spiers is a different ou, an otherwise bastard, who gets the hell-in if he's menaced, it's part of his craft. Even if he himself is supposed to go to his gym this afternoon, he clearly feels under threat of aggression from the entire staff of this prison, which they can't shut down until final tally, with every single man locked in his cell, including me, at present sunbathing in the exercise yard. Threat and aggression are two things Spiers is impervious to. As I say; that's part of his craft. He is especially impervious when he has the regulations behind him. He's the hell-in now.

So I'm trying to run counter-clockwise around this little yard, and Spiers is strolling clockwise, jangling his section keys behind his back and whistling a jingle under his broken nose, and as we come to pass each other I ask him Meneer, what's this guitar music coming from the cells here? I thought this boep was supposed to be silent. No, says Spiers, those are the condemned, they are allowed to have a guitar.

Is this B2? Ja, the middle floor there.

B2 is opposite the punitive part of A1 remote from me, solitary with no food, and the preventive part, Seg. A1 is separated by the width of this little exercise yard from the Death Section one floor up. I'm glad I'm on the further side of A1, where one can't hear the guitar.

Eventually Spiers says That's an hour, come! I put on my shirt.

As he goes about locking me up I say Thank you, sir, and he lays a disapproving glance on me straight and says Look, I don't need you to congratulate me for doing my bloody job, I get paid for it, okay? and locks the cell, the grille and the metal-covered door.

That wasn't the last I had of sunshine in the Madhouse. At about month five I'm already into shirt-sleeve time as I work on my mound of mailbags, and on one particular day, as it's getting a bit middagete-ish, I can tell by the signals coming from my gut, I realise that the radiation inside this two-metre home of mine is getting a bit extreme, and as I drop my mailbag to stare about and wonder at all this brilliance, there appears on the wall opposite me a small smudge of sunshine. Not too big, about the size of a thumb-print, but it's total sunshine, photons, and it hasn't even come through glass. There is nothing between this wall and the central star of our system. It takes but a single step to get my hand there. I am in touch with the universe.

A scratch with the mailbag needle in the middle of this beam at each event of the day will give me a good clock, and I won't need my stomach and drooping eyelids so much, but it seems no time at all before the daily patch is so big it's hard to find the centre, and I'm able actually to take off my shirt and sunbathe, just a patch at a time, about a breadplate-sized patch, while working on the bags. I reckon soon enough I won't look so ghostly, and I stop my work every now and then to look at my limbs so vigorous, and feel the youth in my body, and now and then do a few push-ups and the like, and work up a good sweat and really feel triumphant and cocky because of the fullness of my life after that brutal winter.

Work on the Tiger has gone well too. I've completely stripped the airframe, wings and fuselage, and tested every load-bearing member. Also I've had the Gypsey Major out of the kite with a block and tackle and on to a wheeled trolley in the hangar, and done a complete engine overhaul in two months.

Just replacing her fabric covering remains. You can't actually find anything in this world that's entirely a waste of time, not even mailbag sewing. I realise as I pull the fine linen over the rear fuselage that I'm using a sewing technique under her belly that is in fact the mailbag stitch, and here she stands, as new. She has a new pair of tyres, too, low-pressure nice squashy things; what we don't want after all this love and care is that a bloody tyre should burst on touchdown and wipe out both wings on that side. I spray her end to end with a grey lacquer primer, ready for the heraldry and a blaze of striking colour with her final paint job. But not yet.

First I get her out there on the grass field on a nice Sunday morning, all grey and sombre in her primer paint, and do a tail-up wheels-down run into wind, then a flight the length of the field a few feet up, testing the controls, then a whole circuit, wide, wide, with some adjustment to trim-tabs afterwards, and now we're ready for the whole thing, the real thing.

But first the painting.

I get the priming coat smooth as porcelain with fine waterpaper and much further spraying. On to this I spray two coats of really good quality silver lacquer, bright as bright, over the whole aircraft, and over that two coats of prussian blue, the darkest and most transparent blue you can get. With the light reflecting off the silver and coming through the blue she is the colour and the tone of the sky at the very merest hint of dawn down on the dark dark beach there, almost black, yet full and rich and glowing inky blue.

The upper side of the top wing and the underside of the lower wing I divide end to end into squares: a chequerboard. The fin and rudder and rear end of the fuselage too. Starting at the wingtips I spray alternate squares full cerulean blue, sky blue, with a touch of white. With each successive set of squares I leave out much of white and some of the cerulean and add a bit of prussian blue, so by the time I'm two-thirds inboard the squares have become barely distinguishable from their background, like the spots on young lions. The fin and rudder too are full-strength chequerboard contrast, but as we come forward along the fuselage it fades, and at the rear cockpit we've got to the lion-cub spots again. The remaining areas of deep prussian blue make a stunning contrast.

Her engine cowling I've had off to a panelbeater to get it absolutely smooth, without the smallest dent, and full shiny metallic silver, polished brightly, unpainted. Just aft of that I have sprayed in her name in firm angular letters to match the character of the checks: INDLAZI, a mousebird, in white.

Test flights are over and she's absolutely ready for everything. The greatest thing of all things is aerobatics, of course, and that's what I must work on now.

Perhaps you have been to an air show and there come across an aerobatics competitor going through his flying sequence on the ground. He has it down diagramatically on a little sheet of paper, which will be sticky-taped to his instrument panel later, but which he now holds before him as his free hand carefully flies through the routine. In competition he's restricted to the air above two kilometres square, marked on the ground, and now on the tarmac here he has chalked off a square two metres by two, and his flying hand is equivalently restricted to that. His body movements are slow and considered and formal. For points in the air his manoeuvres must be precise, and each part in the sequence always at right angles or parallel to the last, so here he stands with his feet precisely together, and when he moves them he does so only at right angles or straight forward or about turn, and his paces within the square are small and regular and precisely all of the same length.

The flying hand is the thing to see, though, twisting about at the wrist as he does a four-point vertical roll, bending back at ninety degrees as he goes into an inverted half-loop, another half-roll as he now goes into a full outside loop-and-a-half, ending up with a stall turn at the boundary and rolling into the most difficult thing of all: a full 360° horizontal circle exactly within the square, with four full rolls along the way. All that stuff.

It is all an advanced Post-Modernist Ancient Egyptian dance; you could win a prize with this dance unchanged at an Eisteddfod. It is what I am doing a couple of nights after the test flights. I have waited for the lovely summer moon to give me my breadplate of beams on the wall when the sun has left off, so I can read my phantom slip of paper with the sequence on it. My peter is roughly two metres square, so I don't need any chalk. My flying hand is into a six-point hesitation roll without loss of a single foot of altitude when I hear the midnight special coming to shine his ever-loving light on me.

With my Dobermann ears I hear him way down the passage, opening the section gate first, and peering at each sleeping ou through his spy-hole. I know he's at mine now.

That's all right; regulations say nothing about flying, even at midnight, as long as it's not noisy. He stays at the spy-hole, tjoepstil, but I know he hasn't moved on. Suddenly my ever-loving light comes on and he barks Wat maak jy daar, man? Ek het jou 'n hele rUK hierso dopgehou! Wat maak jy?!

Nee, ek vlieg, Meneer. A long silence, maybe half a minute. Jy WAT? Ek vlieg, Meneer. He's staring at me as I pace about and writhe my wrist.

Nee, God, man, jy's vokken mal! Ja, Meneer, dis van die tronk. He stays another half-minute or so, there must be some contravention of something here, but he can't think of what, nor anything to say, and I hear the spy-hole cover closing. I hear him muttering as he switches off my light and his trouser-legs swish away. Yirra Yissis, man, ek weet w'ragtag nie!

Next night I decide to do the actual competition flight with a certain Lt Brown in the front cockpit. He's the bloke who shot down von Richthoven in WW1; the Tiger flies better with a bit of ballast forward. We talk during the sequence, over the primitive hosepipe intercom of the Tiger, while I'm flying it. It's a strange experience: I have twice as many hours as he has, but he's twice the pilot I am. No, Richthofen is twice the pilot I am, and Brown is four times. He's so eager after my ten minutes in the air he can't wait to fly the sequence himself.

So it's the night after that and we're having a little celebration of our flying success; nothing big, you know, just a couple of Pernods and a bit of dancing with French girls maybe. Smashing, the moon is doing her tropical best for this jazzy New Orleans evening in my peter, and I'm making blues, a bit of Sonny Terry, and sort of kwela-ing in the middle of the seven-foot floor there with the blues harp huddled up to my mouth and half swallowed, and wa-wa-ing silently away with the music all inside my head:

When you dance like that,
In your pants like that,
Baby you could make a blind man see,
You're a chocolate cookie and you bring out the boogie in me.
My liewe Here Jesus! Jy vlieg alweer! Nee, Meneer, vanaand vlieg ek nie.
Nou ja, in God se naam wat maak jy dan, man?! Ek speel bekfluitjie, Meneer.
Jy WAT? Ek djaaiv, Meneer. A long staring silence. Jy's skoon vokken moerse
mal, man, weet jy dit? Ja, Meneer, 's vannie vokken malhuis. Yirra Yissis, nee,
man, ek weet nie! I picture him shaking his head again as his broeks swish off
away down the corridor. Ja, Meneer; mooi loop, Meneer.

You take me back to nineteen and forty three,
You're a be bop baby and you bring out the boogie in me.

Lt Brown is a bloody sight better company than J. Christ any day, the
Glorie-Paradys notwithstanding. Maybe one of these evenings I'll ask him if
perhaps it would have been a better idea if he'd knocked off Hermann Göring
instead.

Thirteen

AFTER FURTHER WEEKS, OR MONTHS, I don't know, I've lost count, my peter is slammed open one morning and Vatjougoed says Kom, oefen, and the narrow passage with its little cat-house light-bulbs is waiting for me and my exercise, and as I move out he pushes me to the left and says Gaan staan daarso. I go to that end of the passage and wait to see what will happen. Way down there I see the Opper, the Chief Warder, Stephanus van Rijswater, standing at the other end of this passage, and I wonder what the hell now is going on around here. Van Rijswater has substantial buttocks, and walks leaning curiously forward from the pelvis. He is known hereabouts as Here'smyheadmyarseiscoming.

Vatjougoed goes to a cell down that end and opens it and out steps a bloke called Ben Turok, from Joburg. I've seen his picture in *New Age*; he wrote a sort of ideological analysis of the news. VJG takes him to the Opper, who speaks some words. Ben turns and starts his exercise walking towards me, and I towards him. I know by now why the Opper is there, so when Ben comes past and raises his hand in greeting I do no more than wink an eye. When I get close to the Opper and Vatjougoed they beckon me to stand there with them, and when Ben comes along from the other end they pull him over too. The Opper raises three fingers of his right hand. Vatjougoed says We told you not to speak and you spoke. Ben is bewildered. We didn't speak, he says, we smiled, but Here'smyheadmyarseiscoming is stuffed if he's going to take down his fingers and lose face and authority. I say to him Better tell him the three fingers mean three meals, Meneer. If I tell Ben this interesting thing direct three fingers of the Opper's other hand will go up too, for me.

Ben is flabbergasted, but it's a good introduction to this place, and after a couple of weeks he's into survival mode. In spite of the absurdities of never making more than eye contact for fear of loss of meals, and that sort of slick tyranny, it's nice to know there's someone else around.

But there's no such thing as stasis in this entire universe, and after no more than a month or so our doors and bars are included in the general whamming open one Sunday morning after inspection, and there's Spiers again, who hauls us out with all the other fifty or so ouens of the madhouse, and holds us back a bit as all others are off to the exercise yard to walk around in file in a big circle, and then says to us You two walk the other way round, and if you talk to those ouens sal julle gat sien.

Can we talk to each other? Balls, man, he says, I haven't got time to see you buggers don't converse. And can we take off our shirts? You can take off the whole bloody lot if you like, but when you see me leave this door put it all back on again fast and walk separately.

A curious experience! But no need for me to feel strange about the forgotten techniques of conversation, because all I have to do for the present is listen to the the the flood of news, the avalanche of information that Ben has for me, the recent history of the Struggle. Even gossip; I haven't seen a newspaper in more than a year.

How, though, does the Party persona of Jack Hodgson come to follow me about so? Ben tells me of the Hodgson commando's adventures in the revolution trade in Joburg, and whereas I'd felt and still feel embarrassed about the Mallun sink, well really...

'sBlood! 'sHaemorrhoids! They had set about the making of gunpowder, no less. I mean this is real REAL Guy Fawkes stuff, bru.

So the Joburg Jacquerie are off to plant this infernal machine all ready primed et cetera at a site of their own fancy, though they haven't quite got round to fancying any particular site yet. And as they drive along there examining this site and that, this thing done up in a brown paper parcel starts to sizzle and emit smoke, and they get proper anxious as indeed anyone would, and since they're in a nice quiet suburb just now they decide just to dump it, so they open the door of the car and chuck it out, what a relief.

Well I shoudn't say it again, I mean really I shouldn't, for fear of repetitiveness and boredom, but life really isn't predictable, and that means everything isn't, for life is all we've got, so I must say it again.

From absolutely nowhere in said quiet suburb appears in the rear-view mirror a single headlamp and a single flashing blue light, and as this blue light hauls up behind the rear bumper of the Vee Dubs Beetle which the Resistance are presently navigating the urgent repetitive howl of a police vehicle siren is to be heard, and a speedcop motorcyclist draws up alongside and beckons them over to the verge.

He pulls up ahead of them and switches off and puts down his side-stand to park the bike and comes over to the driver's side of the Beetle and takes off his helmet. Good evening, Sir, he says, what a fine night now the winter's over. He reaches inside his leather jacket and hauls out a brown-paper parcel. This parcel seems to have fallen off your roof-rack, Sir, he says.

The gunpowder seems to have stopped sizzling.

Oh thank you officer says Hodgson, I don't know how it could have come loose, I strapped it down so securely. No problem, says the officer, as I often say to my wife, who is anxious about my riding about at night when I might run over something which could upset my balance on the motorcycle...

Of course of course, says Hodgson, and I do appreciate your help but I must be off now. It was a pleasure, Sir, says the traffic officer, so glad to.... but Hodgson puts him down flat with GOOD NIGHT OFFICER, WE MUST

BE OFF! Hy trap voet in die hoek and leaves this poor polite fellow wondering why the world is so ungracious.

Five minutes later the brown-paper parcel starts smoking again. They brave the possibility of Rottweilers and chuck it into somebody's swimming-pool.

Well then.

Spiers gives us the whole daysworth of exercise in one whack, a solid hour, and by the end of it I'm ready for my solitary, where I'll have to lie down a bit, exhausted, and wonder at the perplexing frenetic nature of life out there, and why people need to make their lives so complex and confused when mine has become so simple and single-minded.

I don't know that I'd feel so safe out there any more.

But never to worry. Ben is an important figure in Joburg, and benefits are going to flow from this fact. Lawyers have been at the throat of the Commissioner. Ben expects us to have access to the prison library of five thousand books, and study privileges, as declared desirable in prison regulations.

Ben has to push his normal six weeks in the Madhouse first, of course, though I don't want to spoil things for him and observe that my six weeks have taken more than that number of months, and rising. But all wondrous things happen in the fullness of time, and one morning while I'm at my mailbags my door flings open and Vatjougoed thrusts a couple of books at me, from the five thousand.

The first is a slim volume, and tells me how to get a driver's licence in the City of Pretoria in 1932. It has Indian ink graphics in it of a gent in a three-piece suit with a tie and a Homburg hat at the steering-wheel of an open Austin Seven, and I don't mean seven litres, I mean seven horsepower, the power of twenty-eight quarter-hp legs on bicycles, i.e. fourteen pals pedalling uphill.

This worthy is making hand signals over the gun'l of the Austin, across his double-breasted jacket and waistcoat and collar and tie and over his head. The graphics show him from both ends, ahead and astern. From astern one of the signals tells those behind him that he is approaching a wagon with sixteen oxen in yoke, and is contemplating the overhauling of this itinerant stockyard, and the driver of any following Austin Seven, or even an Austin Twelve, had better be careful in the matter of casually following this driver into the overtaking manoeuvre, because there might be a similar wagon with a span of sixteen approaching from the other direction, and the Austin Twelve or Seven driver might get trampled to death amongst the stampeding cattle.

The other book I liked much better. It was the story of a Pom admiral who sailed up a body of water in Canada to get behind the Frogs in colonial days. I wasn't sure where the body of water was, nor what it was called, because that part of the book had been smoked. It was a serious piece of history, well published and printed on good paper, though that had been its undoing during its shelf life, and presently its covers looked like the mouth of a pensioner whose false teeth had gone overboard from the Ile de France on a rough Atlantic crossing.

Later in my career I learned what was meant when some bandiet came up to you as you were having a quick illicit read standing with your broom there during that fifteen-min expectant spell before section inspection in the morning and asked Is it a good book? Not bad, you might remark, or even: I would recommend it, whereupon the eyes of this bandiet would closely follow yours, for there are gentlemen even in this rough community, and as you were done with that leaf, before you could say Jack Robinson whomever, and turn the leaf over, it would be gone from under your very nose, literally, and up in smoke, also literally, into somebody else's nose. Some of it, that is, most being folded away for further skywe.

The pages had been randomly smoked, of course, all being of equal quality, so most of the gaps were one or two pages long and easily handled, but my best was the big gap of fifty-four pages, where I could employ and test all my Rorschach and Tiger Moth ingenuity, and construct a piece of history convincingly to bridge the gap. To this day I think it was better than the normal dreary history of the Royal Navy and most colonial wars.

At one point I had the surviving crew of one of His Majesty's Ships wrecked on a great riverine shore amongst the surviving individuals of wrecked native nations living cunningly amidst the limitless pines, where between and amongst them all they were able to fell and plank the timber to construct and launch and sail away a ship entirely of their own intuitive design. What construction, and where to? I work on it yet, from time to time. And why not? Most history seems to be such prostheses anyway.

My mind tends to wander, generally, and at this time I make a point of letting it stray off thus. Encouraging it. It will come home.

Ja, I remember now, this must have been about month seven in the Malhuis; I know this because I remember noticing at that month that I was better at fantasy than I was at reading. You want a story, I'll make you one, like a pavement scribe with his typewriter and umbrella on a Bangladeshi street. Letter, story, obituary, manifesto, what you want, I got it. Same time.

But I'm not so good at reading any more: I get stuck on words, quite often, as a stammerer gets stuck on spoken words, and I don't know how the hell it works, as stammerers don't, otherwise I would stop this bullshit. It's just incipient, and not too much worrying, but by the time Ben and I get to study at month eleven, twelve, or so I'm what you might call illegerate; not mute, for I come from a family as talkative as a treeful of Indian mynahs, nor unable to write, as you see from this present welter of words, but incapable of the physiological act of reading without compulsively running hands over eyes, and going over and over two or three words five, six, seven times, as if wondering how on earth they come to have any abstract meaning at all as scratches on a flat surface. Even when reading what I have myself written it is so, and it's weird. I have it yet.

But that's not bad luck. Bad luck is what a bandiet called Ginsberg got, who after his unexplained time in seg, and deep seg too, measured in years where mine is mere months, stuck razor blades in his eyes, and now makes his way daily to the sunny side of the main corridor of A1 with a stick nobody need paint white since all know the story.

He was moved from the punishment half of A1, that part called Solitary, after the razor blades, of course, and transplanted to the Madhouse part. I suppose there was fear the story might get out. But he's not a Madhouse patient waiting for the psycho and sedulously locked up at all times. He is allowed by Spiers to stand near the gate for a bit each morning until the floor polishers come. Other sections are emptied and closed each day as the ouens go to work; only this one has a boer on duty all day, which Ginsberg needs for going about his daily life. Spiers exercises him with the other seg bandiete, his hand on somebody's shoulder as they amble round and round the little yard.

He is not allowed to talk to the owner of the shoulder, of course, for this is a silent section. This must be bloody hard for Ginsberg, he's a great compulsive talker; maybe that's what got him into seg in the first place, saying the wrong thing to the wrong person and getting suspected of being in some ring of smugglers or sodomites or something. Who knows?

Later, Ben and I became the polishers of this floor, that's how I know about such sorry things.

There he stands then one nice warm Christian Sabbath morn when v.d. Beestekraal and the visiting predikant of the Much Deformed Church come by, doing their Christian bit of unpaid overtime, and Beestekraal asks Would you like to join us in prayer, Ginsberg? and Ginsberg says No thanks, I'm not much given to prayer these days, and anyway I'm a Jew.

Remember, says the Dominee, that our Saviour the Lord Jesus Christ himself was a Jew.

Ja? says Ginsberg, so if Jesus was a Jew, how come he had a Mexican name?, and Beestekraal gets proper irritable at such blasphemy, and makes to go and find the Opper and take away some meals from this crim, but the Dominee takes his sleeve and tells him it's ungracious to punish a blind man on Sunday, though true's God, I myself to this day can see neither moral nor logical connection between this guy's eyes and his gut and the day of the week.

Ja, so at my month eleven or so, maybe a year, I forget, Ben's six weeks are up after nine months, and we do Beestekraal's psychologicable test along with a few dozen other madpersons whose only purpose in this life and on this planet is to get where the snout is.

This test typed out by Beestekraal has many symbolical questions, like
1: Do you dream you are flying?
2: Do you dream you are climbing up a Great Big Christmas Tree?
3: Do you dream you are swimming in a beautiful lake of clear blue water?
4: Do you dream you have murdered your mother?
5: Etc. up to 16.
16: Do you hide in the lavatory when guests come to your house?
17: Do you masturbate?

Well so far my answers to all these are clear. I think I'm flying even when I'm wide awake. Father Christmas can stuff his tree, my dreams are differently heathen, asleep or awake, I dream I'm fucking women. I swim wide awake in this clear blue lake every lunchtime during my little lay-down on the mailbags, with my missus and nice new baby, all three of us naked, teaching her to swim, it's the great sensuous moment of my every day. Most days of my waking life, furthermore, I've felt like murdering my ma, except I'm not a psychopath and she has this irritating habit of generosity.

Never mind the lavatory, if Beestekraal came to my house I'd turn the Pit Bull loose on him.

What do you want I should do in bed anyway, other than masturbate and sleep? Dream of mailbags?

But I don't write all these things down, naturally, you're supposed just to put a little tick in the yea or nay box.

Each ou gets a pencil and this sheet of questions, to be collected by Blackbeard in the morning. Psychoanalysis is a fearsome thing. We've all heard of it, mostly in stories about the loony patient on a horse-hair-stuffed leather-upholstered sofa, the shrink with the Mad German Scientist steel-rimmed specs all crooked on his nose and stuck opaque with dandruff, and his pretty receptionist with the Cross-my-Heart bra; but now it's actually going to happen to us we realise this is no joke, because we've got to get all these answers right if we want to get a good analysis and anywhere near the tobacco, and maybe get put on the building span and work out of doors.

So after dark Ben and I hear these desperate hoarse whispers down the passage, through the ventilator: Fanie! Hey Fanie! Fanie man!

Ja?

Fanie, wat maak jy man?

Nee, ek skiem kraaim.

I mean fer God's SAKE, he's into only his second month of his five-to-eight or nine-to-fifteen years and he's getting ready for the next number when he's out of here, only more shrewd this time.

Fanie, man, wat is die antwoord vir nommer twaalf?

Nee, says ou Fanie, ek skiem dis 'n trep. Skryf mos jy weet nie, dan is jy mos veilig.

Nee, ou Fanie, dan skiem hulle ek is mos otherwaais, en kry ek vokkol.

Ja, 's vokken swaar. Vat maar 'n kans, man. Ek skryf mos Ja.

Oukei ou Fanie, dan skryf ek ook mos Ja. Dankie, jong!

Okay, so by lunchtime next day everybody's psychoanalysed and off to various employment, with or without tobacco. Ben and I are taken off to some unidentified office where a fat man beside himself with personal hatred tells us that we have advanced backwards, to D-group, punishment group, where we've just come from anyway. He doesn't seem to know I've been here almost a year. He doesn't seem to know that anyway we've had only one letter and one visit per six months and all the other vengeful stuff he wants to hit us with now.

Do you know of a word better than Nu?

Nu?

Well, you see, ultimately you can't get away from Lorenz's Butterfly. This Lorenz made the point that the eddies in the air from one mere flap of this gogga's wings in the Amazon forests could, by the ongoing accretion of random events, end up as a meaningful sequence and a hurricane in the Bay of Bengal. There may seem to be laws of meteorology, but forget it, mate, what you're looking at is in fact fractal geometry, the geometry of the infinitely unpredictable, the only recognisable characteristic in its whole nature being its self-similarity. As with the weather, so with boep: never even try to predict more than three days ahead, no logic can construe probability beyond that.

Boep is a self-similar place.

So four days later, for infinitely unpredictable reasons, Vatjougoed is shunted off to another section or another boep, on promotion perhaps, or maybe Beestekraal has found the flagellant stockwhip and covets things his rank does not allow, en Ferreira is gedump. And who takes his place but Spiers.

Ben and I realise within the next four days or so that the whole punitive thing of our solitary is entirely personal, there's no single thing about it in regulations. From the Officer Commanding this place, the Super, right down through intermediate ranks to the psychos and the section boer, it's all been personal and punitive. Maybe from him upwards to the Minister. Maybe they had instructions from the Security Police, but that would be a feeble enough excuse, since the Prisons Department is independent of those pricks. Maybe it came through the Party, which means the Minister, of course. What about that, hey?

Spiers has curious stature in the male community of the Prisons Department. Nobody wants the middleweight boxing champion of the Transvaal to say, or even think, that he is petty and manipulative and vengeful and small. Some resent silently and sullenly this presence of Spiers.

Beestekraal resents it noticeably and sullenly. Mielies seems to find it a great relief.

Spiers is most aware of his power in the Department, make no mistake; he has just been made Head Warder, a sort of sergeant, and this, make no mistake here either, is his section, as of now, and he's on his way up and knows that, and everybody else knows it too. Specialists whose work brings them to his section must do their work here, but never cross his path, whatever their rank, because he has the Regulations behind him, the referee is watching, and the referee there at head office knows who he, Spiers, is.

There appear strange nuances of behaviour, of the sort to which captive creatures are deeply sensitive. I wake up alert one midday in the middle of my dream, my quick ziz, because I hear Mielies' duck feet coming down the passage. That's all right, he's not dangerous. Curiously, he stops at my door, which even more curiously is not locked. The grille is, of course, and Mielies opens the door stands there and smiles at me through the bars as I rise from my mailbags. He has in his hand a Crunchie bar, which he has brought along with his lunch-time sandwiches, but which will increase the girth of his belly, he explains, pinching up a handful of epicurean paunch to demonstrate this truth. He would like to know if I would like this chocolate. It is a relaxed and genuine offer. It is very bizarre.

I take this Crunchie bar from Mielies and ask him if he has a knife, because I have only a spoon for my food, and he opens his pocket knife and hands it to me. I carefully cut the chocolate in half, and give one half back to him and say Will you give that piece to Turok?, and Mielies starts to weep, and I have to give him some sheets from my toilet roll to wipe his eyes.

After pap next morning, I don't know what time it was, one doesn't think of hours and minutes in boep, only the periods between food; after pap then my cell is opened, both doors, and there stand Spiers and Ben, and Ben is wearing nought but a pair of navy blue soccer shorts for his comfort, and a big square polishing hanky of red cotton stuck in the elasticised waist.

Spiers hands me similar section-cleaners vestments and says Trek aan, kom!

He locks my cell, habitually, when I'm out of it. What would somebody steal in there? My spoon maybe.

We're in the big main corridor of A1 now, seventy, eighty paces long, about nine or ten wide, I suppose. This corridor has had fifty years or so of polishing done on it. You can literally see your face in it. If it weren't black you really could shave in it.

Down the centre of this corridor run the little tramlines for the trolley with graze and katkop, that small loaf which is half your day's ration of bread, as coarse as it's possible to get flour coarse, with the small dark crust on it just the shape and the feel of a cat's cranium. I don't understand why I have to find in this miserable place the best bread I've ever eaten, except of course the Department would know where to find the cheapest and least-processed flour, hardly processed at all, and baked by the bandiet kitcheners themselves, who know there's one good thing going, and it's the katkop, and bake it at that time of day that will give each unhappy bandiet in the boep his katkop so hot sometimes that he has to toss it from hand to hand a bit before the first beautiful bite, and be of good cheer for a minute or two.

But los these sentimentalities; I am told of one of our comrades in the struggle who had his knob nailed to a table by the Security Police, and it is in these terms that one should write definitive history of the Struggle, and not dwell on the delights of bread-eating in this evil systemic place and concede humanity to the ogres who run it.

Well okay, I lack commitment, and only picture this victim going for a pee with his fingers on the holes like he's playing Bach on the Blockflöte, otherwise he's going to piss in his eyes and shoes when he starts to urinate.

But never mind.

Nobody at all walks anywhere in this corridor outside the tramlines. Nobody, that is, but Beestekraal and his cricketers and the Doge, Il Duce, the Superintendentgevangenisbeampte and his entourage on their Sunday Special, the Big Inspection. They walk wherever their feet may fall. That is their weekly ritual of power, to scuff up an entire week's work of two men.

When I say nobody walks there, I mean almost nobody, for Ginsberg parked by Spiers down near the Section gate scarce counts as a body. He's standing there for the sunshine, though I must explain there's precious little of it, light in here is reflected, it's three storeys deep with a glass roof over steel mesh. He's standing here to listen to things, that's what for. He won't trudge about here and scar up the polish with his bandiet boots, what's the point?, there's more to hear if you just stand still. So nobody sees him. It's unearthly, he's become an apparition whom people perceive only when there's a certain accountable number of rations on the katkop express.

Spiers takes us to a collection of floor-polishing things down the corridor. There are the expected tins of black wax polish and rags and big oval brushes, those you use for grooming a horse, also those wads of old blanket called taxis that you place your bare feet on and move over the floor with a skating action, to give the final high gloss, right at the end. There's also an invention here for use right at the beginning. It's a great rectangular block of concrete with a steel pipe embedded in it as a handle for two men, and it's bound about with a coarse copra floor mat, the sort that is supposed to say Welcome, fixed with wire to the concrete slab. Spiers explains its use. It is to remove all boot-scrapes from the Sunday inspection and take the whole passage back to uniform primal unpolish, ready for the week's elbow-and-knee grease, and uniformly flat so one can almost shave in it by next Sunday.

Okay, Meneer, we're keen to get active in the great outside world again, we'll get cracking right away with this monolith.

Ben Turok is of Lithuanian stock, the people of stone, a Lapith. He looks like an imbhokodwe, one of those igneous easter-eggs the size of one's head, that has thumped and polished its way downriver in flash floods all the way from the Drakensberg to the sea over a million or so years. I myself am built like a piece of wire sculpture, steel wire and habitually springy.

Orraait, push it! says Spiers, and Ben and I spit on our hands and grip the shaft of this gravestone and heave, and nowt happens. We're unmatched, says Ben, you're too tall and our centre of gravity is too high; you must bend your knees a bit. Ben is a short-arse river-rock, and if it were logical to suggest that he should walk on tip-toes I'd have done so, but he's right in the matter of physics, so I bend my knees and shove and nowt happens again.

Spiers is not really much of a laughing man, I suppose, but he gets close to it now. No, he says, you got the wrong action, and takes the handle of this thing and walks away with it about twenty paces down the corridor, ewe gerus, and turns it about and back, and when he now talks to us I notice that he hasn't even had to rearrange his syntax or grammar to give himself a few extra commas and things for that quick extra secret puff and pant.

I realise I am not the piece of steel wire of narcissistic reverie, but like one of Count Dracula's staff a translucent wraith of spectral skin stretched over a frame of second-hand coat-hangers and old walking-sticks and broken brollies, this polythene skin traced about with bumps and tints of blue veins to offset the crimson of the eyes and pallid pink of lip and gum.

Ben Turok is but a balloon, a head-sized easter-egg of used breath, who might leak if strained, a long slow whistle like a mosquito, until all left were some eyebrows and receding hair and stuff amongst the blue soccer shorts and red cotton hanky of his prison issue clothing.

Better just start with the taxis, says Spiers, and that's what we do for two hours, by the end of which I'm just about ready once again for a further spot of solitary confinement, please, I'm so pooped. I eat my fish called mermaid with the boiled brinjals and fall asleep slumped over my small table, never mind illicitly lying on the floor. By the time I've got the four pee em soup down I realise I'll have to phone Lt Brown and tell him I'm off sick for a couple of weeks.

With the morning bell I remember the last time my legs felt like this, and it was when I first rode a horse; the adductor muscles of my thighs have become biltong, atrophied and incontractile, and I find it difficult to squat on my balie. But I remember enough from the athletics, and teaching drawing the classical anatomical way, to know that we can give the legs a relative rest today and get stuck into the wax polish and use the torso a bit.

Ben staggers out of his peter like a landmine victim and we get down on kneepads all sewed together from reject mailbags and bits of blanket, like great big doughnuts, and set about the eight hundred or so square metres of black floor with the rags and the wax and the horse-brushes. We know what our upper bodies are going to feel like tomorrow, but bugger that, we're really into relish of the exercise just now, side by side down there, rhythmically swaying from furthest left to extreme right, like ngoma dancers, or if you want to be serious, galley slaves at their oars, but DOING it, man, and nice to be alive again.

Our first foray takes us down the northern side of the A1 corridor tramlines, and we cross over to the southern side to make our way back with the polish and rags.

Howzit, kêrels? says Ginsberg standing there with that strange bentforward posture that some blind people have. Howzit, we reply, but bad luck, boet, we're not supposed to talk to anybody. No, says Ginsberg, that's all right, you don't have to talk, I just want to tell you a good joke, all you have to do is listen, and he lays on us the first of numberless Yiddishe jokes that drive us out of our bloody minds in the next while, man.

Moses is up on the mountain, says Ginsberg, and suddenly God says to him MO-O-Oses, says God, Behold, I have inscribed for Mine People Laws upon Tablets of Stone, and I send thee hence that thou mightst take these Laws unto Mine People, and shew unto them the Ways of Righteousness, and lead them therein, that they mightst walk in Fear of Me, the Lord their God, evermore.

Yea, O Lord, says Moses, ... er, ... uuh, how much are they?

No, they're free, says God.

Oh, says Moses, in that case I'd better take two.

Please, Ginsberg, says Ben, we're trying to polish this floor, man!

It takes a while to cover such an acreage with wax, and we have not only to get it waxed, but to shine it up with the horse-brushes, and all within three hours, with our aching bodies.

An hour or so later these aching bodies have taken us back to the top of the corridor and we're down the north side again, this time with knee-pads and horse-brushes, and at the bottom we pick up all this apparatus and cross over the tramlines to come up the south side and here still stands Ginsberg with his ears.

We're down on our knees again and into serious polishing, and only an hour left of aching physical fortitude to get it done. The rhythm is the only thing that keeps our suffering selves going; the joy of sheer physicality is all used up.

So this mama is in the doctor's surgery with her boy, says Ginsberg, and she says Doctor, vhat can I do mit mein kind, he shvallered ay chisel?

Oy mein Gott! says the doctor, clutching his temples, vas it ay wood chisel or ay cold chisel? No, says Mama, it vas ay cream chisel.

GINSberg, we chorus, fuck OFF!

But we get the whole great corridor done, I don't know how, by supreme courage I suppose, and we leave only the final flourish, the shaving reflection, for the morning, and wait for our soup and lights-out with some eagerness, and collapse into bed. On to floor, rather.

Next morning, instead of being healed in the legs and injured in the torso, we're crippled all over, our muscles still pumped full of lactic acid, and we walk about clutching this part and that as if we've just been run over. But we reckon with guts and careful movement we'll get the whole corridor done in the three hours before inspection. We set off oh so gingerly, and we're halfway down the northern side on our taxis before we have enough breath left over from gasping to have a conversation, and Ben says Never mind, Comrade Jock, as soon as we've got used to the exercise we can use this time profitably, and I'll start a series of short lectures on Scientific Socialism, and if you like I'll set for you a series of short oral tests, so that you can gauge your understanding of Marxist Theory, and improve it a bit, I see it's weakish.

Ginsberg hears us starting to talk, and makes his way across the tramlines to the wall on this side, tapping his stick and reaching for the wall with his free hand, and scarring up our nicely polished floor with his cardboard sweet-potatoes. Hullo you blokes! he says, I've got a good one for you today. GINSberg! says Ben, Can't you see we're trying to polish this floor, for Chrissake?

No, says Ginsberg.

So Mrs Rapaport pulls into Katz's Butchery and asks How much your fillet steak there?, and Mr Katz says nine rands fifty ay kilo, and Mrs Rapaport...

Fuck

OFF

GINSBERG!!

Spiers comes along to see what the hubbub's about; I told you ouens not to talk to other prisoners. We're not talking to this man, we're telling him to fuck off, look what he's doing to our floor!

Ja, says Spiers. Shit, Ginsberg, I said you can come out of your cell if you stay in one place, now you scratched up this floor these pore buggers trying to get ready for inspection just now, man!

No, says Ginsberg, I just wanted to tell them about Mrs Rapaport in Katz's butchery... So Mr Katz says nine rands fifty ay kilo the fillet steak, and Mrs Rapaport says Do I look stupid? Do I seem like it's my honeymoon? Cohen's Butchery over the road there has it eight rands fifty ay kilo. Mr Katz says Nu?, did I invite you in here? Did I kidnap you in here? Why don't you go to Cohen and buy it eight rands fifty ay kilo? Because he is sold out, says Mrs Rapaport. Missus, says Mr Katz, if I was sold out I would give it you seven rands fifty ay kilo.

Spiers looks at Ginsberg in utter incomprehension, blank surmise, silent as on a peak in Darien. He really doesn't know what on God's Earth he's talking about.

Goeie genade! he says, shaking his head, Stand where you are, Ginsberg.

So Ginsberg stands where he is and we taxi off a short way, escaping in silence. Spiers is back presently with another pair of taxis. Take off your shoes, Ginsberg, and hold them. Put your feet on these taxis in front of your toes. Ginsberg ties the laces of his spuds to hang over his shoulder; he needs his hands for feeling his way about. Ben and I have got a bit ahead, as I say; about five paces, but Ginsberg soon catches up with fast skating, touching the wall with his fingertips at each slide to the left, and we can't retreat fast enough and still get a shine on the polish.

So this group of Japanese tourists come up to the little old Jewish lady in the street in New York, and the group leader bows and asks her Prease, can you tell us the way to Grand Central Station?

She nods knowingly; Pearl Charbour you knew the vay?

Please, says Ben, please Ginsberg, for pity's sake, in the name of mercy, won't you just fuck off?

Me, I've become crafty in recent life. I realise Ginsberg's jokes might just save me from the Scientific Socialism.

Fourteen

WELL OF COURSE YOU CAN'T ISOLATE individuals in silence in a community as small and compact as this one. Apart from those actually locked up in their peters, that is. The Super came early for that first inspection of our handiwork and leggiwork, and since we were at the top of the corridor when he arrived, in the middle of our final polishing, we just stood to attention with our brooms alongside a bandiet called Koelie Myburgh because he was darkish of complexion, and whose job it was to stoke up a boiler in a little room there so the ouens upstairs in A2 and A3 could shower when they came in from working on the spans. In A1 we had only cold water, all year round, as befits a Christian penitent.

The Super talks only of his hypochondriac health, all the time, and he's bellyaching about his headache as he comes past and notices us there and asks Spiers, Aren't those the political offenders? Ja, says Spiers, coming straight to the point, where status and power are behind the facade of rank, I put them to hard labour because of their bodily condition. Status because Spiers knows all about bodily condition and the Super only the lack of it. Spiers looks straight and innocently at the Super's face, and at that moment Mielies comes out from his office. I wonder What's he doing here on Sunday? Looking at his cunt drawings maybe.

The psychologist agrees with me, says Spiers, and Mielies stands dumbfounded because he's clearly never spoken any single word at all about this, never ever discussed it with Spiers. Oh yes, he says, I foresee a probable preponderance of psychosomatic imponderables if they don't have this hard labour.

If you think those are long words in English, try them in Afrikaans.

There's one thing in which the Super has great experience and it's psychogenic disorder, and what if one future day the world and the press outside find we opblasers are getting certain inspuitings for lunacy and others for somatic collapse and we walk about in strait-jackets as Ginsberg did while his eyes were healing over, and he had to be taken twice a day to the toilet by one of the cleaners, who would have to wipe him afterwards too? The Super marches off complaining about his dedication to his wards and the lack of gratitude in the Department. The World.

Within the fortnight it took us to get, well not fit exactly, but mobile without pain, we had become integrated into the Madhouse convict community: four section cleaners, I think, apart from Ben and me, two psychos' clerks, a small weasely man called McGray who did something I can't remember, and Koelie. Then Ginsberg, of course.

Problems of unauthorised conversation became boring; Beestekraal looked silly when he tried to enforce silence, we would reply Ja, Meneer, and just look at him. Also he couldn't really get round Spiers, who would say Ja, Luitenant, and look at him. But it took most of our three hours a day just to get the corridor polished anyway, after which we were locked up again, so we didn't stand about conversing, we hadn't time.

Ginsberg was actually a help, he was making a contribution in the polishing and knew it, it was work he could do, and he tapped about with his back straightened up, and sang quietly to himself when he'd run out of stupid jokes. I therefore thought to encourage him, as I say, so he might stick around and save me from possible withering away of the state and people's poetry on the clipboards, though I must add my feelings towards Ben were very warm indeed, and I'd have listened affectionately to a lot of swan lakes and Leninist glorie-paradyses and all that goeters in the cause of companionship, if not actual comradeship.

Latish one morning Koelie comes to Ben and me and asks our advice on an important thing, and we nip off from our taxiing near the gate with our foot rags, to buff up the top of the corridor where there's a tiny patch of sunshine. In this sunshine stands a small cardboard box, and as we come up close we see that inside this box is a white rat on an old floor rag.

She is called Muis van der Kombuis, explains Koelie, because she sleeps in this secret box behind the nice warm boiler in winter, and behind the coal bin in the boiler-room in summer. Well, that's the plan; he's had her only six months. She is a fine rat, explains Koelie, and holds his hand down to her. She leaps on to it and reaches up her head there to recognise him, to sniff him, and twitches her whiskers. He asks if we would like to hold her, and we would.

It is a strange feeling: you never ever touch anything alive in prison, without fear of punishment. There aren't even insects in this one. I haven't touched a warm-blooded body in a year and a half, and that last was only the palm of senior counsel in a farewell handshake. This is a very cuddly rat.

Koelie is not sure of a diet for rats, he explains, and though from what I've heard and remember about rats they're happy to eat the insulation off electrical wiring in factories amongst other things, and start short-circuit fires, I don't tell him this, but nod my head receptively, and give it much thought.

How the hell did he get this creature in here? Inside these walls somebody could have found a brown rat, however unlikely where even mosquitoes can't make it, but this white one must have been brought in from outside, and what does a bandiet have to trade with a boer for an illicit pet? Not tobacco, not arsehole, not kinky stuff; there's not really anywhere to do it, not in the Madhouse anyway, and the risks for the beampte are too great. But here she is, Muis van der Kombuis.

Koelie saves nice little nuggins and nibblies from his graze for Muis v.d. Kombuis: a small piece of mermaid, a spoonful of brinjal or mealie rice, also katkop for in-between snacks. Does that sound about right? We intellectuals should know. He doesn't want to make her all fat and ugly with eating between meals. Then, also, he's worried about the lack of exercise, and of course she doesn't get nearly enough sunshine.

Ben points out that she is an albino, and direct sunlight must hurt her eyes like hell, even damage them, because there's no pigmentation in her irises to protect her retinae from ultraviolet light, and they'll get badly sunburned inside her head.

O vok! He snatches her up and thrusts her inside his shirt. Do we think she might go blind? He takes the cardboard box and stows it back in its secret place behind the coal bin. He gives her various tests from time to time to try out her eyes, like wiggling his finger behind one or the other hemisphere to see if she will turn her head that way.

Life has become comprehensible and manageable, though never predictable, as I say, and still bloody lonely, of course. I have an assortment of relationships, all pretty slight excepting Ben's, but the important thing for all apes is that they are social species, so I'm at least a normal ape now during three hours of the day. I look forward to Lights Out and getting to work on the new sixteen-foot bay-boat with Lt Brown, then the big moment, which I've now made the very last, for relish, and that is the sentimental bit about Jess and Susie, so sentimental as to be unreal, why should I picture us as bathing the baby all our spare time? But I need the sentimentality, there's nothing else to be tender about. It works for me.

Well maybe I can score a white rat. Koelie comes to me with his own sentimentalities. He takes from his pocket an old toothbrush which he has just replaced with a new one with nice straight bristles, but he's kept this one for grooming M. v.d. K. Would I like to see how sleek she is these days? Of course. He sits on the edge of the coal bin and puts her upon his knee, where she shuts her eyes and goes all dreamy while Koelie polishes her up. He has a problem with her tail. Surely she should have hairs on it, to keep it warm like the rest of her body? No, that is her radiator. The blood-vessels in there lose heat as it circulates through her system, like a motor car radiator. Koelie is astounded speechless by this piece of biological wisdom. Not my wisdom, that is, but hers. How could she know to do that with her tail? I tell him I have had the same sense of wonder about my missus; how could she be so clever as to make a baby inside there with so little equipment? I mean another existing person suddenly appeared amongst us here where there was nobody before, and made out of ordinary supermarket food, nogal.

Koelie goes off and comes back with a wad of damp bog paper and wipes down her tail. That should help the cooling along on a day like this, shouldn't it? Ja, it should. And maybe in winter I can get another piece of blanket for her tail so it doesn't get all cold at night. Ja, try it.

Daft bastard.

Anyway, there's no stasis in this Universe, as I say, particularly stasis in tranquility. Though I am having a nice calm time Ben is sore distressed and irritated about his study privileges, which have just come on stream after threats outside of a judicial order on his behalf ordering the Department to show reason why he should not have access to that which their own regulations declare to be highly desirable, regulations enabling bandiete to get standard eight, nine, even matric on occasion, rewarded by office jobs in the boep. I'll get the study privileges too, of course, but for now I'll just wait and see how it goes with Ben. Anyway, I find reading difficult, and on balance I'm as happy with the bay-boat and weekend aerobatics in the Tiger. You must never add further, personal, discipline in an overdisciplined place like this; you must do what makes you intuitively happy, if ever you can grab the chance.

I'll tell you about the bay-boat presently.

Ben opts for a degree. He could have chosen something less fraught with hazard, I dare say, than what he has selected for study: the History of English Literature, Economics and other things unlikely to give anything but frustration. He has nine books in his cell, for this degree. He expects others to arrive as specified by his tutor at the University of South Africa, but they don't get this side of the reception office. He stands out for the Super on inspection; he believes in going straight to the top, and cut out the frustrations with underlings in an office.

The Super looks at the list, a couple of dozen. This is storybooks, he says. No, they're novels, says Ben. The Super looks at him sideways, with a small lupine smirk, insofar as he knows how to smile at all. Novels is storybooks, he says. We got five thousand here, you can have two a week.

Just for a moment there I hope Ben will say No thanks, I don't smoke, but he says Well, in a way one might say that a novel is a storybook, in the broader sense of the word....... but he can't get beyond this second comma when the Super gives a sort of thought-you-could-get-around-me-did-you sour smile, and looks again at Ben's list. There he sees Galbraith's economics stunner: *The Great Crash.*

No motor-car racing, no novels, no storybooks, he declares, and moves off on his tour. Ben is losing control, and I signal to him to shut up if he wants to eat ever again on this earth. Trouble, of course, is that a novel IS a storybook. As for the motor-racing, he should take up aerobatics, no permission required. Probably better fun than memorising the Marxist Glory-Paradise too.

I tell Ben about our new project, the bay-boat, and he thinks I must be barmy to waste time, as if I'm short of it, on imaginary construction of something meaningless enough even if it had real physical existence. For that matter he sees no point in angling anyway, it seems a hell of a way to get one's nourishment and a hell of a way to spend a valuable afternoon otherwise available for the contemplation of dialectical materialism and socialist theory. And what's the bit about the imaginary bloke, what's wrong with real people? What about comrades in the Struggle? No, I say, I think about them often, and I quote the guy who had his cock nailed to the table, except I don't specify my imagery in that regard.

If I weren't so dedicated to Ben I'd tell him that, whereas socialism in my opinion is all about compassion and altruism and generosity, there's one thing it sure as hell has got nothing to do with, and that's science.

So let us pray that come it may,
As come it will for a' that...
That man tae man the warld o'er
Shall brithers be for a' that.

But one finds the scientific label stuck to all kinds of fancy faiths and scriptures, to make them incontrovertible, since they are governed by some system of Universal Laws, like Newton's, and you can't disagree about a Law of Nature, man.

As if that were ever what scientists did.

The best Isaac Newton could ever do about this was to say God arranged it all, better ask Him why it works this way, then dust his hands off on the tails of his coat and get back to his English scepticism and the maths of pendula and planets, with reversible time.

Ideologues and bigots need laws of nature to stave off argument. When scientists looked for laws it was always to explain some set of phenomena, or make some idea a little more comprehensible, or to disprove it, never to defend it. I want to say this to Ben, but don't, because I want to stay comfortable, and I want him to like me. Affection is fundamental here.

So Ben and I are down on our knees in the passage and giving it rhythmic blazes and working up a good companionable athletic sweat with the horse-brushes, and we're so fit now that we can converse the while, and he's telling me all about some economic phenomenon which is as self-evidently true as the classical laws of the conservation of energy, but which similarly took genius equivalent to that of Isaac Newton, the genius of Karl Marx in this case, to perceive and formulate for us modestly middle-IQ citizens.

Ben is defending Soviet socialism with Newton's Natural Philosophy.

You ouens Jewish? asks Ginsberg. He is, I'm not, I answer. Go on, man, you argue like Jews, both of you do, says he, for Ginsberg has ears as sharp as a bat's, where did your old folks come from, eh?, he asks me. One of my great-grandfathers came from Amsterdam, I say, where he worked with diamonds some way, I'm not sure. Then you're a Jew, says Ginsberg, not a valid one, it should have been your granny, but you'll do.

GINSberg!, says Ben, we were having a private conversation, man, as socialists.

Ja, says Ginsberg, they're Jews too.

So Solly and Abie are on tour in the United Kingdom, and they're taking the air in Windsor Great Park and arguing the proper pronunciation of the name of this place.

It is Vindsor, says Solly.

It is Windsor, says Abie.

And at that point they come upon the Queen, exercising the Welsh Corgis. Good morning, Your Majesty, says Solly. Good morning, replies the Queen. Your Majesty, he asks, is it Vindsor or Windsor?

It is Vindsor, she replies.

Thank you, Your Majesty, he says.

You're velcome, replies the Queen.

I like the idea of the Queen of England being Yiddish, like all those Afrikaner right-wing witous being Shvartzen if you go back far enough, and Jesus a Mexican. She probably got it from Victoria and the German connection. Ginsberg and I have a cackle. It is the end of Scientific Socialism for today, which is half at least the cause of the cackle, I must admit, but sorry to be so cynical.

Ginsberg, says Ben, you have fuck-all sense of occasion!

Ja, says Ginsberg, it's a bugger.

We're so bloody deft at the floor-polishing these days that there's a half-hour or so to wait for the Super's inspection, during which Koelie shows me the bit of blanket he has scored for a total cover to the home of Muis van der Kombuis, instead of just a little lappie for her tail. Winter is approaching. He has cut a sort of hatchway in this blanket, a small hatch with a flap, so she can go out for a pee at night. I've never heard of a rat or mouse that doesn't pee where it stands, or sleeps, but Koelie wants to believe this is a hygienic animal. Maybe she does pee elsewhere. Rats are very intelligent. Maybe he has trained her.

I tell Koelie about the boat I have in mind after the Tiger Moth, but I don't want to make him too nostalgic, because he has a long stretch to go yet, decades, so I stick just with the structural details. I tell him about my decision to use marine plywood and indigenous hardwoods instead of fibreglass for all but the hull, they've got more character, and the copper nails and brass screws give it all such a nautical air. The polyurethane varnish you get today gives such protection it's as good as fibreglass anyway. Inside the marine ply cabin, fittings and fixtures will be of dark indigenous wood, umThombothi and the like, offset by pale yellowwood, but not too much of it, and if we can get it.

I tell him about Lt Brown and how he enticed von Richthofen down to deck level where Brown in his SE 5 had had the aerodynamic advantage in climbing away from the red Fokker triplane, and how he stall-turned and nailed the Red Baron to the floor and shot him dead downwards through the thorax with one burst.

Koelie asks me to tell him each day how far Brown and I have got with the boat. He was a housepainter outside, and maybe he can help with the colour scheme, even the painting, he's handy with a brush. He can paint a dead-straight line with a three-inch brush, he says, that's the test, and I agree. Also, will I ask Lt Brown, please, to send him a daily instalment on his flying adventures, especially details of the sortie with Richthofen, and pegging him to the ground with bullets. He's so dillied up, he really believes the bloke is around somewhere.

Come to think of it, so do I.

So over the next while, three, four weeks, it's a long time ago and I'm not sure, I ask Ben if he'd like to come along to story-time with Koelie, but he's not really into such bedtime stuff, he's grown up now, and I wonder what he's going to do about Conrad and Hemingway and their storybooks, if he ever gets there, but that's irrelevant.

I get about fifteen or twenty minutes at a snatch for story-time, and Koelie gets Muis out of her kitchen and sets her upon his knee for toothbrushing, with her hemispherical eyes all dreamy, and makes himself comfortable for the yarn, the two of us on the floor of the little boiler room, leaning against the wall, while all others kick heels around the section, and yawn, waiting for the Super's Inspection. I get a new system going: my nightly enterprises with Lt Brown and the boat and the kite are designed for compression to fifteen minutes with Koelie, and if we have some minutes over, that's fine. He always has many questions about circumstantial things: will we have windows on the boat, or portholes? What is the air temperature at sixteen thousand feet? He gives me a set of questions for Lt Brown each night. Does one need a matric to learn flying?

If he has any snout Koelie makes a skyf first, for the luxury of the occasion, and naturally I have a pull, thank God I don't need the stuff, as this daft bastard grooms his rat.

We're getting well into winter now, and even the three hours' aerobic exercise on the corridor aren't enough to keep us warm, and we wear our corduroys at work. Otherwise it's the same old routine. The Super comes every Sunday and ritualistically fucks up our week's work and we start all over again. What the hell, we did it for fitness anyway, and there's neither art nor any pride involved.

Always complaining, his particular complaint one Sunday is the lack of appreciation shown him here, by everybody. The more intense the complaint, the slower he walks with Heresmyhead and a head warder whose name I don't know, I think he's the Super's clerk, who carries another clipboard with paper and a ballpoint, to write down all offences and the names of the offenders, for later punishment. By the time he's opposite Ben and Koelie and Ginsberg and me, standing to attention there with brooms and polishing rags and things at the top of the corridor by the boiler room, he's come to a dead standstill.

He says to Heresmyhead: As you know, I've got this weak heart. But never mind. Nev-ver miiiind, I say to myself. I stay up every night until twelve, later, later, studying, studying, to help these people. He makes a gesture of generalisation towards us four. Why else would I need criminology, but to help? and what do I get? DOGS' ABUSE, that's what I get, he declares, Ek word soos 'n HOND misbehandel, as he moves along a bit and starts once again to wipe his hand over things, to see if there's any dust. Do you know, he asks Heresmyhead, that I could drop dead here this very minute, such is my physical distress and the state of my health? Are you aware of that? Is anybody in this place mercifully aware of that? Neee, O Neeeeee!, shaking his head.

Like the Super in Die Rooi Hel inspecting the shower area for sinful water, he inspects the boiler room now for sinful coal dust, like in normal moral circumstances he might find goddam gold dust there in this his criminological El Dorado. He runs his hand over the walls and the asbestos-lagged boiler itself, even the outside of the bin itself in which the coal is stored. Nothing! No dirt! There must be some somewhere. Put your mind to it, you'll find it; he looks behind the bin for an unpolished place, and there sees Muis van der Kombuis on her blanket in the cardboard box.

He comes gasping and triumphant out of the boiler room. Who cleans the boiler room? he asks Spiers. Koelie speaks up, I do, Meneer. The head warder comes forward and writes down Koelie's name. Wat is die oortrede, Kolonel? he asks the Super, What is the offence?

Go and look behind the coal bin, says the Super, glaring at Koelie the while with thin white lips and staring eyes and righteous deep breathing. The head warder comes out of the boiler room and says It's a rat. No response; the Super is staring criminologically into Koelie's face. What must I do? asks the head warder.

Kill it.

The head warder comes back from this duty shaking his hands in some hygienic or symbolic way, in need of a rag to wipe himself, for rats are filthy carriers of disease. He takes Koelie's red kerchief from his waist, where a bandiet cleaner keeps such a thing with a little knot in a corner, so it doesn't slip out from his broek. He wipes his fingers on the cloth and hands it back to Koelie. He further symbolically wipes his hands on the arse of his pants and takes back his clipboard from Heresmyhead, and the caravanserai ambles off to the plaintive litany of self-denial and injustice coming out of the Super.

Koelie moves not a muscle. As the entourage leaves the corridor he says, ewe gerus, Make a skyf, man, says Koelie.

I don't need to tell Koelie what I'm doing. I go into the boiler room and look in the coal bin, and there's Muis in her kombuis with her head wrenched almost off, attached only by a skinful of blood. I put her in her cardboard box with her feeding tin and the blanket with the peeing hatch, and and chuck the lot into the furnace.

Bad luck, Koelie, man.

It's going to get him three days' ricewater, for sure, four maybe. What's more, it's going to count against him in the matter of remission or parole, by years, maybe. He will also lose his snout privilege.

Man, if he drop down dead here in front of me I just turn him over like that with my foot, says Koelie. He demonstrates to us how one might roll over with the outer edge of one's prison patat the carcass of a mongrel found dead on a road, dead of dogs' abuse. If it were small enough. Otherwise don't bother.

The first thing you learn to live with in prison is injustice.

Koelie is here for murder. Unlike Elston in die Baai, though, who made the plea in mitigation that he was out of his passionate mind and drunk when he went to look for the guy, Koelie took his time calmly and seriously, as he had loved his woman calmly and seriously, a couple of months' time he took, and worked it all out premeditatedly and coldly, as indeed his victim had done in his quest for yet another scalp, another sexual triumph over another man's sexuality, and Koelie got the guy as he came up the staircase to his flat where Koelie was hidden and where Koelie nailed him to the floor as he turned in vain to escape, and shot him deliberately dead with nine mil pistol fire downwards through the thorax, that's why he got life instead of twenty like Elston, and maybe that's why he's so interested in Lieutenant Brown.

I hear educated folk often enough say how curious it is that criminals always get the compassion, whilst the victims get forgotten. Well, those are educated folk who haven't been to prison. Criminals in prison don't feel themselves to be recipients of compassion from anybody, nor deserving of any, not even from each other. They don't see each other as poor disadvantaged lads, whatever that may mean, as if it's normal to be advantaged, they don't think they're lads who understandably went astray and ended up as a whole lot of persecuted innocents in a distorted culture.

Arrive in a long-term boep and say the judge or the magie made a mistake, you weren't guilty, and I tell you what you'll get, you'll get fingers pointed at you, that's what you'll get, and cries of derision: Yah! First offender!

Moenie sug nie. Fundamental prison wisdom. Don't sigh. Moenie met my kom sug en blaas nie; you push your time, and I'll push mine.

Curiously, in this regard they are more honest than most. Any. But don't take it further than that. If they're candid about their criminality, that's the only thing they are candid about, and it comes from simple cynicism, not moral rectitude, nor any self-examination, except in the matter of committing the crime with more craft next time.

They're candid enough only to recognise the equation: society needs us here, to scare the living corporeal hell out of its deviants, since the scriptural Hell is all well and good but it's for mañana, and anyway you can't demonstrate that it does really exist beyond the grave.

We criminals don't benefit from the other half of the equation, of course, the sociologists do, they study us assiduously, and the reformers do, they suppurate sympathy, they sleek themselves up all plump and shiny with righteousness.

Okay, we'll play out this rôle because we're trapped in it, but don't patronise us, because you'll get only scorn in return, and we'll roll you over with the outside edge of the prison patat, like a dead mongrel on the N3.

Let no post-graduate student lady pose as a prostitute so she can get arrested by the police and locked up amongst the whores for a weekend and write a thesis on it all for her Masters.

Let no liberal come to a bloubaadjie with condescension. Let no liberal come to a bloubaadjie. Let the Prisons Board come to this bloubaadjie, the former mayor of Pretoria, the seventy-year-old Predikant, the retired Advokaat and the rest with their pursed-up Calvinistic mouths, and their level suspicious stares, and moralise at him while he wrings his fingers obsequiously, and makes his ingratiating gatkruip plea for remission or parole. These are the terms of the masquerade, the ballet, the charade.

Frans Hals got it dead right. Go and have a look at The Governors of the Alms House, all of them at the long table there, unsmiling at the supplicant before them, who is you, the viewer, not a smile amongst the whole committee of them, and the matron with the tight lipless mouth and the curmudgeonly purse of money in her extended hand, and teach you to be poor, you bastard, in a decent Protestant country.

But don't start being rich, whatever you do, because then we won't have anything to frighten our Calvinist kids with.

A true bandiet understands the terms of all this, and that's the only thing he has in common with his fellows, apart from his general criminality.

The victims got all their compassion in court, and didn't they just deserve it? But they're dispersed now, they don't constitute a community with anything in common. Here we're a defined community, aint we arf ay; we've been very purposefully defined, and all in the hands of another defined community of men rescued from poor whitehood, and these men are going to have their will of us. They need the power of it, as the citizen in the street needs them to have the power to do it, but you'll have to ask a different sort of scholar about that, and why.

However beauteous the terms of the Prison Regulations, such as to bring a tear to the corner of the eye of each dear soul who drew up the United Nations Charter about such regulations, these regulations are but a crude palimpsest of nice words over a coarse code of brutality amongst these saluting men in their menacing military clothing.

I believe the women are worse.

I'm sure in other parts of the world where they're fresh run out of poor whites they will find other suitably abject communities viciously to provide the man-and-womanpower, but the righteous scholars will be the same, and the liberal reformers will be the same, their sentimentalities and compassions will be the same, because they're the same other half of the same equation. They feel the same guilt because their decent democratic society, whichever, needs the equation:

We need the Devil
Your true bandiet is a true living devil
A bandiet is not nice
I should be surprised if he were
Even Koelie.

Fifteen

BEN AND I HAD A STRANGE EXPERIENCE ONE DAY. Funny, you can go days, weeks, months without anything happening that you could by any stretch of the imagination call Experience, and then suddenly you get your whole year's supply of it in one monstrous moerse whack.

We had Adios Amigo one night and the expected tensions and delays to the timetable next morning, but hell, man, it was getting on for the main meal, the middle meal, and clearly no time to polish our floor, and we were still closed up. I could hear that nothing was happening elsewhere in the section either; I mean I could understand that it wasn't just that Ben and I had been dumped from floor polishing for one of those imponderable prison reasons; nothing whatsoever was happening in the section, anywhere in it, we hadn't even had breakfast, nor emptied our balies. Nobody had.

A smart screw can have both doors of a cell open in three seconds flat, and on to the next, with the help of a smart head cleaner, and I hear Spiers doing that now as he comes down the passage with Blackbeard. Kakbakke! calls Blackie as Spiers is on to the next cell, and we're all out together, all fifty madmen, and fling our faeces down the drain there, and flush out the balies under the big garden-size taps and wipe them with rags we have for the purpose, and fill a small basin with water for hand washing and stand it on the lid of the balie, and another smaller one floating in the basin with water for drinking, and back to the cells, and all within ten minutes.

CLACK CLACK CLACK CLACK CLACK!! as the Madhouse cells are all locked again, excepting the cells of the cleaners, and Spiers includes us floor-shiners amongst them. Ben and I creep apprehensively from our peters, for crisis is what prison life is about, and we smell it in the air now; we're accredited bandiete by this time.

We creep down the passage to the cell set aside for the storage of wiping and cleaning and polishing things. It isn't locked, of course, so we can get in and out as we need to collect our taxis for the brief morning buff-up, but as we go to open it we see that the outer door of the cell next door is ajar, and that is a thing always of primary interest to any bandiet.

So before we get our polishing stuff, we open this next door to see what's inside, and inside behind the locked bars are six men sitting on the floor, with a pot to piss in. Spiers has left the outer door ajar so they can breathe in this little space. They wear normal prison clothing, except they have tapes on their jackets instead of buttons, they have no laces in their shoes, and they're eating whichever meal it may be with plastic spatulas instead of metal spoons, and out of soft polythene bowls, because these are condemned men, the White Condemned, they're dead, and we find ourselves in conversation with the next lot for the gallows.

Howzit?

Only a priest has an appropriate greeting for a dying man.

Yous ouens want snout? one asks, in a sudden shocking inversion of the normal.

Wouldn't mind, if you can spare a bit. He smiles and gives us a whole twenty pack of cigarettes, I mean Jesus, I haven't seen a ready-made cigarette since the single farewell one at the Baai. With this currency it's like being in Berlin in 1945; you could have your will of the community with this tobacco. For a day you could be the Mayor of the city. Gauleiter. I skiem it might be a nice memorial gift for Koelie.

Do you want matches? I mean for fuck sake, this man is for sure a first offender; his first offence must be his last. Ja, please, if you've got matches to spare. You mean whole matches? The most match I've seen in two years is a single one split into four, and never more than a tiny piece of slatch, that black stuff on the side of the box.

So I'm up the passage to unload this lot smartish in case some beampte runs his hands over me, or even strips me naked, which is a thing you can expect at any moment in boep, and I find Koelie in his stokehold, and put the twenty pack and whole box of matches in his hand when nobody can see me doing it, and I say Muis said I must give these to you, and I fuck off smartish too, knowing that if any boer finds these things on Koelie and he snides on me, puts my pot on, to save himself six meals I can just say I don't know this man at all and he's lying.

One of the condemned actually looks like a murderer; red hair, green eyes, cruel mouth and great knuckled hands, he sits cracking these joints and looking like Erasmus van Vuurwapen at interrogation in Die Baai. My thinking is very confused just now. I find myself wondering which of the two has killed the most people.

They've been explaining to Ben while I'm away to Koelie what the delay is about. I come late to the speculation between them. A grapevine is a slow-growing thing; news in boep is a static discharge, it is sheet lightning. Some sensitive soul, and who could it be other than Blackbeard or McGray, Spiers seems unlikely to talk like that, it's against regulations; some kindly person, I say, has told them the delay is because one of those hanged today was found to be yet alive, not entirely dead rather, undead and jerking about at the end of his rope, and the District Surgeon has had a problem down in the tiled pit there with its ceramic drainage gutter along the centre for the muck and effluvia of death; snot and blood and urine and strange smelly stuff from bursten bowels and ruptured sacs.

What does he do? Does he wrap his arms around the legs in a good Blou Bul rugby tackle, and heave down? Does he take from the pocket of his white lab coat a hypodermic with stuff he's got from a friend of his, who's a vet? With others watching? Don't be silly, that's murder. You can't murder a man who's been unsuccessfully hanged. He has civil rights.

Okay, so we'll just cut him down, while the District Surgeon calls an emergency ambulance with its electrics all flashing and hysterically whooping through the early morning commercial traffic of Pretoria to take him off to the intensive care ward of the Hendrik Verwoerd Provincial Hospital, where they'll give him a transfusion and a neck brace and much Valium, and a little light will traverse a graph on a computer monitor, and they'll make him well enough eventually to come back to the small hospital at Pretoria Central and get all recovered and fit and fattened up so they can hang him again. It's unlawful and indecent to hang a sick man, whatever he's sick from, even unskilled hanging.

But the law says this scoundrel shall be hanged by the neck until he is dead, and makes no mention of the number of times you may hang him to achieve this.

Come on, man, what's your guess? Mine is that the District Surgeon took the time necessary to ponder this moral problem, and when he'd finished pondering and went to the survivor after the cutting down and laying flat on the tiles he found, good gracious, golly, he had meanwhile died of suffocation, the cutting-off of blood supply from heart to brain. Oxygen death of the brain, instead of muscular death of the heart for lack of neurosignals from the brain because the spinal cord was severed, the proper way to do it. The heart is supposed to stop first, and then the brain die, and this is back to front. A fine legal point, but who the hell is going to debate that, other than the six guys sitting eating porridge with plastic spatulas here on the seven-foot-square floor in front of us?

But I'm sure it took further time, very much further, for the District Surgeon to fill in the death certificate in such a fashion as to make it compatible with what the hangman and other beamptes in attendance had seen. I mean there must have been others there to handle just the sheer physical bodily bulk of six dead men, which I believe is the usual crop, though perhaps they use special bandiete for this jovial job, also hosing down the floor and walls stuck about with the death-squirting, and neatly winding the hosepipe back on its wall drum afterwards.

All the more reason then to make sure the death certificate is safe; for what hell would break loose if some convict or beampte corpse-remover got a statement out of this place to some paper or person, to some new young enthusiastic woman district surgeon perhaps?

Maybe he'd smuggle out the yarn in return for money anonymously deposited in an account outside. Of course, if it's for money it can't be true, especially with his being a criminal anyway, or an ill-paid eighteen-year-old, that he'd seen the District Surgeon take a syringe from his pocket and stick the needle into a dead man. But what debate, what confrontion, what litigation, and what a mess with the liberal newspapers, eh?

So it means they use older white warders for cleaning up the shit of black corpses?

All these absorbing aspects of their future and the clinical process of dying are topics of discussion for the breakfasters here, or is it lunch? Of course, the pace of conversation is leisurely, and there are long gaps of silence and contemplation in this conversation.

We ourselves, Ben and I, don't really get time to shine up the corridor, and we're soon slammed in our cells again, each with two meals in two stainless steel bowls, pap in one with a mug of the same old coffee made from the beans unknown to agriculture, and mermaid and boiled beetroot in the other, for the brinjal glut on the prison farm is now over and this new glut of beets is coming on stream. I wouldn't mind a glut of apples. And hell, can you just imagine a glut of cheese? And what about an egg, hey? A glut of hens?

I'm not a happy lad as I give myself a nice set of red lips from the beetroot lunch, like Greta Garbo. I don't actually want some people to kill other people on my behalf in this way. I don't want them to do it on my behalf in any way, but whether I'm a bandiet or not I'm still a citizen of this shitbegotten country and they're doing it on my behalf.

It occurs to me there's one point for despotism. Dingane is the hell-in to some miscreant who has offended his, Dingane's, personal opinions, and Dingane says Take this sod outside and pound in his brain with a bloody big club, and it happens there and then, and nobody even tries to suppose it's done on behalf of some dumb umfana herding goats over the hills and far away. The trouble with democracy is that it equitably distributes malfeasance amongst the entire populace.

Not that there's much democracy around here just now, think I, but we'd better be bloody careful when we get some going, or we'll end up like another great democracy that's around just now, injecting and electrocuting and hanging and shooting certain citizens on behalf of certain other citizens herding cows over the prairie and far away, and all unbeknownst to these decent cowherds, for our citizens must not personally be exposed to the indecent burden of guilt of this murderous quandary, it's not good for healthy-minded folks. It's so ugly the suitably paid official killing specialists must do the guilt bit.

Q: What do cowherds pay taxes for?

A: So that government will bear said burden, and of a family evening the cowherds personally can spend time thus saved glooming at anthropomorphic movies about lion kings and bambis and elephants flying with their fucking ears, and weep when they see one about a dog saved from a drain by Rescue 911.

But I don't know why the issue is so often debated arse-about-face. Sure and good enough, there's disgust at the procedure of hanging; an abattoir pneumatic bolt would be more decent, especially if the appeal judge did it. But how anyway can we permit any one of us such debasement as to shoot the bolt or pull the trigger or throw the lever or kick the stool? Also, can there be any limit to sympathy for any sentient animal that knows it's going to die? Even though he asked for it, of course, the swine, and serve him right.

These things don't come to the point.

The point is the profound hypocrisy to which you and I are party when our representatives go to whichever governmental assembly in whichever may be our land, and there after due moralistic debate decree that certain behaviour by any individual in this community will entitle us, you, me and them, to kill him, and that's exactly what the murderer did, only he did it on his own behalf, and not yours or mine, and in a way that's less disgusting. He doesn't assume our rage is as great as his, and thus feed himself this moral bullshit about the murder being a decent civil item on an administrative agenda.

Maybe it was better when we all put on our Sunday garb and went along to watch. It hadn't all been rendered so smug; you went to enjoy the cruel spectacle for straight vengeance. Just the plain cruelty, perhaps. The murderer was cruel, here's my chance to enjoy a bit of that too.

Me, I'd rather be killed by passion than smugness, any day.

Shit, any day I can handle the loneliness and the physical hardship of this place, my Marathon resilience has stood me in good stead. The mediaeval exorcism and the primaeval aura of death I can't handle though.

As I say, however, one's experience in this world seems to come in big dollops, and the very next morning Spiers opens my doors at cleaning time and says Trek aan jou baadjie, kom, and my heart just sinks because, as also I say, those ominous words mean only trouble, and you've got to put on this jacket because you're going to Heresmyheadmyarseiscoming to be charged with some piddling offence and have your food taken away for some time. I think of Koelie and the fags. I comb my memory for other sins, but can think of none. It must be that.

But Spiers seems relaxed enough as he says Bring your toilets too, and I stuff my shaving and toothbrushing gear and soap in my baadjie pockets and step out of the cell, and there down the passage stands Ben with his toilets also in his baadjie pockets, and a cardboard box at his feet with his storybooks in it, plus the Galbraith, the acquisition of which has caused him great yichas, which is a sense of triumph, or status.

We're stood at the Malhuis gate, waiting for Spiers to find a moment and take us off to another section where we'll become normal bandiete and maybe get a real job and privileges for good behaviour, like a monthly visit and all that goeters. Ginsberg is down there, waiting for us to start the day's polishing.

He's able to manage the taxi part of it okay on his own now, with his stick and his extended fingers, and he's slowly waltzing about near the gate. With his bat's ears he hears us speculating about our future, and skates over to us. Aren't you ouens working today?

We're off to another section, I say.

There's a bit of a silence, while he wonders if he'll keep his taxying job with new polishers, I suppose. Pity, says Ginsberg, I'll miss you.

I'll miss your jokes, I say.

Fuck, says Ben.

Well Spiers opened the section gate all right, but it was a strange foreign warder who took us off, and not to another section, but to Reception, where we are given our property bags with the shirts and ties and jackets and whatnot we were wearing when we got sentenced, and we sign for all these things, and we get led out to the reception yard with its external gate, where stands a Prisons Department van with steel mesh over all windows and on the door a hasp-and-staple locking system which is proof against any hacksaw blade, plus an Abus padlock, similarly unassailable. Never mind another section, we're off to another prison.

We get handcuffs and leg-irons and that chain connecting feet to hands, and bundled into the back of a truck. Through the meshed windows we see the driver and his shotgun-rider signing for handguns, and fixing these sidearms to their sides. Doors slam, things click and clang, the great oaken doors open and we're out of Central and off down the main road of the great Prisons Reserve.

Jock, my old comrade, says Ben, sitting there on Galbraith and George Eliot and eight other great thinkers excluding Charlie Marx, We're off to Robben Island and the other politicals!

Ja? So where are our salmonellaburgers and the cold black diuretic khakibos coffee in a milk bottle, without sugar ?

No, declares Ben, they will take us now only as far as Zwartkops Air Force Station just around the corner here, and there place us upon a Dakota, and off to Cape Town before lunch, maybe even direct to the island, for they must have an airstrip there by now, such is the importance of the place, politically.

We don't get as far as Cape Town, though. We get as far as the main gate four hundred metres down the road. We turn left at the corner there instead of right for Cape Town, and just about a hundred metres down a public road into the main gate of another prison on this reserve, not nearly as romantic as Central, which was modelled at Union in 1910 on a prison in Manchester or Antwerp or somewhere. Maybe the basilica of Santa Sophia in Constantinople, come to think of it.

This one's modelled on a brickyard.

This brickyard, however, is real steeped in history. It goes back to the old Republic. Presently it is a kaffir prison, with a bit set aside for white remand prisoners, but it has seen better days.

When we're eventually settled in, though I wouldn't say comfortable, on these our new premises, a row of cells sealed off for prospective white politicals, it turns out that Ben occupies the cell of Robey Leibbrandt, and I the cell of the present Chief Warder, the Opper, a boer called McTavish, which gallants spent some days of WW2 here as Ossewabrandwag freedom fighters, which Imperialist cynics called terrorists: guests of Jan Smuts and pals of Adolf Hitler.

Leibbrandt especially. Leibbrandt went especially to Germany to learn the techniques of random bombing of public places, to make the country ungovernable and thus ripe for National Socialism, and he and McTavish did the Germiston Post Office, if my memory serves me correctly, and killed nineteen people and got sentenced to the rope.

If my memory serves me correctly Leibbrandt ended up unhanged as mayor of some dreadful Transvaal city when his people came to power.

That's nothing. Once I get established and work out when there's nobody lurking outside my door and know that it's safe to put my bankie on my table and climb up to window-level and peer out, there I see six newer red bricks built into the old pinkish ones at the end of the reception yard. The clay deposit that made these pale sienna things was all used up in the old days of Oom Paul.

The red bricks, it turns out, were replacements for those pink ones shattered when Jopie Fourie was shot against this wall. Jan Smuts wanted there to be no shrine, no martyr's memorial for believers to come to after the rebellion had failed, and maybe stick their fingers into the bullet-holes in the pink wall as if into the side of Christ, and imagine our Jopie sitting there on the government varnished meranti chair, handcuffed to its back legs, and when the rounds ripped through his heart and lungs leaving fragments of his flesh and blood and bone and soul on the bullets, these sacred relic bits then getting left in the craters on the wall as the ricochets whined away.

Put your finger into one of these and your warm living flesh is where the hot dead flesh and fiery spirit of our Jopie have been. You're in his presence.

A stone's throw wouldn't quite make it from where I am, but a biggish mortar throw would, to the Voortrekker Monument, where people belong who stick their fingers into things, and believe in them.

Said monument is in line with one of the Zwartkops runways. I sit and remember the days of Robey, 1944, when a typed order appeared on the Standing Orders noticeboard at the Air Force Station, saying The dropping of practice bombs on the Voortrekker Monument is irregular, and will cease forthwith.

I mean, you know, this bloke would take off with twenty of these eleven-pound things on wing racks, not much to them beside a hell of a lot of white marker smoke, but bombs nonetheless, and after getting airborne, whilst going to raise the wheels with a finger of his right hand, would accidentally with his left elbow lift the red safety cover of the Jettison button and push the button, also accidentally, with this same elbow.

Building had been suspended during the war for want of materials and labour. Though the community, I suppose, had become patient and resigned to seeing it get no bigger over the long years, it must have been some cause for dismay, I dare say, to see it getting noticeably smaller over those years, albeit slowly.

Well, anyway.

I'm yet in my mid-thirties, but I seem to have been around for a hundred years.

In this cell you could play squash. It's also seven feet wide but it's ten long. Here I mean to do not only aerobatics, but cross-country navigation. Also figure-skating when the winter comes and I need the exercise for warmth before the kip on the concrete; the music will be the passionate piece of Rachmaninov from that shmaltz movie called *The Red Shoes*. These are the private personal things of course; the boat is there, coming along just fine with Lt Brown, and a pity about Koelie, he could have made a contribution.

All the details of my intricate personal life I plot out and fit into an ordered daily schedule. There's a couple of extras now. There's no way they're going to make this a silent prison. The hubbub at night is that of a small town with all its citizens on the market square; this is a local prison, a short-term prison, stretches less than two years, and most of its occupants are average male uncriminal inhabitants of the world out there, Pretoria. Well, its townships, naturally, for this is a black prison. It's easy to pick up a few months for being around the streets after ten without your ID, your dompas. Or any time of day, now I remember it. After ten it was a crime even with your dompas.

On another later stretch I am taken with Hugh Lewin through this main unpolitical unsolitary part of Local for some reason I can't remember, to fetch something or other as cleaners, I think. Here we look into cells empty of everything but a dreadful stink from a great galvanised shitbin in the corner which has been emptied of the metabolic waste of thirty-six men, we count the felt mats stacked in the passage. Of course this bin has been all hosed out and had carbolic dip chucked into it, but that adds to the general nausea, for they're airing it with the lid off while the lodgers are off to daily labour. We agree we're lucky not to sleep next to this thing. Five or six have to, though, for we calculate roughly the measurements of this place, and it turns out that each man has a floor area eighteen inches by six feet, and that's exactly slave-ship accommodation, man.

You've seen the deck plans, the accommodation dimensions, the printed layouts for investors of Liverpool or Barbados, and before these prospectuses there were things drawn on sand by dhow captains for Arab dealers of Zanzibar and Dar es Salaam.

So with such population density you can imagine the nightly social din from a few thousand of these Ethiops, Nubians and Blackamoors, men of Prefter John'f Land and Monomatapa, Land of the Unicorn and the Pushmepullyou, here be Monfters, and the crescendoes and cries of violent struggle and buggery and mayhem as frustration and rage are worked out man on man.

All those things, I mean, when they're not singing, which the black peoples of Africa do most of the time, so one gets to wonder what the hell it is they have to sing about, if singing is a thing of happiness, that is, and why there's so much harmony in that and nowhere else in the bitter life of this our curséd continent.

Suits me. I get in an hour of merry Mozart whistling after graze and lockup, and bel canto singing: Uno furtiva lachrima, Donizetti, out loud, with little quality of voice and no technique whatever, but what interpretation!

One furtive tear. What a treat to get away from Sad Movies Make Me Cry and that lot, and especially, of course, the sudden tooth-grinding gut-spasm shock of Adios Amigo, even though you've been expecting it for the last week or two of the usual six.

Adios compadre, then shed no tears, may all your mañanas bring joy to your years.

Here the seksie boer is one Strondjas du Preez, and here, he tells us, our job is to bring this newly brickworked section up to full regulation soulless cleanliness and polish with numberless layers of black wax and limitless application of Brasso to steel rails, and to scrub the walls with blue soap against any chance of sinful dirt.

Fair enough, it's all in anticipation of new companionship and we're out of our cells seven hours a day. We speculate who the newcomers might be. We look forward to seeing personal pals but hope they haven't been caught and tried and sentenced. We're very mixed up, but excited; we will be a community, we will have companions, comrades!

But what the hell now? One morning I hear Du Preez at the section gate and stand all ready at my door for the polishing. But he marches straight past and lets Ben out of his cell and starts him working. I sit down again. After a bit he comes back and slams me open and says Trek aan jou baadjie, kom. Besoekers.

Visitors? I had my six-monthly visit from Jess only four months ago. And why the plural? They must have put me into C Group, or even B, without telling me, and maybe Jess has got permission to bring Susie along. She's two now, and should be pretty mobile, but kids aren't allowed inside prisons without very special permission, one's got to be terminal or the like. Well maybe it's my mother Jess has brought along. Whoever it is, it's going to be a great day.

We don't go to the visiting-room, though. We go to a small office with more of the varnished carpentry. There sits Van Vuurwapen with a Security Branch dude called Wessels from Durbs, with brilliantine on his Hotnot hair brushed flat and straight, and a permanent smile on his face like it's got spectacle-frame earpieces on it, and he takes it from a glass of water on the bathroom shelf each morning, and puts it on under his lipful of neatly brushed moustache when he's finished brushing his piano keys, and there it remains, all day.

His suit is brushed. His shoes too, and his fingernails.

He doesn't have the big face-mashing hands of v. Vuurwapen, and he's a bit thin, but he looks to be pretty deft with the thumbscrew or a bottle of cyanide.

Ja, ou Herrilt, announces ou Rassie, Ons het elke muis gevang en elke muis het gepiep, and they all blame you.

He hands me over to Wessels, who unctuously describes to me the capture of the entire MK leadership of Durban, though why he should be unctuous about it is another of life's mysteries; it is I who should be seeking to kiss his ass. But I have learned to react slowly to these mysteries of life, having much time available to me, also I remember that Vuurwapen knows me as an imbecile, so my reactions to Wessels' story are gradual and pretty dumb, and I notice after a bit that ou Rassie is starting to swing on his meranti chair again, and clatter his great big false teeth, and creak his knuckles.

I dredge up from way down there remembrance of all the old physical gestures of things past, and I remember Rassie's symptoms of impatience, and realise he is impatient right now with the techniques of this suave poens with his suit and tie, for Christ's sake, and his brushed moustache, tinkling away here like a well-tempered harpsichord with all its sharps and naturals showing as he smiles, both manuals, upper and lower; techniques to extract evidence from a prisoner in prison.

This is not Marshallplein where evidence is extracted, like teeth; I am the property of the Prisons Department, and you don't need personality play here with assorted manipulations, nor a bliksems suit, nor even a bliksems smile, all you have to do is declare the deal. The manglings and mutilations come later, on police premises.

Wessels doesn't seem to understand interdepartmental suspicion, and resentment about status, and jealousy. Of course they can get me back into their hands any time, since there are further charges in Durban, but the fact remains, you don't give people the police process on prison premises.

Our department needs no help in the matter of bastardry, thank you.

Wessels babbles on. He reels off a list of names and things these names have provided. He names the names of the nameless revolutionaries who hurtled from the hedges to join the attack on the bourgeois reservoir, and what each name has promised by way of corroborative evidence in the matter of my coming from Die Baai to mastermind things.

He doesn't report any statement from Slim, though, and after a bit it occurs to me that he hasn't mentioned Slim at all, not even his name, and straight away it occurs again to me that this is because Slim has done a Plumbin, and had his passport ready and enough money in banknotes to buy the ticket cash here and now, immediately, for the very first cancelled seat this very afternoon on the very first aircraft of any airline whatsoever to anywhere wherever in the whole wide world, and by now he's done the traditional tour; Swiss Cottage via Tel Aviv.

SHMEITZ!

FLEE!

Erasmus and I have been around so long together by now, he realises that I realise something. He's getting a bit doubtful about my imbecility too, and he doesn't want me to realise anything not provided by him for realisation.

He interrupts Wessels straight, in the middle of a sensitively brushed and polished sentence, with a bone-smashing statement: We want the rope for Govan Mbeki and Dennis Goldberg, he says. If you don't give State's evidence you will get the rope instead.

He produces from a briefcase a loose-leaf resumé of recent legislation for the Statute Book, and opens this file before me. I notice that he keeps his fingers on the pages so I can't see those before or after. Take your time reading it, he says.

It says that in terms of the new Terrorism Act the rope is the full penalty. He watches my eyes at their reading, and when he judges I've read the right amount he says It's retroactive. That's all he says, and leaves me to ponder what's on the pages before and after under his fingers there.

Well, I've never known any legislation to be backward-reaching like this, not in criminal law anyway, but then I don't know what fascist powers the régime may have accrued to itself in the years I've been out of circulation, there are no newspapers here, no radio. My thinking is not very practical these days anyway after all the solitary; my sanity has depended on fantasy; logical, but fantasy none the less.

What was it though that he was hiding with his hands? But then, was he hiding anything, and was this perhaps a device to unbalance my assessment of his menace? If he really hadn't wanted me to know the before and after he'd have unclipped from the clip-file the relevant page for me to read. I mean, he must have realised that I'd immediately notice his clumsy concealment. Or would he have or would I have? So why did he do it?

Games.

Maybe he really would rather like to see me die, for personal vengeance.

He watches my eyes.

At the right moment he says We got the whole bloody lot at a place called Rivonia, looking straight in my face. We've charged them all with conspiring to overthrow the State by force, and Mandela and all his clever comrades are going to die, and they're all talking like papegaais to save their own necks, and all those from PE include you and say you went to Durban to start it all up there. So now it's Govan Mbeki or you. Take your pick. We know he sent you there, we even have the number of the flight you went on. We will go along with a plea in mitigation of sentence if you give evidence that he was the master-mind. Maybe we will see that you are charged only with the Explosives Act again, and you'll get only twelve years, but we need the rope for him, and you can help us button it up, and that's the deal.

I look straight at his face too, as I wonder why he hasn't mentioned Max and while I'm actually still looking at him I realise that Max also has fled, and he's safe overseas from the purposeful cruelty of Vuurwapen's world. Somehow I don't feel so sour about that, because Max was always a modest man, a trusty follower by nature, and never ever had the need for big reputation and yichas, and the power to direct the lives and thought and culture and sensibilities of people, nor indeed ever had use for revolutionary fame, the great driving force.

There's a long silence now, during which I notice Erasmus van Vuurwapen with an irritable gesture of the eyebrows shutting up Wessels, who is just lifting the lid of his keyboard again to say something irritating, and Vuurwapen notices my noticing this, as he has noticed my noticing the absence of Max's name on the Rivonia list, and he's noticed my doubt and quandary, and he's missing nothing, for the Security Branch of South Africa are getting smart at their job, man, maybe the best in the whole world of tyrants at this job. Or the worst, of course, depending.

He has all the cards and knows it. He has the ace. He exposes his epoxy toothwork in a mirthless rictus of triumph. I'll ask the Superintendent to give you time to think about it, says Erasmus van Vuurwapen.

Ja, we know what such time means, and I'm back to my peter to get used to another winter of solitary. But what the hell, man, I'm still a better bandiet than Vuurwapen is a boer and I don't fear loneliness, and though the thought of the rope appals me I reckon I can handle that fear without heroism but as an otherwise bliksem.

It's not different from being thrashed at school for hardegat, only bigger.

Anyway, it's only a chance. I have only Vuurwapen's word for it, and his games. Still fucking frightening, though.

Strondjas clangs me shut and I sit down on my bankie, a bit shakily to be sure, and recite and declare once again the constitutional principles of this cell: anxiety and fear will have only one hour of each day, and that is mid-morning before graze. It is not allowed to be anxious when lying down, and especially it is not allowed to be anxious when looking out of the window, so what I do straight away is get my bankie on top of the table and my eyes above the level of the sill, and see, there is the same old panorama to which I'd become stranger of late: the reception place where Jopie was shot, the hospital yard now empty because the boere are away to lunch, but my old tomcat pal still there spraying his estate, and above the remote roofs now the topmost twigs of a couple of jacarandas, which have appeared since I left, with a community of little mauve doves in amongst them, clapping their wings almost straight up to fifty feet or so, and spiralling back to the jacaranda branch with that strange anhedral glide they have.

I will take at least an hour for looking at the sky and birds and cat, then, and calm down, and afterwards sit seriously for an hour or so and try to make a couple of rational decisions, and not fall into that dreadful condition of obsessively, fruitlessly, going over and over one's critical situation without adding anything as a possible solution of the problem, because there's no further information available on which to base any new thought, no input, as recent jargon has it.

That's like taking out a piece of sculpture and compulsively going over the surface again and again, polishing and polishing, over and over the existing form without adding any new detail, nor making any formal change, and to fill one's time with repetitive behaviour like that is very bad for the mind and indeed the body in a place like this, especially when it's all about the dread of death.

Well, I'll have to ponder the trees and the turtledoves in the abstract again for a bit, it seems. I remember the biblical image of peace; And in the land the voice of the turtle shall be heard. The next morning Strondjas slams me open when he's back from his breakfast, and I'm ready and hopeful that perhaps there's polishing today, but he says Bring your toilets, and I know there isn't.

Nor was there ever again.

It was the old ghost chains again. If Strondjas had had a sense of humour I'd have asked him if maybe he'd like me to carry my head under my arm. The same old escort was there too, a brace of beamptes buckled about with pistols in big holsters and ammunition clips in small holsters, and watching dutifully the Abus lock on the back door of the van from their following car.

Sixteen

BACK AT CENTRAL I ONCE AGAIN hand over my court clothing in the stale-sweat-smelly suitcase, and Salie Vermaak the screw running the saal takes me over and delivers me to the grille of A1. There is Ginsberg still, as chance would have it down this end of the great corridor, waltzing about on his taxis with a couple of new floor cleaners. All is silent. My gut is in free fall.

DANKIE HEK! cries Salie Vermaak, and rattles his keys between the one-inch bars of the A1 grille. No answer. Is dit nie Ginsberg nie, Meneer? I ask, and Salie Vermaak grins at me cannily, for he knows I'm calling over Ginsberg with his vespertilion ears, and Ginsberg is going to come over here where he hears my voice and speak to Salie Vermaak in my presence about things that don't matter a shit to him, Salie, but which might be overheard by me.

Ginsberg has saichel. He assumes I'm back here because I'm in trouble, and you don't speak to a bandiet in trouble. Meneer, he says to Salie Vermaak, I want to tell you a good Jewish joke while you're waiting at the gate. Okay says Salie, because he knows this incommunicado thing is in the main a bag of bull, and Ginsberg is not going to give me secret encoded messages and all that. So long nobody sees Ginsberg looking at me while he speaks. But then Ginsberg doesn't point his face at anybody in particular, anyway, when he's talking.

So this visitor comes to ring the doorbell, and there is the usual mezuzah nailed diagonally to the door frame: that little capsule with a little paper inside bestowing blessings on this happy home, and blessings also on visitors. We all know what's in there, but this visitor waits a long time and gets pretty bored before realising eventually that everybody's out, and in his boredom he opens up this mezzuzzah, and there on the little slip of paper it says Help! Save me! I am a prisoner in a mezuzah factory!

Salie Vermaak waits politely for the rest of the joke. After fifteen seconds or so he realises it's all done, he's heard it, and his gaze sort of drifts off to the rest of the insides of Pretoria Central, not that there's anything for him to see there that he hasn't seen before during his ten years in here, but he's got to look somewhere to find reality, in God se naam.

I dunno, Ginsberg, he says, You better go and polish the floor.

Meneer, says Ginsberg, It's the oldest recorded Jewish joke, it's from the Dead Sea scrolls. It's used for emergencies.

Ja, says Salie Vermaak.

Spiers emerges from way over there next to Koelie's boiler-room, and walks his elegant balanced way down to us between the little rails of the katkop express. The metallic tumblings of the great greased lock bounce back in echo from the other side of the saal a couple of times, and I know I'm back in Central.

If I have shown Spiers as a fair man, it was my intention to show him so only because it was more efficient for him to be fair and have no untidy hatred around. He didn't need hatred to win in his boxing, it muddies things up, and why should he then have use of it in his employment?

I didn't mean to present him as a man who likes bandiete. Anybody who likes a bandiet is making a grave mistake, he's a bloody fool; a bandiet is not nice.

So Spiers is at no great pains to greet me, he's not going to smile all over his face and fall about and ask me how my life is going because he cares about my life and is surprised to see me back. He does not pump my arm now and say Welcome Home. He says Kom! So ek gaan, and would you believe it, the only unoccupied cell in the Madhouse is the one I had before, and as I enter it I remember the Spike Milligan song I'm Walking Backwards for Christmas.

I get an undeclared concession: Spiers tells Blackbeard to get me a pot that doesn't have its enamel chipped all over, and I get a nice new one from stores, even with a factory stamp on it saying Batch Somenumber, because Spiers knows we intellectuals are dainty about our defecation.

I sit at the little table and lean my elbows on it and miss my little platform for the pot there, with the nice Apache basket decoration all about and the pot in magnificent display up top. I go for a walk around my premises and compose my mind.

I am a bloody sight better bandiet than Erasmus van Vuurwapen is a boer. My Oupa Van was a Boer, a Kommando Boer who drank a cup of water a day in thirstland while the horse got four, over towards Upington se wêreld in the hellish heat, and ate biltong made of horsemeat when the animal was ridden close to death and slaughtered and butchered and eaten to the point of nausea by starlight, so the riders would be well away by first light when the carrion birds awoke to give away their position, and strips of its flesh were then hung under the saddles to absorb salt from the sweat of living horses, and later hung outside the saddlebags to dry a bit before getting eaten over the next week or so.

Living off the country meant no rich pickings.

This pig and his swine friends in their loony porcine fatherland don't even know what a Boer is. Their Vaderland Boer is a piece of bad sculpture on their Fascist moerse monument. All they've ever done is persecute anybody of decency within the community, including decent Boere. Anybody of compassion is fair game. I would really rather die than do what he wants, and that's no act of heroism, it's from hardegat otherwaais vok jou, man.

It is what the Zuid Afrikaansche Republiek had the final pleasure of saying to the British Empire: Nou ja, Grootbek, kom vat my!

Nou kan jy maar gerus ophou kakpraat. Come and take me, Big Mouth.

I've tried walking sideways, and walking to the front,

But when people see me they just say it's a publicity stunt

SO

I'm walking backwards for Chriiiiistmas across the Irish Seahea.

No mailbags, no Blackie with a porn proposition, no polishing, no taxis, no Koelie, no Ben. The Minister has spoken.

Well, his minions have spoken on his behalf. The Minister is too important to do duty down at this level of course; but feel reassured, he is still with us, up there, distant and dignified, to represent the majesty of our security laws. Just very busy, that's all.

Solitary, solitary, solitary. Think about Vuurwapen's proposition, nothing else.

I try to think of everything else, anything, but it's difficult. If I'm not careful I will lose touch with Lt Brown, but it's hard to concentrate on spray-painting just now, when all I want to do is stave off thought about the menace of another bloody trial, when I don't know what the hell is going on politically out there, nor what legislation the bastards have available after the couple of years of my absence.

I know I'll have to leave all that to the defence team, and though Defence and Aid is banned they will still get overseas money to such a team somehow; but come on, man, I'm the bloke whose head is on the block, or in the rope maybe, is this an impossibility? Have these pals of Adolf Hitler got round our capitalists as Hitler did his, and established their tyranny? Has the economy collapsed to such an extent that fascism has become possible? I haven't seen a newspaper in more than two years.

As things turn out, it doesn't matter for the present, for I haven't seen a dentist in three years, and my teeth hurt something cruel. Nobody knows about fluoride yet. Many long-term bandiete have toothless gums like a garrick, I notice.

Never make the mistake of getting bitten by this fish because you believed for biting you need teeth. A garrick can crush a three-pound shad in two with its toothless mouth, so that only skin and scales hold it together. Bandiete have gums that could crack nuts, like a macaw. Not that we get nuts in boep, nor pineapples and the like, of course, nor anything on a bone, that needs gnawing. All food here has the nature of porridge, styf or slap, but always porridge. In UK boep is called Porridge. Here they can fry a pig and make it come off the stove like porridge. Maybe they do it for all these ouens without teeth. In boep you don't get fillings.

If your teeth hurt, they pull them out.

You can shut your mind off to most things if you're clever at it, most pains of the body too, but there's one thing you just can't exclude, and it's pain in the head: ears, eyes, teeth, migraines, gunshot wounds I suppose, though I haven't had that particular experience yet, the shottist missing my head by a centimetre some years later.

The rest of your head is too close to the brain for exclusion. I calculate it's worth a tooth or two to get rid of the pain, and hand my prison card in to Spiers for seeing the District Surgeon in the morning, after the beampte breakfast break.

At eight or so Salie Vermaak rattles his keys between the A1 bars and cries Dankie Hek!, and the sick, lame and lazy are marshalled into yet another stripe down at this hek. The lazy don't stand a hell of a chance on this parade, as they might with skill on a sick-parade in the army. There's a dankie hek at the other side of the hall too, and we trudge out to the hospital yard. Here I am instructed to join the dentist queue over there.

Probably there's only one queue in the world that you can barge into at any point you like without provoking outrage, and it's this one at Central, where an ex-Transvaal Rugby man, the District Surgeon, is the dentist. People fight here for a place at the back of the queue. There I espy Tokkie from the Baai, and I make my way over to him and say Ekskuus tog and push into the line and the bandiet behind Tokkie there eagerly moves back for me.

We whisper. Tokkie, hoe gaan dit jong? Hullo, ou Djok. Nee, ek sukkel mos, man, whispers Tokkie, five-to-eight is mos vokken swaar, jong. Die boep is up to shit, man. Ek gaan vokkol remission kry nie, ek stoot net maaltye, man, elke week is dit three meals. Ek gaan die hele vokken agt jaar stoot.

I see he's boring into his stretch the hard way. And you? he asks. No, I've got toothache. I don't want to load my woes on to his already heavy burden. Moenie sug nie. He's got no devices for handling his stretch.

There are gaps in the conversation, and we're supposed to be silent anyway. In these silences we hear clonking sounds, about one a minute, and as we get ahead in the queue we realise these sounds are coming from the room where this Transvaal Rugby man is at work.

Klonk! Klonk! Klonk! One a minute, roughly.

Tokkie and I come to the door soon enough, too soon, and we peep round the frame, and there we see Lock van Druten in a two-man scrum, and he's covered neck-to-knees in a white plastic apron with blood smeared all over, for fucksake, like he's running an abbatoir, and he's got his left arm around the head of his patient seated on a government varnished meranti chair, his left hand gripping the forehead, and he's hauling out teeth one a minute and flicking them from the pliers into a galvanised-iron bucket in the crooked arm of a bandiet in his boep corduroys and sweet potatoes, who leans over with ghoulish fascination written all over his face to stare down the gums of the victim and breathe all over him.

Nee vok! says ou Tokkie, and turns instinctively as if to flee.

DO IT, TOKKIE! I say, and grip his arm, and he does it, and I look away as his molars clang in the bucket. It didn't take long, which I suppose is a plus for this type of dentistry. This ou doesn't keep you in an agony of suspense. This bloke don't fuck about.

I march in and sit on the varnished chair, and Van Druten squirts me full of local anaesthetic and lets it brew up a bit while he washes himself and the tools of his trade with Lifebuoy carbolic soap under the tap at the basin over there.

He comes back and gets a grip on my head and wrenches six teeth from my upper jaw in six minutes and chucks them in the bucket, while I stare aghast at the ghoulish face of the bucket-bandiet, where in other dental surgeries I have stared at the bright theatre lights. We don't need such illumination here, of course, for the chair is pointed at the sun outside the window there. That's why he pulls folks' teeth out in the morning.

At tooth number six I pass out, and come to with my head between my knees and the great line-out left hand of the District Surgeon holding my head like a rugby ball to keep me in position, so I don't fall out of the chair. Okay he says, and gets the grip on my skull again and wrenches another six teeth from my lower jaw in another six minutes. This time when I come round there's a couple of bandaged convalescents from the yard lifting me out of the chair, and blood all down my shirt. Five years on bits of bone are still working their way out of the flesh of my mouth.

Well it's an ill wind and all that, for these bandiete are led off by the hospital boer, who unlocks a hospital cell, wherein these two deposit me in a bed, for Christ's sake, a bed. The great symbol of status is a bed. You don't get a bed just because you're A-group; you must be more special than that, you must be the librarian or Somebody's Clerk or the like. Additional to such appointment you must be a non-smoker; you've given it up so you can pay some C-group moegoe with your snout issue to tidy up and polish your peter every morning, and especially, to make the bed. Status, this bed.

A Section Boer knows about such irregularity, of course; by rule no prisoner may enter the cell of another, ever. But that's power; the boere like certain bandiete to have such status; it helps them in the matter of intelligence and control.

Well anyway, this isn't quite as you may envisage hospital accomodation, with here a young man who's fallen off his motorcycle, his leg all in plaster and hung from that sort of trapeze thing, lazing about there with flowers in a vase, eating chocolates from a box as he listens to cricket on the radio, while opposite there is the geriatric who's had the prostate op, eating grapes as he studies the boob 'n bum magazines. This isn't really a hospital, it's a sickbay in a long-stretch boep. This cell is also solitary. Naturally.

But I'm in it! I am going to score something from this: a bit of custard, maybe, and some of that standard Provincial-Hospital-type poached fish that looks like a boiled sanitary towel, and a cup of tea with sugar. While I am here I can only score.

Sure, this bed is a real pit; my head and heels are at equal altitude, and my arse sags a good foot lower than that, and if I were to roll over I should appear as someone in erector spinae spasm after taking strychnine. So I don't think of that, but of navy lads in their hammocks, and how the hell could I ever want to roll over and lie face-down in my present condition anyway?

Don't be silly, man. Where from hospital food? The mermaid I pulp up in my mug of water with my fingers so I can swallow it without chewing, the beetroot I abandon, and the pap goes down a mixture of porridge and blood, like that dreadful stuff the Masai feed on: milk from the udder of the cow mixed up with blood from a hole in its throat and wood ash from the fireplace, the whole lot turned to a nauseating pinkish-grey junket with a spoonful of the cow's urine. That's really disgusting parasitism, hey, one species feeding off another, directly, body to body.

Here I'm largely feeding off myself, a sort of perpetual motion, energy-wise, like that guy in satirical French literature whom I should remember but can't, who fed on slices of his own buttocks in a time of vital crisis. I think it was on a raft at sea, some such circumstance. I think he was Candide.

Well by beampte after-breakfast-time next morning I'm starting to think it might be nice to straighten my body a bit, and there's a small hint there that I might actually enjoy a flat lay-down on my felt mat. The shock of the anaesthetic's wearing off has passed, though all is yet sore, and I'm starting to look around for something to occupy the mind, and to notice these smaller additional discomforts. I turn my head to the left, and there under my mug of water I see a sheet of newspaper, a sort of tablecloth.

My God! Newspaper! I'm going to find out what's going on out there!

On this side are advertisements for the sale of old motor-cars and pedigree puppy-dogs and the like, while on the other are pix of the Moroka Swallows laying hell into Bushbucks, three goals to nil, but I'm going to interpret something from it all to give a hint of the state of my nation.

All I learn about is the state of the American Nation, from a really poxy Dagwood cartoon at the bottom of the page, corny complacent suburban humour at its worst, but I read it, look at it, gape at it, there are people drawing cartoons out yonder yet, and I even raise a smile at the drawing of the dog Daisy stealing the top storey off a Dagwood sandwich, a foot high and symbol of American Affluent Ill-Health.

My concentration has wandered off a bit then, and I let it go and drift about where the hell it will, we're on holiday. The sheet of newspaper is on my lap as I see visionary junk-food before my eyes, and randomly recall the doughnut and hamburger story of Sir Launcelot Kennedy; his visit to West Berlin to defy Soviet arrogance at its worst, up there on the outdoor podium with an audience of one million, such as hitherto only Onkel Adolf could raise, to declare his solidarity with the populace of this place, and with passion to declare himself a citizen of Berlin. Only he doesn't say Ich bin Berliner, he says Ich bin ein Berliner, which means he's a sort of local doughnut with jam and sprinkled sugar on it, and the Mayor of West Berlin puts his cupped hand to the ear of a senior alderman next to him there and mutters It's just as well we're not in Hamburg.

I'm lying with this piece of newspaper on my knees, then, and looking at the ceiling and thinking I should really try to be more generous, and remember less sarcastic things, like how JFK got his name in the Guiness Book of Records as being the only US president to visit the village of Kilkenny in Ireland, where ancestral Kennedies and cats come from, and where he wrote his name on a wall of the Catholic Youth Centre with a felt-tipped pen, and didn't introduce himself as a bowl of stew.

I'm so absorbed in this irreverent thought that I don't notice a furtive eyeball at the spy-hole, but there is one there, and the rest of the body it belongs to whips it away from this hole, and before you can say Morris Boris O'Horrorsky Ugh Ugh O'Toole the whole body/eyeball assemblage has click-clacked my cell door open, nemmine Walt Kelly, and wheeghed the sheet of newspaper out of my fingers and declared: If you can read you are ready to fuck off to your section, like I read with my gums; a sort of oral Braille, mandible and maxilla mumbling over bumps on the paper.

Ja, Meneer.

You wouldn't believe it, but I feel so insecure in the foreign culture of this place that I quite look forward to the privacy of my own old one-out bachelor flat with personal toilet and face-washing facility. I look forward to old Rorschach pals, the feathered dinosaurs and the Tante Jus of Goering's transport Luftwaffe. But hell, man, I could have played it all with a bit of boepcraft if I hadn't been so slow, and scored a hot shower before going home.

Well, I don't go home. Not to stay, that is; I go there only to collect my toilets.

This time it's not the Madhouse, boet. This time there's no glorie-paradys, Calvinist or Leninist. Messages from the Security Branch have arrived on the Super's desk. This time it's Ginsberg's old habitat of three years, his half of A1, die yskas, the deep-freeze, the deep seg and isolation and punishment half. The only reassurance around here just now is that Spiers will give me my solitary exercise out of doors each day, I can depend on it, in the sunless winter light, half an hour mornings, half an hour afternoons.

This place is dim. It is the Antarctic SANAE Base with the generators shut down. No straight sunlight ever enters here; it faces south and there are two floors of cells above me and three also on the other side of the narrow little exercise yard between. In the middle of the day a forty-watt bulb burns so you don't bite your thumb whilst eating your graze. Other than that there's no point in having the bulb burning anyway; I mean I'm not really doing much in the next while, and if I need to sleep I know where my wireless is and if I need to pee I know where my cock is and where the balie is.

This place is but fucking cold, man, and it's only the beginning of the Highveld winter.

The usual furnishings are here. Blankets don't get washed in prison, not those I've been in anyway, and these as also the felt mat smell of other peoples' bodies; that strange bitter stink of old sleep and old semen. Then there are the small table with two bowls of water, one for drinking, one for washing, and the small stool. And the pot. With a lid.

I realise that my choices in life have once again become limited, and the only choice I have now is whether to stand up or sit down. After some thought I elect to sit down on the bankie, with my nice unchipped balie at my feet so that I can dribble into it from time to time, for my gums are still oozing stuff though the flood of blood stopped yesterday.

I really really look forward to lying down, though.

Buddhist meditation bollocks, and all that West Coast Californian crap of physical posture and the positioning of the hands and balancing of the head and emptying of the mind therapeutically. I can make myself brain-dead as an act of will in any bodily circumstance, like an Emperor Penguin with an egg balanced on his feet under the fluff of his belly in the dead dark of a polar winter, and nothing mystical about it: when the time comes signals of food will wake him and me to some hours of life.

This is what I do when the dribbling slows down a bit. I loll my head against my left shoulder in the corner of the cell, and unplug all systems. I sing myself to sleep with a sentimental lullabye inside my skull:

As I was walking through Dublin City
About the hour of twelve at night,
'Twas there I saw a fair pretty maid
Washing her feet by candle light.

Various prison thumps and curses bring me halfway to the surface, but they are not for me, they are not about food, and I drift down again.

First she washed them, then she dried them,
Round her shoulders she tied a stole,
And in all my days I never did see
Such a lovely lass, upon my soul,
and I'm gone!

Well, it's not the rumblings of the katkop express that wake me, nor the rumblings of my intestines, it's the hubbub of the condemned over the way, over the width of the little exercise yard. I suppose they've been sleeping when I was sleeping, something like that, but they all come alive at about rumbling-gut time, a rowdy ruckus in this dead-quiet place. With what punishment do you menace one who's going to die, who chooses to yell crazily with cynical mirth, or howl his head off with rowdy missionary song as the days relentlessly dawn and decline?

There are many many condemned indeed in this the Condemned Capital of the World. They seem to pack them in pretty densely. It sounds as if there are six or seven separate communities up there, that number of cells each with its own mortal cacophony. I suppose there is the same number on the other side of their corridor.

It is inexorable horror up there in B2.

Critically I get working on a system to exclude all this lawaai from my perception, for reasons of plain personal survival. I will make it part of the general background din of nature. I know the trick, I've done this thing before with prison racket.

I will do the same now with the simian din of Central, the din of the murderous monkey, the din of its victors and its vanquished both. I will not give a damn about the dying, I will see to it that I don't die myself, of dismay. This is survival. I will listen only to those sounds that were necessary to my continued supply of food. I will do what those sounds indicate I should do, and make myself as unnoticed as possible while I bore my way through the remainder of my stretch. It is only a matter of months now, less than a year, and I know I'll make it without giving in to Vuurwapen and Wessels if I can just create a peaceful place in my cell here, and get on with some new construction, or building for a change.

I've had a wooden house in mind for a while, with verandahs. I'll be able to escape back to this from Security Branch visits if I can only keep the cell a calm place. I am not going to let my neighbours' tumult destroy this calm.

Well I'm busy in the evening with some of those leg-stretching exercises that runners do, a good habit though they're supposed to be followed by running, of course, but better than nothing just now, when in amongst the din of the dead I hear a faint distant sound from the past: the submerged sound of a guitar and the sound of somebody singing Xhosa folk songs and ANC songs of struggle:

We will not relent, though we are imprisoned,
Only give us freedom.

It's Max.

God Almighty. Nobody's going to help me now, nobody's going to come to my aid with the building of boats or houses and the painting of Tigers,

184

nobody's going to invite my indignation at the death of his rat. I myself am going to die.

No, I am going to come out of this experience like the man tied to the post blindfolded, waiting in cold sweat for the sergeant's final command to the firing squad, then only clicks coming from the breeches of the rifles, because it's all been just another sick trick of torture, and the rifles aren't loaded at all, what a joke.

I mean, they can't hang a bloke like Max, man, he's not hanging material, he is innocence itself, he's a lovely man. They're not really going to do it, don't be silly.

Well, they are going to do it.

So never mind purposefully shutting this clamour out of my mind, I realise the horror has suddenly become personal to me, and I must now veer through 180 degrees and concentrate on the inclusion in my awareness of everything, every last little detail of sound coming out of B2, and build up from these minutiae a view of the minute evanescent society in which Max is to use up the brief fag-end of his being upon this earth.

It seems to me that if things are as tranquil as they now are, sorry about the sarcasm, with even guffaws of desperate laughter every now and then, and the still fairly controlled singing of last-hope hymns and a general background of babble, that they must quite recently have had a hanging, and this lot must know they have six weeks or so of life left in which desperately to guffaw and babble.

Only their species has imagination, a capacity for the agony of death a thousand times; only this species knows what its instinctive dread means.

When the antelope see the big cats coming they don't imagine the great claws pulling them down in full flight and the great teeth shutting off all blood to the brain, nor the suffocation, nor the numbness as their glands pump the anaesthetic fluids prior to death. When the kill is made, each victim has a first-time unknown unexpected experience. They can't know about it beforehand, for they have no culture. They know only the nameless fear of instinct.

Only Max's species can fantasise, construct the scenario of the moment of death, but further; only Max's species can rationalise, and what they're now doing, I'll bet, is expanding six weeks into six years, or sixty years, it depends how intensely you live, and death is not actually upon us yet. It is like being at the back of the dentist's queue.

Blessed are they that die in a bomb blast.

Over the weeks I sit and listen to this pervasive babble, then, with my remaining teeth clenched, there's no dodging it even if I want to, and I don't want to; I'm going to grind through these last six weeks of Max's life with him, my comrade, at whatever cost; it will be a personal act of defiance, I will make a positive thing of it. I will not submit to the triumph of those SB bastards. I will tough it out.

So after tally and lock-up and shut-down of the basilica behemoth when the whole place is in the care of two warders and neither of them in A1 here, I do the old window thing with the wooden stool on the table, but now it's not for the study of tomcats' spraying nor the aerodynamics of wildfowl, mate, it is for the sombre business of finding which cell Max is in, and making a guess at the length of the bit of life left to him.

Well I've seen the B2 windows during my exercise time in the little yard there, but now it's dark I see that the last three are without lights, and on peering at them awhile by the floodlights of this exercise yard I can see that these windows are bricked up behind the bars. This must be the triple-size Execution Cell. You can't hang more than one person comfortably in a seven-by-seven-foot cell. Maybe it's wider too, to give more than seven feet depth. Maybe it goes right across the B2 passage.

Down below in B1 I notice the last three cells also without lights, and I calculate that those three are where the corpses dangle when they've jerked to a stop after the drop from B2 above.

There's no telling; people who go in there seldom have the chance to come out and describe the architecture of the place, except the staff, of course, who may explain it all to their pals, but I can't help feeling that pals not in the department would rather on balance talk about rugby, perhaps, and those in the department aren't allowed to discuss it, and especially nobody may discuss it with prisoners.

Maybe others in the department don't want a vok to hear about it anyway.

Over the next month the character of the daily din changes day by day; every day less a formless mixture of individual rackets blended to a background hum; every day more singing, more harmonious presentation of themselves as a community, not to me nor to anybody else out there upon this earth, but to God.

The African voice is full and deep and unstrained, and music is the great substance of African culture. I often feel, ignorantly I dare say, that the great music of this world comes out of Germany or Africa, via this or that route.

Go back far enough and you'll hear this music in the Olduvai Gorge, where hyenas hunt your children and Death comes upon you statistically, it's got zilch to do with your moral behaviour, as if morality has anything to do with it in a world of hunters and prey. The moon peers dispassionately down at you by night, and the sun seethes at you by day, and there's no explanation of anything at all as you arrive alive and conscious upon this planet, and what the hell is a planet anyway, and what on earth is this consciousness for, that I've got?

So the statistical time for your death is here.

But thank God the Christians told us about God. Approach God therefore as you would the Prisons Board. Hunch your shoulders up a bit and confess the evil within you and wring your hands a bit and raise the pitch of your voice a half-tone or so when you speak, so it's nice and wheedling and whiny when you plead for mercy.

Remember, though, when you make a sacrifice to the Superintendent in the Sky, a sacrifice of Song, let it be a sincere sacrifice of great quality, let it be the best, full, passionate, deep Olduvai voice, the voice of mysterious Death. The process of your dying starts in your larynx.

I'd like to hear these condemned in the Lower Church at Assisi, singing that music, and maybe take all the sanctimonious Jesus-creepers of the brotherly choir there and put them here in B2; that should please them, since they want to be near to God.

Nearer my God to Thee, let them sing, as the navigation charts and the Champagne empties start to float.

The end of it all is too dreadful; they start squirting the hangees full of sedatives two days before the moment, you can hear it. But what are we talking about, amigo mio? The sedative hasn't been distilled yet that can dull the brain to this thing, distract the mind from the imminent moment of death, Death, defined, precise, precisely defined. The B2 bedlam hymns don't stop at all for forty-eight hours, more, three, four days and nights, however exhausted the voices, the singers; Let it be, Lord let it be.

3.30 a.m. on the Day. The big section gate clangs as the White Condemned are shunted into A1; the B2 death cell door clatters open, I hear it with my mind and whole body in spasm, and the last frenzied psalm of the living dead disappears in steep audioperspective down the corridor, then silence. It is systematic. It is efficient.

It is over.

It's all over before six, prison breakfast time. My wireless is done up in its totem, my pap has been shoved under my grille. How can I sit and eat porridge at a time like this? I get back in my corner and pull out the plugs. Try to sleep, you didn't get a hell of a lot last night.

I suppose it had been like this after the last execution, though I hadn't been here in those early days of Max's moving to the front of the queue. Everybody over the way there seems about as stunned as I am. I suppose the din will take a day or two to build up, but when it does this time I'm going to be ready for it, and move into voluntary deafness, and hear none of it.

So it's a silent day, though of course you can hear the odd ou taking the lid off the shit-bin over the way, and that sort of domestic clatter, also a bit of talk now and then, of course, but not the great raucous racket as of the last weeks.

But it's been a long, long day, and it's good to get the old head down at lock-up time in the crushing crystalline cold of this place. That's at four, so of course you want to wait until lights-out at eight before actually falling asleep, otherwise it will make the night just too long and you'll be awake again in the middle of it. At four I'm on my mat then, wearing every fabric thing in my possession, my head wrapped in my dish-cloth showering towel on my potato pillow and the blankets pulled up over everything. Calm. It's over. Sleep will come with a little warmth in four hours' time, and knit up the ravell'd sleeve of care.

It is the time for fantasy, imagination, though I must confess I'm a little afraid of my own imagination on this night, and even more so of my capacity for fantasy. Los 't. Just concentrate on the warmth.

The four hours went well enough, the eight o'clock bell shrills and I start to shut up shop. It will take the duty boer half an hour to get over here and switch off my light, and that's the time allowed for recounting the day's events, filing them away and closing the cabinet, locking it; it is not allowed to go over the contents again when the lights are out.

Then the trick I learned in the Drakensberg, sleeping rough on tufts of frozen grass and fragments of frigid rock and loose earth; settle yourself into these shapes inside your tiny tent and bag, though here in boep it's all dead flat, of course, but just as cold; then wait for that great sensuous moment when heat is no longer draining out of you, and go over your entire body bit by bit feeling the warmth of life returning. The best bits are the feet. Don't wriggle about, it wastes heat, and fold the feet together in your socks. Don't waste the heat of your breath; breathe under your blanket.

I'm doing all these clever mountain things then, and just at that first stage of dropping off, about nine o'clock I guess it must have been, when I hear the song;

Oft hae I rov'd by bonie Doone
Tae see the rose and woodbine twine,
Whiles ilka bird sang o' its luve,
And fondly sae did I o' mine.
Wi' lightsome heart I pu'd a rose,
Fu' sweet upon the thorny tree!
But my fause luver staw my rose-
And och! he left the thorn wi' me.

and I stiffen, body and soul, I go rigid under my army blankets on the concrete floor as all my suppressed primal survival instincts burst to the conscious surface: OH HOLY JESUS FUCKING CHRIST, MAN, WON'T YOU JUST DIE? GO AWAY?

What right does he have to do this to us? I just want to thrust into B2 and HIT the bastard, true as God; what the hell was wrong with him, couldn't he just make his stupid brain tell his stupid bloody body just to march in there and DIE, since he knows it's got to happen and it's going to happen, so why not do it NOW? He knows for whom the bucket clangs. It doesn't take long. Just DO IT, MAN!

So gaan dit mos.

Well I realised soon enough why Max's group couldn't have been at the front of the queue for that last hanging: if they don't allow you laces in your shoes on Death Row, how the hell would they allow you guitar strings in the final death cell?

In fact it seemed strange that they allowed a guitar in there at all, except for the fact that someone who thinks suicide by steel string strangulation better than execution by rope will delay it to the very last, in that final cell, and get what relish there may be from such meagre life as is left him in this gruesome habitat.

But I realise next morning that they're in there now, just moved in, and they're only the political condemned, four of them, alone. The singing of songs of struggle is without accompaniment. Also, these songs are not interspersed with other stuff. No nameless repetitive tribal singing measured by time, by the yard, as it were, by the metre, that you can cut off at your convenient length.

Nor of course the same sickening old Protestant hymnal nursery-rhyme-level rubbish, dished out to humble believers around the world, as if to love good music you have to be of class, and rich, and O! intelligent, what condescension.

So this political community is separate, it is single malt, as it were, unblended with the general mix, even their times of song and talk don't coincide with the others'. They do their singing when others are sleeping, after the main middle meal. Maybe they want to hear what they're singing about, maybe the words are important, they're not just offering a sacrifice of song so they can score a bit of mercy; with their last words they're telling the world a great truth.

We will follow Luthuli, they sing, and other such, songs become by now songs of historical heroism. Strijdom, You Have Struck a Rock.

But there's a limit here; too many of South Africa's songs of struggle are facetious things about a man in a Bantu Administration office stamping dompasses, that sort of thing, too many are trade union songs of demand for better wages, and so on, though that's good political health, of course.

Few are heroic enough for this moment, and you can sing them just so often, and even in this awesome crisis you can eventually get bored.

We fall back on the old stalwarts: Bandiera Rossa, the Red Flag, sung in Italian, nogal, the Internationale sung in any language of choice, they're all there, and Nkosi Sikelele iAfrika, which takes five full minutes in the singing, in the matter of time the best so far for people in our circumstance, and which anyway gets round to the matter of God and his Protestant hymns. Come, O Spirit. Woza Moya.

Sorry, you comrades out there, but within the week the same old Protestant hymns are what they're singing. Sure, there's discussion about it; I can tell

Max's voice I'm so close, now they're in line for the rope and he's directly opposite me in B2, and though I can't distinguish his words, I know that these guys are explaining to him their need for the Spirit to Come, and he's doing the democratic thing and going along. But what the hell, who gives a shit, so long you can sing with great beauty, and leave this world a true African. No wonder one talks of the Breath of Life. It's the timbre, it's the resonance in throat and mouth and sinus and antrum that is the essence of your being, and that's the way it should end, with your head and your heart full of sound and song, whatever that song may happen to be.

I'd come to feel rather guilty about my sentiments at the last execution. How genuinely stricken had I been at Max's plight? Hadn't I been playing out a self-indulgent act? And then my impatience when at the final curtain he hadn't obliged me by being dead, so that now I'd have to go over the whole phoney set-piece again, the whole sequence of formal self-centred postures?

How could I have wanted him dead for my own comfort of mind, just to score a bit of peace for myself? It had been for Max to score whatever little last warmth from the last ember of life that was there, and it was not for me to curse him because he didn't make my limitless life just that little luxurious bit more comfortable.

Well I won't make that cheap mistake again. I will stay cool and make mental vibes for Max this time round, whatever that might mean. Of course it means I will still be making vibes for myself, but maybe I'll be more sincere this time. There won't be that embarrassing falling about because things don't go my way.

Well of course it went exactly as before; the same racket, the same sounds, the same music through the whole community, except without the skill of Max's music. I realise I'll just have to grind through it all as before, but maybe with more decorum, now I'm sort of used to it. But I'm ticking off the weeks, how's that for cynicism? I'm as bad as I was last time round, though maybe differently.

I'm up to one week, one week two days, one week four, one week six, I'm almost at two weeks, then only a month to go, more or less, unless there's some hitch or postponement to the fairly regular six-week cycle. It could be a couple of months. But I'll tough it out without self-indulgence this time, then get back to the creosote poles and the house on the beach dunes. Maybe a dollop of cynicism would be healthy.

On the morning of two weeks exactly, in the middle of that deepest sleep that comes at about three or four, I am awakened all confused and wobbly by the sound of the great A1 section gates clanging as the white condemned are brought in.

I leap to my feet all disconcerted and unsteady and stand as far back as I can in my peter, so I can just get a glimpse there of the northern wall of B2, and I realise the Death Lights are on and Max and comrades are about to hang.

This time I'll see if I can keep control, hou kop. I splash my face at the water bowl and wrap a blanket about myself then sit on the stool and shake my head to clear away cobwebs.

After a while I hear the screws leaving A1 when they've settled the White Condemned with drinking-water and a balie. I also hear Max at one of his old mission-school songs, but this time it's not Who is Sylvia? it's the real Lutheran God stuff that his mates also know. They get going on this thing obsessively, like Bishop Wisdom's flock at his cathedral, incessantly, unceasingly, non-stop, and I go with it until for reasons of exhaustion maybe after twenty minutes, half an hour or so they pause and at an impulse I grab my bankie and put it on my table and climb up to the window and yell, I really bellow MAX, MAX, MAX, it's JOCK!, and I'm at such a level that my nose and eyes are just at sill-level, so I tip up my head like a baying beast and howl MAX!

There, suddenly, unexpectedly at his sill his upper face appears, only his eyes because he's one floor up from me, and he shouts back JOCK, oh JOCK, can it be YOU, oh please Jock, is it YOU?

MAX! I yell, but what to follow? I can't say Howzit? I know too well how it is. There's no time to ponder the question anyway, already I hear feet pounding across the saal to A1 and up the stairs to B2, because of the outrageous yelling. And it's six days' ricewater if I'm caught.

Max, what happened?

But there's no time for an answer.

Oh Christ Max! How...? But there's no time for me to finish the question either.

I can hear the screw at the A1 gate, he's struggling a bit with the keys; there are many of them, and he's new to this section, and that allows me just a few bonus seconds.

How do I use them? No time for Good Luck, nor any point; he's got no luck left in this life, good or bad. It's all predetermined for him, defined in detail. Go well, hamba kahle? Don't be silly. Try Adios maybe? Adieu, mon ami, go with God my friend, my comrade? He can say that to his cellmates, but it's not for Max and me.

BE BRAVE, MAX, BE BRAVE! I shout.

The beampte is actually in the section now, he has only to lock the section gate behind him, that's regulation, and it's during those few seconds of locking up that I'm down from the stool and table and the stool is on its way to the floor and luckily he stops at a cell two before mine and briefly checks in there through the spy-hole and that gives me enough extra seconds to fling myself to my mat and grab the blankets over my head. There's about one second to spare.

He peers at me a good long while. He knows it's me. I lie dead-dog. Is dit jy wat so vokken skreeu? he asks. I dopily raise my head, Ekskuus, Meneer? Skreeu, man, skreeu, skreeu! he repeats, with rising impatience. Nee, Meneer, ek skreeu nie, and I get my head down again. He stays there scheming. What can he do? He fucks off fuming.

I hear him at a cell down the passage, asking something with mumbled replies. It seems, though, that there are only three occupied cells just now in the punishment part of A1 on this side of the passage, and just as well; if there'd been ouens to left or right of me they'd have shopped me for sure in hope of unspecified advantage.

But never mind all that. Over the way I hear the beamptes bursting into the Condemned Cell yelling Get down kaffir! and the sounds of bodies thumping about. I suppose Max was standing on somebody's shoulders; how else to get up to window-height? There's no furniture in there. When they're gone the same Lutheran hymn picks up again where it left off.

Ten, fifteen minutes later, it's hard to tell after all these years, and in the middle of the hymn their door and the grille are opened, I can hear it; the Time has come. The singing stops, I suppose from momentary shock, and Max gives a full-throated cry of existential animal pain, horror, from the floor of the Death Cell, he shouts it for the whole world to hear, GOODBYE, GOODBYE, I'M BRAVE, I'M BRAVE, OH GOODBYE!, and somebody grabs him and he's away with his Christian comrades, and their Christian song fades in steep audioperspective down the passage; Let it be, Lord let it be.

My anatomical clock says it's almost six. I carefully make up my wireless with all the folds regular and the corners square, and put it to one side. I roll the mat nice and tight and carefully place it in the correct corner, and place the wireless on top of this totem all neat and symmetrical, and take my dishcloth towel and fold it twice and put it in the opposite corner of the peter, round from the door, and sit on it with my arms around my knees and my head on them against the wall there, strange how useful a wall is for wailing Oy veh! Oy veh! and I huddle in the grey-enamel concrete corner of the cell in a foetal position and rock myself to sleep, oblivion, I shut down all systems and become brain-dead. Shortly somebody opens my door and somebody else shoves a stainles-steel bowl of pap and steel mug of coffee under my grille and I hear nothing of it.

At eleven, thereabouts, I am awakened by Spiers shaking my shoulder. The cleaner bandiet comes right into the cell and puts my fish graze on the table, along with the breakfast pap and cold coffee from the floor. I totter to my feet and look at Spiers.

Wat die hel gaan hier aan, man? Hoekom kruip jy daar weg? he asks. Hoekom is jou gesig so rooi? I crept into the corner, and my face is so red, I explain, because I am ill from something, I don't know what. Wil jy die dokter sien? he asks. Nee dankie, Meneer.

This time the same doctor may pull out all my finger-nails plus two toenails to make up his dozen.

He backs up to the inside wall of the cell and reaches up his head and looks at B2. He looks back at my face. Rol af jou bed, he says, gaan slaap. Eet eers jou kos, dis 'n bevel.

Roll down your bed and sleep, my God what an order! The eating of fish and beetroot and mealie-rice I do because he has made this too an order, but there's no relish in that part of it. He's back with two aspirin as I'm eating; SlUK hierdie goed, he says. I swallow them as he watches; he has to watch, that's regulation, otherwise a bandiet will accumulate pills for smuggling, any old pills, any old capsules, tabs, all colours, every size, a handful of them, what a trip in exchange for tobacco. Sure, you may end up in hospital, but what an additional holiday! You may die from something in the mix, of course, but who gives a vok about that anyway, and what a way to go.

Heresmyheadmyarseiscoming arrives on Opper's inspection at twelve. He stops at my door because it's closed, and looks at the name up there. Hierdie man het die flu, says Spiers. He makes no move to open the door and I make no move to stagger to my feet. It happens just as I'm dropping off, and I drop off for seventeen hours straight. When I wake up for morning pap and coffee I see my supper there, my soup, I hadn't even heard them opening my door to shove it under the grille. I down it cold with the porridge and bread, then the coffee to wash it down.

Well, one doesn't die of grief. Not in the communities I've lived in, anyway; in the main they just couldn't afford it. Materially, I mean; financially.

Life is not a Puccini opera.

After two weeks or so my elbows are raw from supporting this sleeping head at the table. Bum downwards I'm pins and needles most of the time from bad circulation, sitting asleep on the unbevelled edges of the wooden stool. I realise I've got to find something other than sleep to take me through the crisis. Whatever it is, I've got to find it or make it myself, and the only thing I've got to make it with is my physical body, and as always in the past the great remedy will be to get to a fine pitch of physical fitness, such as will enable me to exclude all, all, everything else from my mind with the process.

Not an easy thing in a gym two paces long, and then too my sleeping is not a luxuriant reposeful thing but a desperate involuntary shutting-off of the mind from a world just too hideous to be awake in, and all my body wants to do, all the time, day and night, is fall asleep and stay asleep. Maybe my glands are squirting the same juices that make the wildebeest go numb before its death, when the eating of its living body has already started.

Maybe Max was numb on the traps.

Well, I can start with the leg-stretching exercises where I left off a while back there. When I've become once again mobile I can maybe try a little running morning and afternoon in the exercise yard, though this will be a comic enough experience in my corduroys and amadhumbi shoes, clumping round and round the brass fire hydrant in the centre of this little place.

But I work out a schedule, and calculate that by the time the warm weather comes and I can get a pair of cleaner's soccer shorts from Spiers with a bit of luck, I'll have toughened up my feet enough to do the running kaalvoet around the hydrant, half an hour mornings, half in the afternoon, and at my plodding prison jog that will make six miles a day, plus a bit maybe, or ten kays by your recent reckoning, ten six-minute kilometres to the hour.

So I hang my baadjie on this hydrant in the exercise yard, and, as I pound my inelegant way around the yard, my shirt too after a bit, and put in the last five minutes barefoot, increasing it over the next month to ten, and after that the entire hour, kaalvoet. I can't do the stretching just before the running, which would be the right way of course; I don't know at which point in the daily routine the running is coming, but back in the peter there I get in an hour a day of what used to be called physical jerks when I was a kid.

In the morning I do the standing-up stretch things, after lock-up I do the lying-down stretch things on my mat, also press-ups and upper-body exercises, so that by the end of two months or so I'm as fit as your normal citizen in the street. Aw come on, let's not be coy, I'm a bloody sight fitter, and I have applied The Technique, and not thought about Max at all, nor anybody else at all in the whole world for that matter, during that time. Well, not too much, that is.

Every available moment not occupied by prison routine is occupied by some sort of exercise; if the limbs and the back and belly muscles are just too tired, kaput, use the muscles of the fingers and toes, the neck.

My entire life is centred on my physical self, and if you think that's unhealthy and asocial, it sure as hell is, but I know the tricks of survival by now, and survive with an intact mind is what I am going to do. I am not going to stick razor blades in my eyes.

I hear no sound from B2. Nor do I hear any sound whatsoever from anywhere else, until after about month two of the new régime I hear the telephone ring one evening after soup and push-ups, and there is Lt Brown. Where the devil have you been? he asks.

Seventeen

BY SPRINGTIME I'VE SCORED THE CLEANER'S SHORTS, reduced my time for the kilometre to five minutes, if Spiers' half-hour timing of my exercise is accurate, and if it weren't for the unevenness of the paving-stones in the yard and the pounding of bare feet on such a hard surface I reckon I could have brought it down to four and a half. All rough reckoning, of course, but a pace more or less enough to give one a standard marathon time of three hours thirty or so on a nice smooth road, with shoes on one's feet, and not running in a bloody circle or figure of eight all the time.

And by summertime I've worked out a system of aerobics to do in the cell, an hour or two, I suppose, in addition to the strengthening exercises of abdomen and anterior leg muscles and quads, whilst clinging on the bars of the door; then the muscles of the back plus the gluteus muscles and hamstrings down the back of the leg done on my rolled-down mats in the evening. I just exercise all day, except for a small sitting-up sleep over the table after the middle meal.

Totally obsessive behaviour, and that's what I want it to be. Get obsessive and stay obsessive. Just make sure it's the right thing you're obsessive about, that's all.

So I start having anticipations in the four months or so I have yet to push of going back to my old athletics club in Durbs when I come out, where Jess has moved with Susie, and having a crack at a marathon after a couple of training runs on a road. All right, a half-marathon then, let's be modest.

One morning six weeks before release I've just downed coffee and pap, and I'm staring philosophically into the mug wondering what on earth it could be made of when Spiers opens up and beckons me out of the cell. I come out with a sense of mixed wonder and dread. Anything at an unusual hour is usually dreadful in boep. It's just after six, man, so it can't be prison business that this is about; that starts at eight after the beamptes have breakfasted. It can only be about travelling, and it's going to be a long haul, that's why we're leaving early. It's going to be to Durban, pending release, I bet – I hope, rather – but then why not just let me out of the front gate of Central with a rail warrant on the day of release? We'll see. Just don't ask what's going on, it will give them the pleasure of saying something facetious, and you still won't know.

At this point I find myself standing next to Heresmyhead in Reception. I take care not to look at him; it's plain he's stationed himself there so I'll ask him where I'm going and he can say the facetious thing. After some silence he can't stand it any more and says his facetious thing anyway: We taking you to Durban to teach you to eat with a knife and fork again. He smirks.

So I know I'm not going to Durbs, and suddenly it all falls into place, how could I be so dumb? Of course they didn't bring further charges after I'd refused to give State's evidence eighteen months ago; of course not, some of the new sentence I am inevitably going to pick up might have been given to run concurrently with my present stretch. They want the lot. They want it as revenge for their fiasco in the Baai. With this twelve coming I'll push fifteen total, no remission, no parole, no privileges for good behaviour. Just punishment. D group.

I'll be charged right near the end of this stretch, with a few weeks in hand for a defence team to get mustered. But they don't want to run to the end of this stretch during the time the judge has given the defence for getting team and strategy together, so they'll have to release me and maybe the judge will give me bail and I'll just bugger off out of the country. They've planned this one carefully.

Maybe they thought a bit of Ginsberg-type deep seg would change my mind for me. But Govan's trial was over fourteen months ago, and I wouldn't have been of any value to them after that, even with a changed mind. The seg was plain vengeance for not changing my mind, most likely.

Ja meneer. Deadpan.

It's the Supreme Court in Maritzburg, then. Nice old building, two storeys, brick and stone, graceful, gracious, as the Law is supposed to be. I suppose I'll like it a bit less when they've finished with me.

Nice to get away from the dying, though.

In the Reception Yard stands yet another wire-meshed van. On the floor stands a cardboard box and in the box are a quart bottle of yet more coffee and something sewed up in a piece of mailbag canvas. Paper bags have been invented by now, but there's nothing like tradition.

That's all; I will sit flat on my backside all the way to Maritzburg, eight hours it took in those days. So what, I'll be able to see the real world outside the mesh window, however dirty the glass. What a treat! Enjoy it while you can, you're not going to see much more of it in the long, long future.

I get the prison jewellery yet again, hands, legs, and boomps-a-daisy, bracelets and anklets, the two chained together, I clamber in the van and we're away, followed by a car containing the Super with a hamper of padkos, not for me alas, and an unknown warder with a huge six-gun strapped to his left tit.

This coffee makes the teeth brown. It causes one to pee out half as much again as one has taken in, so one is always thirsty for more of the stuff, on account of the dehydration. I've already had this great big bladderful of it with my pap, so we're scarce out of Pretoria when I need to relieve myself.

I bang on the cab with my fists and yell, the passenger boer turns round but he can't see anything, the glass is bloody dirty and he's on the sunny side of it. I shout Meneer ek wil pis! I shout it a few times before he hears, then he points to his watch and puts up his open hand; five fingers, I must wait for five minutes. Okay, I can see it's a bit built-up around here, so I wait for ten minutes, then fifteen, and we're out in the veld now, so I kick bedonderd on the cab and yell Pis, meneer, pis! I'm bloody nigh bursting, and we're getting on for Germiston along that old road, and it's more than half an hour I've been sitting here biting on the bullet, and I think The Hell, I'm going to piss in the van. But I've got to sit in this thing for many an hour yet, and it's summertime...

As I writhe about and clutch at my crotch wondering if it's worth another kick on the cab, and gape desperately and randomly about with staring eyes, there I notice a tiny hole in the door of the bak, where a rivet or small bolt has been taken out to remove some numberplate or tail-light or something, and I calculate that my body is now so supple from all the stretching exercises that I should be able to get the end of the old man to coincide with this wee gatjie, even with all the boep chainwork about my limbs.

I do it too. Half rolled over, half kneeling, I manage to crush myself against the door and get everything lined up and dribble-proof and here we go! Heavenly! I open my ecstatic eyes shortly and realise that if I roll them a little to the right my left one will be in line to see out of the corner of the rear meshed window, so I do that, and there I see the Prisons Department car with its windscreen wipers going like crazy, and the two boere looking up at the cloudless sky and at each other and hunching up their shoulders.

I calculate that from a litre of this coffee I should be able to get at least six good pees, it's like loading a rifle magazine.

I clatter over to the cardboard box accordingly, and drink a pint of the stuff, half a litre, and sure enough after half an hour I'm ready again. I let the pressure build up to about two bars this time and writhe over to the little hole and piss all over the car again, and again they look at the sky, and I can see them also examining the instrument panel this time. What for? Nee, God weet. Maybe a red light to say there's no water in the radiator.

Round three. It's a good one this, like a fire extinguisher, and it's just too much. The driver hoots and signals the van driver in his rear-view mirror to stop. They're all out of their vehicles and underneath me now, looking at the fuel tank, I suppose, because I can hear somebody say Moenie rook nie, don't strike a match.

Through multiple thicknesses of dirty glass, plus the windscreen, I spy them at the front of the van. They raise the bonnet and presumably check the radiator and coolant level. Nothing. They shut the thing and shake their heads.

All four of them come round to the back and the padlock rattles, the door opens and somebody says Oukei, klim uit, kom pis.

Way back there I once met at a social do in Northern Rhodesia a District Commissioner whose previous appointments had all been in eastern parts of the Empire. As chance often has it at parties, I found myself alone with him for some few minutes, and obliged to make safe conversation. What is your main impression of Africa? You can't get much safer than that.

All the men piss together on the lawn, he said, rank regardless. Urination is the Great Leveller.

So we all stand in a row there on the yellow grass, and all sigh, except me, and somebody says 'n Lekker pis, en 'n sterk straal, a good piss, and a strong jet. The reason I don't sigh is that I haven't got a teaspoonful of urine in me. All eight eyes turn to look at my knob; I thought you signalled you were ready to burst, back there at Irene? Ja, Meneer, you know how it is when a lot of ouens are pissing together, sometimes you can't do it, for psychological reasons, seelkundige redes.

O my God, mense, hy's skaam nogal! Bellows of laughter in the veld. He's shy! Is jy 'n moffie, jong? Am I a poofter?

Nee, jy weet mos, meneer. They all look away to laugh, and I rustle the grass with my foot and hope it sounds like somebody pissing. I go back to the van saying for all to hear What a relief, and climb in and drink the rest of the coffee as they slam and lock the door.

The van is actually a sort of ginger ale colour. Maybe that's why they can't see where the volleys are coming from, but the next one spoils it all, it's too soon, I've overplayed my hand, and they hoot and overtake the van, and now stay ahead. I still have two rounds in the magazine. What a senseless waste of ammunition. We'll never win this war.

There's a delay at Reception in Maritzburg. The lifer from Central who's been running the place for the last eight years is down the passage with the Parole Board, and the boer in charge doesn't know where anything is. After a bit four Bantoe gevangenes come in one door of the office and exit by another opposite, holding by its four corners a boep blanket, wherein lies the unconscious form of the lifer, who has just been told by the Board that he may go home now after only ten years to his wife and kids, not noticing in his file that his wife went off with somebody worthier nine years ago, nor calculating that his kids are now twenty-one the youngest, and all off with personal partners, and maybe lost interest in their convict father.

But he returns to Reception soon enough with his hair and collar all wet from having a bucket of water poured over him, massaging his eyes and staring around him, and writes me into the system. A frail boer with beautiful eyes like Audrey Hepburn, called Cruywagen, a wheelbarrow, takes me off to the Blanke Seksie, where fifteen men have been removed from one big cell and relocated in an another which has fifteen men in it already. It has to be so because I am a politieke gevangene and an opblaser too, who might teach these enterprising lads some nasty habits with explosives. I have to live alone and there's only one single cell here, and that's occupied by the lifer.

These two are really beaut big cells, hey, though not big enough for thirty. I can hear the ouens groaning next door. I stand in the middle of the vast polished floor after graze and lock-up and have an attack of agoraphobia; it's scary, man, I need to sleep with my back up against something. I take my mat over to a corner and make a bed there.

Sleep is difficult; I feel dislocated and anxious. Somewhere nearby I can hear a radio softly playing; what sort of place is this? Maybe it's the duty boer somewhere, but why in one of the sections? After an hour or two I get up and walk about. Hell, in here with my bare feet on the nice black-polished floor I can get in ten miles running a day easily, and I give it a try there and then in figures of eight and ovals. This trial will take many weeks, months maybe; in that time I'll build up to eighteen or so, four hours slow stuff, jogging. I've got to come out of boep eventually, though I'm not eligible for parole like the bandiet in the blanket, nor remission for good behaviour, nor, for that matter any other reward for good behaviour whilst inside. When that happy day comes I'll stop jogging, I'll be ready to run.

The radio goes quiet, and a voice calls in a fairly relaxed sort of whisper Hey, you running there, howzit, man? Put your table by your window here and climb up, man.

Me? Don't be silly, I'm from the Big House, I know about snides. What is he going to score? What have they told him to get out of me? But I put the table there and climb up. The windows are low down here, I don't need the bankie, the sill is at shoulder-level up here. What's it, man?

No, I'm the ou who booked you in today.

The ou in the blanket?

He, he, he! Ja, man, he says, jis, ek het lelik geskrik, I caught such a vokken spook, man!

I relax, he's got nothing to score, he's going home. Well, he's going out, I mean. Hey, good luck, man! Ja, thanks, hey, you also. How's this boep, man? I ask. Nee, dis 'n lekker ou boep hierdie, he says, die graze is mos bietjie min, maar hy's darem lekker graze. Ek kry ook tee.

TEA? How the hell do you get tea? No, I'm A-group, he says, I also got a bed and a wireless and a letter every month. How'd you get the radio, man? No, my uncle sent me. I write him letters, you know.

What about your kids, hey? No, my kids don't like to see me, just my uncle, but he's a old toppie, and he write sometimes only. I don't think he see so lekker any more. And visits? I ask. No, nobody visit me, man, it's too long ago.

This White part of the boep does indeed look quite lekker; it's just a single-storey row of cells in the prison yard, and they open on to a concrete stoep polished red, which makes the place rather homely. Fifteen or so paces away is the main prison wall, but it's open air from here to there, with a feeling of space, and along the side of the stoep somebody has planted a row of sad geraniums, with a few flowers on them. As a spectacle they score zilch, but the bit of aroma coming off them through the cell window adds to the delight of the balmy Maritzburg evening. It's lovely to go about barefoot and naked and feel the life in one's body on a summer night like this.

What are you going to do outside? No, they gave me a suit to put on tomorrow, and a ticket on the train to Joburg, and I got my old clothes in my suitcase still in the property store-room there. Tomorrow they going to give me some start, too. How much start? No, I think a hundred rand, I'm not sure.

Hey, what's your name, man? I'm Jock, and you? No, I'm Frik. Hey, Frik, you're going to see old friends again, man. He, he, he! No, man, my lekker ou chinas are all in Central, man; ek het lekker chinas daarso, maar dis 'n up to shit boep, daai, jis hy's up to shit!

En hierso? Nee, hier het ek geen chinas nie; dis 'n short-term boep hierdie, en awaiting trial, die moegoes hierso kom net in, dan is hulle weer weg, hulle kom net lank genoeg om die skottelgoed vuil te maak. Dis net 'n paar skoonmakers en ek wat bly, en hulle stoot net een jaar. Maar hy's mos 'n lekker boep, hierdie.

Maybe I'll take a nice Sunday stroll and and a reintroduction to my home town on a sensuous Maritzburg morning; a summer day before the sun is high enough to start its scorching, the air still calm enough to be perfumed with frangipani, and clear enough for the shocking colour harmonies of the mauve bougainvilleas and the magenta azaleas against the pale apricot of her old Atlas bricks. I'll go and sit amongst the willows and mulberries along the Duzi banks and watch the scalies rising to take the fruit, and cross by the old suspension footbridge to watch the pretty girls playing tennis at the Kershaw courts.

I'll let my mind drift where it sentimentally will. What a treat. I'd forgotten the City Hall bells, and the hour of British folk tunes they play on a Sunday morning, ten to eleven. I'll hear them down at the Duzi, far away, but clear clear because the air is so still; The Bluebells of Scotland.

O wheer tell me wheer has my Hielan' Laddie gone?

I skiem if they're so slapgat about growing flowers around here, maybe they're slapgat about catching an after-lunch kip, and I'll roll my bedding down and stretch luxuriantly on my back on the nice cool floor and put my kitchen towel over my face and disappear.

When Cruywagen comes for exercise he has another bandiet with him, very pale-skinned. He explains (I think) that this man also must be exercised alone, it's an order from the police. He now has two prisoners in this solo category. He has an exercise period set aside for that category, and he exercises his solo prisoners in this period according to orders. Both of them, together. It is not for me to dispute the logic of this.

Strange Africance that screw speaks, says the new soloist. His name is Niel Furlow, an Irishman and highly professional burglar working in London. That's why he's so pale, he explains; all his work is at night.

Them aint Afrikaans, I explain, them's English. Cruywagen insists on speaking English, with all his verbs at the end of the sentence.

We chat about this and that and get to know each other. We talk about life in London. He talks of the techniques of breaking and entering, and how to find informants on the whereabouts of things; Most of my personal contacts came from the guards of a security company called Securicor, he says. I'd get them to leave a window unlocked at a certain time, he says, that sort of thing, in return for a cut. Yes, I say, and other teams who were into lorry theft would offer the Securicor blokes at Peter Keevil's on the Edgeware Road there a whack of the profit if they'd leave a gate unlocked and take a blow to the head, know the place? Of course I know it; three floors, c overing a whole bloody city block, stuffed all three to the ceiling with lovely grub, imported, how could I not know it? How do you know it, though? he asks. I was one of the Securicor guards there, man, for a couple of years. The other was one Dave Ashment, from Winchelsea, a bloke with one arm, did you ever see him? Yes, fell into a cement mixer, says Furlow, how did he ever get that right, and he carried bits of his own bones around in a paper envelope to show people, is that him? Him in the residual flesh, I reply.

We feel quite close. He is nostalgic for London. I could never get into Peter Keevil's though, he says, nobody could. I should bloody think nobody could, I reply, not with the pickings as they were for the guards. Keevil's supply Fortnum and Mason's, did you know that? Name any fancy delicious exotic food, and you'll find it there. My favourite was tinned pigeons from Sarawak, very delicately spiced, then Finnish strawberries and Dutch cream. You've got to be bloody stupid to get dumped from a place like that and go to some assignment where you do your clock-punching rounds out of doors in the fucking snow at night in the middle of a London winter. Even if you don't get found for collusion in a lorry theft, they'll still move you to a safe assignment looking after scrap iron or something, just in case.

I'll tell you who did get in there, though, I say, and that was the uniformed coppers off the street. There was a half dozen or so of them that we got to know. Jesus, in the middle of a winter's night there would be this electric trrring at the huge steel gate on the Edgeware, and there was this poor frozen bastard blowing great puffs of breath all around. Just checking up that all's okay, mate, he would say. Oh, just fine! Care for a cup of coffee? Half Tanganyika, half Puerto Rico, nice. Come round to the side door.

He'd come in shaking the snow off his greatcoat and big blue helmet and peel off his gloves and rub his shnoz like Good King Wenceslas.

Can't be long, he'd say. Nice smell of bacon, eh? Keevil's cured their own bacon, the place for doing it was right next to the side door. Danish, I would say, and we've got some nice Danish eggs too, like I'm a shareholder in this place. Time for such a snack, eh? No, no, it would take too long. Wouldn't mind a bite of that cake, though, if there's any left.

Always some left. Every Saturday night I would bake fourteen pounds of Christmas cake in the staff canteen, a pound a night each per week for Dave Ashment and myself, the richest cake ever, just solid with dried fruit and candied peel and cherries and lekker treacly sugar and Dutch butter and cinnamon and a couple of dozen of the Danish eggs and a half-jack of brandy for the fourteen pounds. Keevil's didn't deal in liquor. The dop was the only thing I brought in, and nothing went out. That was the rule. It was called Living off the Country, distinct from theft.

Didn't the management know about it? asks Furlow. Oh, I dare say, but insurance paid for damaged packages and took possession of them, and it meant better security if the guards felt themselves to be shareholders, and nobody more welcome than a policeman popping in during the night.

So we go over many places and people known to us, Paddy and I, and I don't mean the theatres and galleries of London, I mean the Farma Cream Co. at Chalk Farm where they made lousy ice-cream and the American Embassy in Chelsea where the cigars were good and the art students around about undressed at open windows in the summer and you could see their tits; then there was an industrial chemist whose name I forget, at Greyfriars, where things went wrong one night and the Securicor bloke was killed by mistake.

But all old days and old memories now.

Furlow has a generally flabbergasted aura about him. Hell, you can't get a year for being in possession of a small safe, he says. Depends what's inside, dunnit? I reply. Well, nothing, in fact, nothing worth stealing, anyway, as it turned out. You mean you stole this safe without finding out first whether there was anything in it? It's embarrassing, but I was drunk, and I'd seen this thing in the Irvin Johnson office during the day, down at the Trawler Jetty there, and I went back to fetch it after a party. I was making a hell of a din, pushing it over the wooden planks of the jetty on one of those two-wheeled trolley things, and when I saw headlights approaching I thought it was my mate coming with the car, that's how drunk I was.

Most embarrassing was appearing in court in a white tuxedo and a red bow-tie. I'd come to Durban to negotiate a deal about a racehorse, perfectly proper, but when my hosts heard I'd been arrested they denied ever having met me when the police went to fetch my suitcase. You mean you were found pushing this thing with an empty safe on it along a wooden jetty in full evening dress in the middle of the night, drunk? You don't seem a very professional burglar to me. Oh I am I am, he says, I have to find school fees for my daughter; she's at a very good place, you know. But this thing is too too embarrassing, I don't know what came over me, and I just can't stay in this country for a whole year. I've told the police that, and they've said they will speak to the prison people about parole to the UK or something.

What the hell have the police got to do with the prison parole board? I ask. This isn't England. Short-term prisoners don't get parole anyway, I say. Only remission, one quarter for good behaviour. Oh I see, he says, a bit crestfallen; but it was worth a try.

And why are you here in Maritzburg if you got busted in Durban? Why aren't you in Durban Local? I don't know, I never thought about it, really, he replies. Is that unusual?

I've lost count of date and days, and the next one turns out to be a Saturday, and since I won't be charged until Monday that means I have a whole weekend off for sentimentalising about old days in Maritzburg with the Lieutenant, and gleaning what prison gossip and scandal was going, from Paddy Furlow. Surely there's one Irishman not called Paddy? You can call me Sigismund, he said. Why Sigismund? Okay, try Nepomuk, whatever. There's only us two here; I'll know who you're talking to.

Prison scandal we got plenty of in the next weeks.

So where were you busted? he asks. Well, the thing happened in Durban but I was busted in Pretoria. So why are you in Maritzburg? Supreme Court, I say, but yours wasn't a Supreme Court case, and you're settled anyway. Yes, he says, I was sentenced in Durban.

We can't work it out.

After I've told him about the inauguration of MK and our adventures in the explosives trade he ceases to feel embarrassed about the Trawler Jetty. My God you blokes were dumb! he says. I read about it in the London papers and thought How dumb, but I didn't know you were as dumb as that. When I've told him about the traffic cop and the gunpowder he stops dead in his tracks and looks into my face to make sure I'm not joking. I think I should sit down a bit, he says.

He moves on to the skills of the locksmith and regrets that he has no pencil and paper for diagrams. Safe-cracking is his pride, though he can see I'm a bit lost in lockpicking explained only with words, and anyway my interest is probably in the explosives side, but as he opens a conversation about this we see the other thirty whites tumble out of their premises stretching their cramped legs and waving their arms about. It seems our half-hour is over.

I'll tell you about the scientific use of explosives in the next couple of weeks, he says, if we're together again; I see your theory is a bit weakish. We'll start with Newton's Third Law: every action has an equal and opposite reaction.

Take plastic fridge bags with you to the job. You can't take sandbags, but these fridge bags you fill with water on the job; there's always a tap there. Sure, sand has a higher specific gravity and more inertia, and it'll direct the blast inwards that little bit better, but not much... At this point Audrey Hepburn arrives and speaks Africance at us, and we assume our exercise is done.

See you then, says Sigismund/Nepomuk.

Well I need no Ginsberg to rescue me from this bit of science, I'm quite inquisitive about it, and look forward to it; but I don't get much of it, not nearly enough, for other events intervene in the programme.

After sundown when it's cooled off a bit, another lovely hour here in the midlands, I put my bedding in a corner along with the stool and table and strip off all my threads and get in a good two hours' jog around the cell, short short paces; it's just too small for running, but this is a good plod, which should give about twenty kays, I reckon. I rub my sweating self down with the towel; tomorrow I'll wash it under the shower and dry myself inside my cotton clothes.

This is pretty silent occupation, and as I'm about it I hear someone coming cautiously along the stoep. I stop rubbing to concentrate on all sounds with my Ginsberg/Pretoria Central ears. I can hear trousers swishing and the soles of shoes oh so gently touching the polished concrete. My hearing is that of a bat-eared fox after all the solitary. I can hear insects under the ground. This person goes to the cell next door and gently unlocks it. There's the small furtive touch of metal on metal. I hear muted conversation and after five minutes I hear the quiet tumbling of the lock again and two pairs of shoes treading carefully along the stoep. The five minutes must have been for Furlow to put on his clothing. I suppose this must have been at ten or half past.

Before dawn I am awakened by the same quiet tread of feet and tumbling of the lock. No speaking.

When Cruywagen opens up for exercise I see Furlow standing pie-eyed in front of his peter, and we stroll over to the sunshine. I'm not going to ask him about last night though I'm curious as all hell, but he seems to have a need to talk to someone, and that's me. He slept not a wink last night. He went off with two plain-clothes policemen to a house somewhere out of town, where he was deposited in a comfortable chair with a quart of beer and directions to the fridge, where stood numberless further quarts. They came straight to the point.

There was a certain Marty Somebody around, I forget the second name, Jewish though, I think it was Bernstein, who has been a festering thorn in the flesh of the Fraud Squad here in Natal for years. Exceedingly cunning, and wise enough to have much money set aside always for the best defence, he has ever been able to let nothing stick to him, except a bad reputation, which caused him no sleepless nights, in fact caused him some yichas, for he enjoyed notoriety as much as fame and wealth. More irksome to the Squad, though, is his boastfulness, and his use of the English longbowmens' gesture of scorn for the retreating French at Agincourt: the two fingers stuck in the air.

Also, of course, there is plain police business. Marty B's millions were not the pocket money that millions are today. The police are going to get him, by hook or by crook. Well, they've tried the hook.

Marty B owns a couple of racehorses, as might be expected. Horse racing has great attraction for crims and mobsters, and naturally to be seen leading your own winning horse off the course for the photographers is very positive pleasure, unlike being yet again acquitted in court, which is negative pleasure, you might say.

Well, when Paddy Furlow fell into the hands of the Murder and Robbery lads, and they found he had horse-racing business to do in Durbs, they naturally handed him over to Fraud for a few days, who might have something of advantage for him to discuss over a quart or two of beer. There might be established a connection between him and Marty B, with a bit of imagination. What's more, since as far as Furlow was concerned the racehorse business which brought him here was perfectly legitimate, despite the paranoid behaviour of his hosts, he could present the first part of any evidence which he might deliver in court with perfect candour, if ever he were called upon to give evidence in a trial of Marty B.

It is now the purpose of the Fraud Squad to see that a suitable trial should come about, in which Paddy Furlow can indeed deliver such evidence. Only the correct opportunity has been lacking. Fortune has ignored them for some years.

Now the apple has fallen right into their lap. As Fortune would have it, coincidental with Paddy's conviction came the shooting of Beach Shanty. Beach Shanty was the winner of the July Handicap and any other race in sight and within reach, a wonder-horse, phenomenal, invincible. Beach Shanty had been out exercising early one morning when somebody hidden in a cluster of bushes shot him with a rifle. The sniper was one lousy shot, for the bullet didn't kill the horse, it got him in the hindquarters where it minced up a lot of muscle tissue but luckily broke no bones. It certainly put him out of action though, and the charge would be the same anyway, if they found the sniper, because it's not unlawful to murder a horse, only to shoot at your neighbour's livestock.

Now, Paddy tells me, the Fraud lads want him to graft onto his straight story of international horse-racing brokerage a bit supportive of a fantasy they have devised, a fantasy of corruption culminating in Marty B having Beach Shanty shot. It is a story devoid of truth, but his bit is devoid also of detail, and thus easily adhered to; the intrigue is simple and the telling of it includes no background stuff, no hearsay evidence, no loose narrative anywhere. For example, Furlow is not going to say he knew Marty B had asked somebody to arrange the shooting, oh no, Furlow will say Marty B asked him, personally, to do it, first time they met, which was also the last. Marty B assumed Furlow had come from England as an agent for that purpose, sent by his mate over there, a person unnamed, and unknown to Furlow. Marty B personally explained the whole plot, according to this fantasy of the Fraud lads. There must be no doubt about his intent.

That sort of thing. It is all carefully engineered.

Furlow will be a star witness; he can't be shown as an accomplice of Marty B in some way, in any way; the court can see no advantage in his lying, it isn't as if he hopes not to be charged himself if he gives accomplice evidence for the State, since he never became an accomplice.

He's already a sentenced prisoner, of course, but it would not cross anybody's mind, nor would people make so bold as to suggest it if it had crossed their minds, that the Prisons Department and Minister of Justice would reward a sentenced thief for perjury on behalf of the Fraud Squad.

Hell, Jock, I told them I'd never even heard of Marty B, how on earth am I going to sustain my story under the expert cross-examination his counsel are going to lay on me? Never mind, they said, we've got it all simply worked out, we just want you to decide in principle whether you want to go along and we'll brief you later if you do. We'll have rehearsals.

You've got nothing to lose, have you? said the Fraud Squad to Niel Furlow.

We go back to our peters after exercise. Paddy's is opened first. There stands the bed again, now with nice new blankets. Also a pillow in a stripey pillow-case, from the hospital.

I don't see him again for a week; next day I'm off to court to be charged, though not to plead, and after that I'm busy with an attorney and senior counsel for the rest of the week.

He calls me over to the window after lights-out that Monday evening, but I quickly shut him up; How do you know they haven't got somebody standing in his socks outside your cell, I ask, checking to see if you're shooting your mouth off about the deal, hey? He hadn't spent a hell of a long time in any prison, that was clear, never mind a place like Central.

So Cruywagen opens up on the Tuesday and tells me in his Old Icelandic that there's a visitor for me, and there in the Visitor's Room large as life and every bit as beautiful, stands me ol' chum, my Congress of Democrats Comrade Israel Eaglestone, Attorney at Law, Marxist.

Issy! I exclaim, hoe gaan dit jong? Nee, dit gaan mos goed, he replies, elke dag bietjie beter, let's ask the officer here to find us another room which isn't wired. He makes this request to Cruywagen in good Ermelo Afrikaans, that's where he's from; Cruywagen waves his beautiful eyelashes up and down a few times as he thinks, and says something to Issy in Anglo-Saxon. He turns and makes off down the passage. What did he say? asks Issy. It is a spell for charming a swarm of bees, I reply, I remember it from The Old English Reader, one of my library books at Central.

Looks like somebody I know, says Issy, but who?

Audrey Hepburn? I ask.

Yes, that's it! says Issy.

We're ushered into an unused office with a telephone. Issy pulls out the plug. I thought I might see you in court yesterday, I say. No, I had to get an exemption from my banning order to leave Durban; that fellow we had here was a Maritzburg attorney, briefed just for the day.

Family and political news first, of course. I've got quick at body language, it's the only language you have in seg. So I know the family side of things is okay because Issy wouldn't be smiling so broadly if it weren't. I can come back to details of that.

First, first, and urgently: what happened to Max?

The comradely grin disappears from Issy's face. Didn't you know? It's almost three years ago.

Issy, ou maat, for more than three years I've seen no newspaper. My two-a-year letters are censored. My visits are supervised. So for Christ's sake just tell me man!

Ja! says Issy, but falls silent. I don't know what secrets you two in PE had, he says after a bit, but I hear you had one; the rumour got out, and the Party put the disciplinary process on Max to tell all, and he did eventually. He couldn't stand the pressure. Rumour said it was an explosive. Nine people got killed in a post office in the city centre, but I've never been given the details, I was always against MK myself. So all I have other than newspaper headlines is rumour.

I fall silent now. It fits, Issy, I say after a while, and tell him about the ammonal and the MK fuck-up. So Max probably told the others what to do and gave them the bomb. I tell him about the thing that first ever turned my mind to political thought when I was a kid and the Ossewa- brandwag hit a post office in Germiston and killed people in a morning queue. It was the most disgusting thing I could think of, Issy, I say, and now my organisation is in the same league, and Max is dead.

We sit in silence. Issy breaks it: It's a pity he wasn't found guilty along with you, he says. As things turned out you were the lucky one. Well maybe if I'd been acquitted we could have given each other moral support and defied the party, even if it meant getting kicked out or maybe shot, it would have been better than what Max got anyway.

I tell him about Max's execution. He was right in the middle, says Issy. More silence, because there is in fact only one thing to know or to say, but to say it would be platitudinous; if you tangle with the regime and the party you must know you might die. Moenie sug nie. Make a skyf.

Any fags? I ask Issy. Ja, he says, for in those days people smoked, the anti-tobacco campaign hadn't got going.

Eighteen

SO WE SIT AND SMOKE FOR A WHILE, then Issy gives my arm a shake and says First things first, and produces for me a platitude from his personal optimistic stock of such things. He's incurable, he has a cliche for every occasion. There's light at the end of the tunnel, he says, though to me the light is that headlamp of a locomotive coming to squash us flat, as people say, and I tell him so.

Issy wants to put my mind at rest about the possibility of the regime's becoming Fascist. No, our capitalists wouldn't allow that, he says. Anyway, you'll see how Sammy Muller runs his court in this reputedly fascist country, says Issy. Who is Sammy Muller? No, he is your judge, along with two assessors.

My main charge is contravention of the Explosives Act, as it was in PE, only with Slim this time, and his insurrectionary gang. That's not political, but the alternative charges are: Furthering the Aims of an Unlawful Organisation, and Contravention of the Suppression of Communism Act, draconian political laws both that have been the statute book ten, fifteen years. Sammy is prepared for a political trial all right, says Issy, with the prosecutor one Cyril Ries, a happy fascist if ever there was one, and with the Security Branch running the prosecution show.

So where's this light in the tunnel? I ask.

One thing Sammy Muller is bloody angry about is racism, says Issy. The most recent cause of anger was personal; he applied to join the Maritzburg Country Club on being appointed to the Supreme Court here and deciding to move house up from Durban, because he's a keen golfer, you know, but they blackballed him. So he's decided just to stay down in Durbs and motor up each day. Who knows what he does about golf down there? Maybe the Jewish Club has some facility, by arrangement with the Durban Country Club.

I don't know much about the assessors, he says, but I'm told they're okay, you should have them on your side. Now to the point, though; we have work to do. He takes a notebook from his briefcase, and clicks on his ballpoint.

Okay, what's the story then?, and I tell him what I think I should present to the court to account for my behaviour on that fateful night in Durban. If you're going to say that you might as well plead guilty, he says. We fall silent for a while and he chews the end of his ballpoint.

Look, he says eventually, we know how it goes in the Class Struggle; I'm going to tell you what to say in evidence, you just see that you remember it.

Don't write anything down, just listen carefully and remember every detail, and don't deviate from that in court. We might stand a chance yet, what with Sammy's predispositions.

So he unfolds his scheme of things to me, and I really concentrate on each and every point, and feel sure I will remember it all. It takes about thirty minutes, detailed, after which we fall silent. After a bit he says Okay, now a most important thing; it's all very well our conspiring like this as Party people, because we can't afford niceties and legal propriety, we realise the primary thing in the struggle is to keep our comrades out of prison at all costs, but the man who's been briefed as junior counsel, Advocate Nigel Carstairs, is a highly regarded officer of the court, and if he knows this is the way we behave he will pull out of this case, here and now. So not a word, hey? Don't even drop a hint. Right? I'll see you again tomorrow, I've got a banning exemption for two days. We'll go over details, now we've got the framework established. Carstairs will see you on Thursday.

We do that. Next day we polish everything, buff it up, we get every detail right, then Issy goes over it in a mock cross-examination, but he can't catch me out anywhere, man. Good, he says, I'll see you in court. Not a word to anyone, eh?

Issy, do I look stupid?

Carstairs has the confidence of a man who has been to a good school. A good Natal school, it goes without saying. The type of humour too, come to think of it, rather bluff, with the sort of abbreviated chuckle I remember from certain British officers in the war. For a short while I taught art at Carstairs' old school, so we're chums, sort of.

He looks at Cruywagen in utter astonishment. Tell him I speak only English and a little poor Afrikaans, he says to me. He's speaking English now, I say, he's asking if we'd like the same office as I had with Issy Eaglestone. Oh I see, I see. He smiles soothingly at Cruywagen; No thanks, I'll find an empty one along the passage here if you'll be good enough to lead the way, please. Cruywagen says it will only be a pleasure, and when we're finished will we please tell them at Reception, from where he will be summoned to take me back to my cell.

Ah yes, thank you, says Carstairs, two spoons please.

We pull up chairs to the meranti table and with a generous flourish he tips out the contents of his briefcase, like a legal cornucopia, and riffles about there. I recognise this riffling; it becomes habitual amongst lawyers, they learn it originally in court as a means for throwing witnesses off balance, but he's doing it habitually now. He comes up with a wad of notepaper and a ballpoint. He takes off his jacket and puts it over the back of his chair as a coathanger and hitches up his shirtsleeves.

Right! he says, Tell me all about it, and I sally forth with Issy's long story of innocence, as rehearsed. He rattles his ballpoint between upper and lower teeth, that's what he does when he's concentrating, I learn as we go along. He rattles it now as I recite my lines. About halfway through he puts down the pen, turns his torso to look out of the window at a view of the blank prison wall opposite, flings an arm over the back of the chair and rests his chin on his hand. There's a bit of silence, half a minute maybe as he leans on his elbow, then he turns back to his papers.

What a lot of balls, he says, It sounds as if you made it all up. If you say that in court the prosecutor will tear out your guts and you'll earn yourself twelve years.

Well I can honestly say I didn't make it all up. Any of it.

He goes back to rattling his ballpoint. After ten minutes or so of silence he says Look, forget that yarn, all of it. You just listen very carefully to what I'm saying now, and remember every detail when you're giving evidence, and you may yet stand a chance. Don't write anything down, I don't have to tell you that, do I?, he observes with one of his British Officer chuckles. Just remember, remember, remember it.

He doesn't rearrange Issy's yarn, he just erases it. He deletes it. He has a competely new slant, very ingenious I must say, and by the end of some repetition I know it off by heart, and feel greatly encouraged.

He reloads his briefcase after an hour or so, and puts on his jacket and goes to the door. There he turns; I don't need to tell you this either, do I, that what has happened here is strictly between you and me. I mean I must have your gentleman's word on that. Do you give it?

Unhesitatingly, I say.

Frank Heavistone will see you tomorrow or early next week; he's your senior counsel, silk, and on his way to being a judge, and if he picks up even the slightest hint of what has been so improperly going on here he will turn on his heel there and then and walk right out of your defence team.

Not me, not me, I say, my lips are sealed, sticky-taped.

Tell that fellow I'm sorry I couldn't wait for the tea, and with a wave he's off.

Well Heavistone doesn't come the next day, nor do I see him on the Monday, but just as well, I suppose, because it gives me time really to polish up the story and imagine hypothetical questions in cross-examination, and the answers to parry them, and remember it all like anything.

Nor do I see Neil Furlow.

As things turn out, he was down the self-same passage in which I was rehearsing my lines for the SB Pantomime, rehearsing his lines for the Fraud Squad Miracle Play.

During the week, though, I have heard once again the furtive door-opening during the early part of the night, but don't even wake up for the return, I am becoming so used to it.

He comes from his cell for Saturday morning exercise with his bafflement diminished. I remind him that if the Squad find he's been talking to me about the deal, or even just that he's been exercising with me, they'll cancel the whole thing, call it off. Well, it was Cruywagens' choice to exercise us together, says Furlow, and we're obeying his orders. And as for the subject of our talking, we're talking about women. I grin at the idea.

No, seriously, he says; well, one woman anyway. You won't believe it; on Thursday night they fetched me off again, earlyish, and put me in civilian clothes at some house, and took me to a suite at the Imperial Hotel, with a nice double bed and bubbly in an ice-bucket, and as I sit on this bed hoping they're not going to put some tart on to me for one of their funny reasons, the door opens and in comes my wife, true as God, all the way from Inverness Terrace, Bayswater, London W2, England.

Just to get you nice and relaxed for court on Monday, they say, and set the Yale on the door and shut it. I got back just before opening, skin of our teeth. Their teeth, that is. The Prisons people aren't supposed to know about this, except the super and the night screw.

So that's why I didn't hear you coming back, eh?

I dare say, says Furlow.

So he's off to court on Monday.

The story the Fraud Squad have contrived for him doesn't have to be too ingenious. Furlow admits his previous record in London, a couple of short terms for theft; so yes, he is a criminal, he supposes, and he was interested when Bernstein offered him a one-off job, but no, he was appalled when asked to shoot a horse. He is a horse-lover, that's why and how he's in the business of horse-brokerage, and that's how he comes to be giving evidence here. He is not a man of violence, he is a man of subtlety.

He was shown the rifle upstairs at the Riviera Hotel on the Esplanade, he explains. He was impressed by the architecture of Issy Benjamin, that's why he remembers the name of the place. Apart from the type, calibre, etc., he recognises the rifle before the court because it has a pale patch on the varnish of the stock, and a couple of screw-holes, where apparently some metal plate has been removed, a nameplate, maybe, of the rightful owner from whom it has been stolen.

A police witness gives evidence that the rifle before the court was found buried in the garden at Marty's house, under a birdbath. A metal detector found it there.

The accused had made contact with Furlong at the Edward Hotel on the beachfront, where he was staying. Yes, he recognises the man who made the proposition, and points him out in court; He is the man sitting in the dock, Your Worship.

Bernstein is stunned. He has never seen this person in his life before. He has never seen the rifle in his life before. Furlow's evidence corroborates the evidence of another man Bernstein has never seen in this life before, the man who actually did the job and was arrested soon enough, who says Bernstein paid him a fee to do it. He now hopes for a reduced sentence for collaborating with the police, says this second man, which normally would make his evidence suspect, of course, but here it is backed up by Furlow's evidence, which is clean.

Who really paid him, what the guilt of the true culprit was about, the real mastermind, these secrets will go to the grave with the Fraud Squad and the lousy marksman.

Details elude me after all these years. I'm not sure that I was ever given any. I do know that Marty B picked up a good stretch, though. Furlow's evidence had been so simple, the story was so short, there were no sticking-out bits for a cross-examiner to get hold of, and worry at, like a terrier.

I suppose the man with the reduced sentence got even further reduction later on. Much of it, maybe. Maybe all, like Furlow.

So gaan dit mos in die tronk.

The Defence case opens tomorrow, says Paddy. Ja, then there's got to be argument, I say, and time to mull over everything before a verdict, and pleas in mitigation, and another while before sentence, so you've got a few weeks of waiting yet, hey?

My wife is still at the Imperial, he says. Maybe they'll let me see her again.

I never saw him again. My guess is they sent him back to Inverness Terrace, London W2, England, with his missus. Soon.

On Tuesday Advocate Frank Heavistone comes to see me. His suit is pale grey with a subtle stripe, and there's a waistcoat with a gold watch chain across his paunch. I haven't seen such a watch chain since the days of my Oupa Langeberg, thirty years ago. His hair is sparse, and white. He is of august presence, he is saturnine. He stands majestically at the window with his back to me, toying with the golden links in the delicate fingers of his right hand. His left is across the small of his back. This gesture I get to recognise often enough in court; it suggests to the person in the witness box that he has something behind his back there, a knife, perhaps, or a can of Mace.

He is an old Party man, drifted away when he lost belief in Karl Marx many years ago, before gaining stature at the bar.

Tell me of the evening in question, and what went before, he says standing there at the view of the blank prison wall opposite, and I recite in prepared detail the Carstairs tale of righteousness. Heavistone allows me to finish. He makes with his watch chain like he's telling his beads. There's a silence after I've finished, longish.

Bullshit, he says.

Another silence, longish.

You sucked it all out of your thumb, he says.

It seems you want to stay in prison.

Take this pen and write down what I say, pushing a notepad towards me, and don't forget any of it, do you understand?

Perfectly, I say, and write it down.

Well I must admit this is the best version of the truth so far, by far. It is neat, it is succinct, it has no ragged bits hanging out for some cross- examiner to get his teeth into like a mongoose at a snake, and shake it all to bits. This one I really remember. Like anything.

Back in the cell, though, I realise that there's a lot of background stuff to be filled in. In the Baai I hadn't taken the stand, and a good thing too, it meant that the prosecutor hadn't been able to winkle political things out of me on behalf of the Security Branch; but he would most certainly try that this time round.

If I know anything at all about PE it is still that old fermenting hotbed of treason and plot, and there's just a chance that these three years on my evidence will still have relevance to present plottery. But if I'm deft enough with the detail this time round he will winkle nothing out of me. Nothing true, it goes without saying.

Most importantly, there's no previous personal evidence from any other trial in any other court that they can hold up in contradiction of what I might say in this trial, for I've never given evidence before.

The Heavistone interpretation of reality is that I wasn't in Durban at all. Why slash and counter through a thousand minute-by-minute tricks and thrusts about each event of that historic night, when I can handle the whole lot with but one answer; I was in bed with my wife, reading Shakespeare? No, I can't produce witnesses. Few men in this world have witnesses to their being in bed with the missus. Yes, I agree, it is true, if I'd had a witness it would have made my defence that much stronger, but it is still for the state to prove that I was not in bed with my missus and Will.

I work out an entire background to that, and a schedule. The first thing is to take each person I knew in the Baai and give her or him a completely new identity, all except Govan and Mr Levitan. Max, too, of course. Govan was alone when he sent me to Durban, but he was picked up at Rivonia and is already serving the natural life sentence he was given at that trial, no remission. There is nothing more they can do to him for refusing to give evidence in this one, and I know he'll refuse.

Once I've got all these Doppelgänger established, the dramatis personae, they will be locked into a parallel fictitious history of MK, for Cyril Ries to pick at. I start with Plumbin then. The SB mustn't by random search find out who his mates were, and wring information out of them.

His substitute has the body of Col. Nasser of Egypt, who is about the same size and shape. If I am required to describe this conspirator in the PE debacle of three years ago I shall recall every detail of the persona of Nasser. I dress him in a brown leather jacket with copper buttons instead of a zip, he wears denims which look silly on one so plump, his name is either Fiddes, a Scottish name, or Vette, Afrikaans for Fatso, I'm not sure, I never had time to find out and just called him Vette myself. I remember he had no parting in his hair. I can't remember his address, though, but I can remember where his house is: down the main North End road, along a lesser one at the top of the hill, then left here, right there until one comes to an unsurfaced rocky cul de sac with humble coloured housing all around. Yes, m'lud, I assumed Vette was a Coloured Person because of his complexion and his tightly curled hair. I assumed he had no parting because of the tightness of the curls.

It all comes readily, all I have to do is remember ole Gamal Abdel, even his smile. Vette too smiles a lot.

Every detail is in position, even the appearance of neighbours' kids. Easy, and of course; this was where our washerwoman lived, where I'd take our bagwash every week in the gladiatorial Fiat. It is not an imaginary place. It just has new inhabitants, that's all. My disremembering Vette's address is a good touch of realism; it makes it look as if I'm being cagey to protect him.

Nothing's quite imaginary. I go over every single ANC person I knew. Some Liberal Party folk, too, with new IDs, who guessed something was going on and helped out where they could, with accommodation and the like, no questions asked. They are relocated in the homes of Progressive Party folk I remember from canvassing in some election at the other end of Walmer. Every friend, everyone we ever visited for a cup of tea, gets a new ID and address and new employment.

All this I have plenty of time to rehearse, and rehearse it I do, ten hours a day, fifteen kays round the nice big cell and a couple more round the exercise yard. I think of every catch and dodge, my responses are immediate, and I'm ready for any cross-examination.

In fact, during the trial which starts soon enough ou Rassie comes to me one day during the tea adjournment: Jis, ou Herrilt, says he, we dead tired driving all over New Brighton looking for that house of the trade union woman, what's her name; are you sure you remembered everything right in evidence?

Maisey Dube you mean? Ja, and that's where her place is all right, you just didn't look hard enough, that's all; it's a small house.

Stupid git.

So it's soon enough then. The case opens in the colonial Native High Court building in College Road, opposite the rugby fields of my old school; I remember riding my pushbike past this place, with its gabled tin roof and pale Venetian Red brick walls, and the deep front verandah, all so homely and inviting in its appearance for a place of such unhappy function. I get a first view of its insides now, the fine furnishings of indigenous timbers and teak and oak, and the great open carved beams of dark hardwood; the art, all this, of the colonial cabinetmakers who found their place in the building trade a hundred years ago.

There must be some softwoods up there too, perhaps the tongue-and-groove of the ceiling, for we sit in a constant drizzle of cryptotermes woodborer pellets. Sammy Muller is lucky, and so is Frank Heavistone; they have little hair.

I see some PE journos there amongst the press, and old Maritzburg faces. One of them belongs to a pushbike classmate from the days over the road, who is now a policeman of some rank; he looks at the ceiling in distaste and gets some of the woodborer manure in his eye and exits the court backwards and bowing to Sammy Muller whilst weeping tears all over his police-blue hanky, and sneezing. Not too many political faces, though. I remember Brecht and the burial of the agitator in his zinc coffin: only his wife goes along to the graveyard,

denn wer da mitgeht, der ist auch erkannt;
those who go along are now also known.

Jess has come along, of course, accompanied by a large youth who smiles artistically and gives a thumbs-up. She has moved to a nice little house in Durban, Issy tells me. But I'm not allowed to speak to her, nor kiss her nor Break the Rules, because I'm still a sentenced prisoner and entitled to one visit of half an hour every six months, and no kissing at all for three years, and if things go as expected, and soon, not for another twelve in addition to the three. As I say, Erasmus van Vuurwapen is along too, to give evidence about the sinister PE beginnings of this crime. Ja, ou Herrilt, says he, but only figuratively, Joe ken kies your waaif en femielie goodbaai thus taaim. She wool be a oul leidie when you come out.

Also present are some of those who are already known politically but have not yet got a banning order, which forbids one's entering any court premises except as an accused or witness, a circumstance likely enough to come about in their lives.

But we really only get things started here. I suppose it was okay in days when both judges and natives were hardier folks and a couple of open windows and a few chains around the natives' legs made things comfortable and safe. And the borer hadn't established their fast food enterprise, of course. Right now it's hot as hell-in here and the wheezing of antique air-conditioners makes the spoken word inaudible, while the monsoon mix of insect crap and turbulence from the creaky old ceiling fans makes ludicrous any pretence to majesty the Law may ever have had.

So we get in the queue for accommodation in that other lovely old building, the Supreme Court opposite the City Hall, in whose grounds stood a prefab way back there, a recruiting office where I joined the Air Force as a kid.

In time to come its pale Burnt Sienna bricks will house the Municipal Art Gallery, all chi-chi and sacred and silent as art galleries are, full of pretty indifferent painting except the impressionist Sisley, and unskilled sculpture of fairly crude intuition which must be good because it comes out of the townships and putting it in the presence of the Sisley is part of empowerment. Outside, the kitsch marble monuments to other, earlier, Imperial empowerments will still stand silent as they do now 'midst the trees, and the iron cannon still menace all who doubt municipal virtue.

We manage to jump the queue appreciably, this being an Important Case, and those nignog subspecies who are waiting to get the rope and the rest of that which such folk receive in this world will just have to put up patiently with it all, however eager they may be to get on with their lives.

This hodge-podge of court accommodation will soon be tackled by The Authorities, and Made Proper. Never mind the huge pressure for simple floor space, it somehow seems improper that warmth from a black bum should be left in a wooden seat by one accused, there to be absorbed by the white posterior of the next accused. Such heat energy is made by the eating of maize porridge, all mixed up with oxygen inside and turned into kilojoules which find their way through the buttocks into this or that surface, whilst Caucasian energy is made out of meat and two veg, with gravy, and finds its way through tremendous enterprise into the economy and the production of wealth, which eventually filters down to the benefit of all via the Receiver of Revenue.

The new C.R. Swart Regional Court highrise block back of the new Railway Station in Durban will be a model for the world to see; a separate floor for each type of South African and Gastarbeiter from foreign Homelands, like a twelve-storey layer cake baked by Mev Swart, and connected one floor to the next by fire-escape only. Separate lifts here, stopping only at floors two, five, eight, or three, six, nine, or four, seven, ten, and so on, according to elevator ethnicity.

Ethnasia will last a thousand years;
Our sages oft proclaim its glories.
Its attributes are separate stairs
And segregated lavatories.

I forget who the poet was of this epic work back there in the sixties, and can't find out, but thanks pal, anyway, if you're still around and didn't end up as jam between the layers of Auntie S's cake.

Nineteen

BUT LET'S GET ON WITH THE YARN, MAN! It's clear from the beginning that I'm even deeper down the drain now than I was first time round in the Baai. Being innocent is a great help in putting up a spirited defence, and I'm a hundred per cent guilty, at least. But there are a few advantages here, however meagre; at least I don't have to sit sweating in gut-spasmodic anxiety as the evidence unfolds. Since I know what the outcome is going to be, I might as well relax and enjoy masochistically the process of thrust-and-parry litigation. See it as a holiday from all the prison cells you're going to be in till you're middle-aged, my mate.

Cyril Ries kicks off by establishing the facts of Slim's torrid revolutionary brotherhood in Durban. He calls as his first witness a seedy hollow-eyed pharmacist of broken spirit, name of Brian, who attests that he was a Red and sold chemicals to Slim. Cyril Ries hesitates, whispers, every time the word Chemicals comes to his lips, as if it is just too vile to leave his decent Christian tongue, like Brian has been seen selling hypodermic syringes to standard three kids, or offering them a feel of his penis.

Maybe the table salt and sugar that Cyril Ries sprinkles on his nosh are spiritual.

Heavistone's turn comes next and he gets stuck into Brian with the utmost sarcasm, and I sort of wish I could catch Brian's eye and gooi him a bit of a wink or something to say Never mind, bru, don't take it to heart so, you poor silly nit, this is only a court of law, man; but Brian averts his head and feels just so guilty, not for flogging chemicals to Leninists, that's just regret, but for caving in when somebody offered to suspend him from the rafters by his balls.

He has a seedy wife and hollow-eyed baby to provide for. He avers that he has a sense of responsibility towards them. He has realised that what he did was wrong. Revolution is not the way to conduct one's politics anyway. That is why he has agreed to give this evidence.

Ah come on, Mr Felix, says Heavistone with studied scorn, you must have thought of your responsibilities before you started, and if you felt guilty thereafter why did you not go to the nearest police station that very day and confess the error of your ways, why did you wait until you were in a Security Branch cell?

But Brian cannot say that the SB threatened to moker him in said cell then give him time to heal nicely afterwards and fatten him up a bit with pap so he doesn't have those ghostly grey bags under his eyes, and iron his broeks and tell him to smile in court when he speaks to the judge, or else. If he says all this he will become an unreliable unco-operative witness, and be charged along with me.

Heavistone moves on to character assassination and general insult long after he has pretty well slain the witness. He produces the can of Mace from behind his back and aerosols him so thoroughly he just stands there wanting to weep, and I find myself wondering why, if this Brian should have thought of consequences before embarking on the MK venture, should not our MK leadership also have given a bit of thought to the consequences of recruiting such pump-up pneumatic rubber-duck personalities as Anatoly Mallun and Brian Felix, without spine or guts?

He goes on with the cruel questioning until Cyril Ries rises and protests irrelevance and Solly Muller agrees with him and sits Heavistone down. Objection sustained, to be American. It seems clear to me that this is how long he intended to go on, and I wonder why.

But it occurs to me after a bit that Heavistone is not a name I have heard in the big political trials. Maybe this has to do with his moving out of politics earlier in his career, as explained; I don't know. Anyway, he is an unknown quantity in this court, and that's an advantage. He wants the news to get around that he is a pure unalloyed twenty-four carat shit, von Oben bis Unten, top to bottom and side to side, with every device at hand to put you down by your own admissions, and wantonly mash up your self-regard. Even if future state witnesses are being held incommunicado, the SB will prepare them for this his bastardliness, and that should predigest them a bit for easier cross-examination.

Things move but slowly in court. They always start late; the witness has been taken to the wrong trial, a policeman has got a borer turd in his eye, the recorder isn't recording, it's morning tea-time, that sort of thing, so it takes most of the first day to put Brian Felix through the processor. By the time he's suitably liquidized by Heavistone it's afternoon tea-time and that's it for today. The Court will rise! All do, and Sammy Muller with assessors bow and exit right.

A lot of circumstancial stuff follows next day, requiring neither cross-examination nor swinery. An old Zulu security guard appears in his specially washed dark blue overalls, with badges over the deltoids of the upper arm, a broad leather belt and shiny black boots with anklets attached. He places his cap on a bench at the door and leans a mighty wooden club against the wall. He makes his way to the stand with that Zulu gesture of obeisance with the knees and back slightly bent, the left hand in salute in front of the face and the right in salute over the head. He stands to military attention and takes the oath. The interpreter tells him to stand at ease, Father.

He hauls on a cheap chain and a great glittery tin watch emerges from his pocket, so as to prove to the court that he comes on duty at such-and-such a

time at the Bantu Administration Offices. My mind turns via the watch and chain to white rabbits. Other details of his routine are established. On a certain night, he declares, he was patrolling behind the offices at twelve, and demonstrates to the court how a sleepy man walks at midnight, though we can see only his top half above the oaken panelling of the witness-box. His language is idiomatic. Idiophonic. Suddenly he heard a sound which said
HLUDUDUUUUUUUUUUUM!!!

A sound of blasting with reverberations. He shows us how he put his hands over his ears, and ducks behind the panelling. He ran round to the front of the building, he says, and there saw fire coming from the ground and much broken wood and glass. He blew on a whistle, which he shows to the court, and other men came running. They called the police. There was a great umtitinyo, a close questioning, with the police, and now he is here.

Heavistone has no questions.

Nor has he questions for the next few State witnesses; ballistics and explosives experts from Pretoria, an Airways booking clerk, those sorts of witness. Factual stuff. We don't want to waste the court's time.

But Heavistone wastes no time in another sense when the next State witness takes the stand. Surprise, surprise, it is none other than Major Op't Boud with his asynchronous eyes and hectoring voice.

So Van Vuurwapen and Wessels have just been doing the leg-work with me since Pretoria, to attend to detail. They are understudies to O'Backside, the Male Lead in this true-to-life Human Drama. He will now be led through evidence of political conspiracy already in the court record of the Baai case, though that evidence ended up as being only against Govan. No association between Govan and myself was ever established down there, save in Siza's invalid evidence, otherwise Govan would have been found guilty along with me. So what here is the relevance?

Whatever that may be, they seem seriously to want it included in the court record here. This court must be made aware that I am a person who plotted political violence in one place and is probably likely to plot it again in another place. But this is a strange way to set about it. I am still baffled.

Heavistone seems equally baffled, and gets to his feet a couple of times to protest wastage of court time, but Cyril Ries with much vulpine darting of the eyes assures the court that relevance will be demonstrated when a certain witness appears, from Robben Island, and Sammy Muller lets him continue.

Surely he doesn't mean Govan? They must have done some bloody awful things to him to get such co-operation, and am I worth it? I doubt that.

Well, what is their plan? As I see it, all they need from PE is an explosives man to say they found this and that at the bomb-site and Rassie or Jorrie to say they found similar things in the garage and my flat; simple, circumstantial, no opinions, no interpretations, no politics. When Wessels' Durban mice have all squeaked the court will see that Durban circumstances are like those in PE; pretty suggestive, and supportive, but no more than that. All additional evidence would leave hanging-out bits for Heavistone to get his canines into, and shake.

Maybe also Mr Levitan should attest that he rented his garage to me.

But apart from Siza's invalid evidence, as I say, none connects me to Govan, and they seem to want that, seriously.

The next step, by my guess, would be to connect the PE evidence to that from the Rivonia trial. That would show the nationwide nature of this conspiracy, which included Slim and his merry men, and Govan. Connect me with Govan, and voila!, I am now connected with Slim via Govan. Something like that, I reckon, is the plan.

But O'Bum wasn't in the Rivonia investigation, so he's not the one here to present police evidence already in that court record.

That means they'll have to bring investigating officers from that case down, plus other witnesses, to give evidence here tallying with that court record, and it would be difficult to prove relevance if objection were raised by Heavistone.

This thing is always a bit tricky, too, of giving minutely matching evidence in more than one court, the trickier the longer the gap of time between testimonies. In going over the same evidence again after a longish delay, you can be cornered by a swine like Heavistone into contradicting yourself a few times, so that increasingly bits of your testimony become unreliable. I don't think this would be a bargain.

So the only way they can connect me with Govan and the Rivonia conspiracy is to get Govan to take the stand, and to try to corner him into saying he was associated with me somehow. He couldn't deny I did cartoons for his newspaper, they were all signed by me, and they wouldn't want a great deal more than that if he were still a little hesitant after the persuasion they'd applied to him.

Well forget about that one. I know Govan, and he's the toughest man I've ever known. He is so tough he used to frighten me at times, and I'm on his side. A pity for them Max is hanged; he'd have been near the end of his stretch if he'd been settled with me, and they could now have slammed him about a bit to make him talk. Try to make him talk, that is. Forget about that one too.

Also, of course, one mustn't forget that as usual they want to puff up the old Rooi Gevaar bogey balloon, scare stupid the white electorate of the country, prepare them for whatever grim legislation may be coming their way, make them receptive to whatever grim militarism. A ranking Security Branch officer is what you need here; NCOs can fill in the mechanical details of garage contents and the like.

But I remain perplexed, and so does my defence team. Heavistone says this is not the bad part, let them blather on; it's the Durban mice that are going to do for me.

Time comes for cross-examination of O'Bum. Heavistone has abandoned knife and Mace, and now has only a knuckleduster behind his back. It is clear he doesn't actually have a lot of questions, if any. But never lose a chance to be thoroughly disagreeable anyway.

He speaks very gently now, though, for starters.

Major er.... he says, and looks on pieces of paper for the name. Majoor, he says, but very politely; in Afrikaans it's quite polite to call him just by his rank, it's the equivalent of Sir. But he knows that O'Bum will see the name-forgetting as a clumsy old device of insult, and he wants O'Bum to know that he's purposely insulting him thus clumsily. He wants him to know he is unworthy of subtlety.

Majoor, do you ever put those people you have arrested and charged into solitary confinement?

Sometimes it is necessary to keep a person separate, in case he interferes with other witnesses.

Understandably. And if no other person in the place of detention is a witness, do you then not keep him separate?

Other people awaiting trial can influence the way he is going to give his evidence, even though they are not witnesses.

I see. And this is particularly true in political cases?

I don't know of political cases. The Security Branch deals only with crimes against the security of the State. We do not prosecute people for having political views.

Do you prosecute them for persuading others to have similar views?

Only in terms of the Suppression of Communism Act.

So you do sometimes have political prosecutions?

No, communism is against the security of the State.

Cyril Ries is on his feet, protesting irrelevance, and Sammy Muller concedes this.

But the words are on the record.

As your Lordship pleases, says Heavistone. Majoor, if I were to put it to you that the accused was put into solitary confinement at the Pretoria Central Prison, at the request of the Security Branch, for five months in a cell seven feet square, what would you say to that?

The Prisons Department and the South African Police are two separate organisations within the Department of Justice. I don't know what board and lodging the Prisons people provide for their prisoners. Heavy humour here.

I see. So if the Court were to order the Prisons Department to produce their records of such board and lodging, and the date of the commencement of solitary lodging for the accused coincided exactly to the day with the date of a visit to the accused by two members of the Security Police, as recorded also by Prisons documentation which could be produced to the Court, what would you say to that?

I am not obliged to express an opinion on that.

Oh but Majoor, you are. You are indeed under obligation to express such an opinion to the Court, that is what is meant by The Whole Truth.

Cyril Ries is on his feet again; M'Lud, M'Learned Friend is continuing with the same line of questioning as before.

M'Learned Friend misconstrues my line of questioning, M'Lud, says Heavistone. I have moved on to the physical and mental condition of the accused on his appearance in this court, and whether solitary confinement was applied to him to soften him up, as it were, for trial.

Continue, Mr Heavistone, says Sammy.

Well, Majoor, was it?

Was what? asks O'Bum, but it's clear he knows what. He is starting to hedge.

Was solitary confinement applied to the accused to soften him up, as it were, for trial?

I can't tell the Prisons Department what to do with their prisoners, snaps O'Bum, testily. It's not my job, I don't care what they do with their prisoners! It's not my responsibility!

Well it is, in a way, in this case, says Heavistone, wouldn't you agree? Since it is you who have brought the accused to trial you want him to be in full possession of his faculties when giving evidence, I'm sure. That is what you want, isn't it, Majoor?

O'Bum hesitates, frowning.

Heavistone turns somewhat absently to Eaglestone and confers quietly about this or that. They smile a bit, and nod their heads. O'Bum waits for them to finish, quite a while. They are unhurried. Heavistone looks up eventually, and still somewhat absently.

More hesitation, much more frowning.

So? asks Heavistone. Is that not what you want, Majoor? Please tell the court.

O'Bum is speechless with irritation, and sullen.

Well, never mind. Heavistone sighs theatrically, shaking his head. Let's move on. Did you or anyone under your command ever assault in his hospital bed a man called Siza Sigcau?

Siza Sigcau was found to be an unreliable witness when he made such allegations of assault in a trial of the present accused in another court in Port Elizabeth, his evidence is worthless! yells O'Bum, flickering his daft eyes, flushed, his teeth clenched.

Yes, Majoor, yes, says Heavistone, sighing still, sarcastically patient; the Court is aware of that, but I am not asking for your opinion of somebody else's evidence in some other court, I am asking you to give your own evidence in this court of your own personal behaviour and experience at a time approximately three years and a half ago.

He continues his smiling whispers with Eaglestone, and riffles papers on his table. O'Bum waits for him to finish. He waits a long time, longer than before.

Heavistone suddenly looks up. Majoor, he asks, still with purposeful patience, Why will you not tell the court whether or not you assaulted this man Siza Sigcau in his hospital bed? We have his hospital record available from that time, saying that he was admitted unconscious with symptoms of brutal assault, that he would respond well to treatment but relapse repeatedly, until finally he was removed from medical care by a policeman who refused to sign the discharge papers. Would you like me to produce this record as a court exhibit, and call a hospital matron as witness? He goes back to his consultation with Eaglestone. They riffle papers, and exchange some document.

HOW CAN I ANSWER YOU WHEN YOU KEEP ON HAVING A CONVERSATION WITH SOMEBODY ELSE? shouts O'Bum.

But Heavistone is already into the next whispering, with Carstairs this time. He smiles in Carstairs' direction and hands him a document. Carstairs riffles it. With equanimity Heavistone takes a fountain-pen from his briefcase and unscrews the top and puts it on the back of the pen. He takes back the document from Carstairs. He writes something on it with the fountain-pen. He holds it up to his spectacles and studies it while he tells his beads. He shows it to Eaglestone. They smile. No smiling nor riffling nor fountain-pen appears in the court record. Just the silence. Appeal judges have only sounds or lack of them on a tape, and the transcribed word; they are at a disadvantage in gauging demeanour.   •

O'Bum stands on his dignity. He will not reply while Heavistone is talking to someone else. He is enraged.

With timing of great experience Heavistone looks up from the piece of paper and snarls WHY WILL YOU NOT ANSWER MY QUESTION?

BECAUSE YOU KEEP ON TALKING TO SOMEBODY ELSE WHEN I WANT TO ANSWER YOU! YOUR MANNERS ARE BLIK...VERY BAD!

YOU ARE NOT HERE TO COMMENT ON MY MANNERS, MAJOR OP'T BOUD, NOR TO RECTIFY THEM, YOU ARE HERE TO GIVE THE COURT A SIMPLE STRAIGHT ANSWER TO A SIMPLE STRAIGHT QUESTION; DID YOU OR ANY OF YOUR SUBORDINATES EVER ASSAULT A MAN CALLED SIZA SIGCAU IN A HOSPITAL BED?

O'Bum turns to Sammy; I CANNOT ANSWER THIS MAN IF HE SHOUTS AT ME!

WHY SHOULD I NOT SHOUT AT YOU? DO YOU HAVE A MONOPOLY ON SHOUTING? yells Heavistone.

He times the ensuing silence dead right. It is total, stunned, as they say, not a murmur in the whole room. If that person who carries the pins about for dropping on such occasions were to drop one now, everyone would hear it.

Major Op't Boud, says Sammy, you have to answer this question.

O'B has breath for only one word, and short, such is his rage, and venom. His eyes are in rewind.

No, he says.

Thank you, Majoor, thank you, says Heavistone quietly, and so sincerely, breathing on his specs, and rubbing them with his hanky. Presumably you are talking only of yourself here, and not of your colleagues, insofar as you know of their behaviour at the time in question?

It is not for me to explain other policemens' behaviour. They must get on with their own jobs, and answer for their own behaviour.

Indeed, Majoor, says Heavistone, Indeed. He stands silent another good long while with his specs in his hand, as if visualising said gentlemen under cross-examination by himself.

So, then, Majoor, he eventually says with yet another sigh, To put it briefly, which we could have done in the first place, you neither know nor care what happens in the hands of the Prisons Department to someone on whom you have drawn up a docket, you feel no responsibility for this person who will have to defend himself in court when the stakes are very high. You accept no responsibility for the behaviour of your staff in the matter of possible assault on someone in a hospital bed, in their custody, nor even do you feel any inquisitiveness about it, yet we must accept you as a responsible Security Branch police officer; responsible, that is, for the security of the State? Is this what we must do?

Fuming, blinking silence.

Never mind, says Heavistone, wearily, to Op't Boud, Never mind, Majoor. No further questions, M'Lud.

So we grind through the miserable list. Vuurwapen and Gruweldaad give evidence as expected, about the grys vetterige stof they found in this place and that, which is the aluminium powder, of course, and that sort of thing. I expect Heavistone to hammer them as he hammered Op't Boud, but he doesn't. It occurs to me he doesn't want to overplay that particular trick of uncouthness. He doesn't want to dilute his nastiness. Also, it occurs to me that he's got the O'B stuff on record only so that he can fall back on the matter of ill-treatment, if necessary, when I'm on the stand, if my story starts falling apart.

Besides, Rassie and Jorrie will have learned from O'B's mistake of falling into the emotional trap. They aren't emotional men anyway, they're zombies. So Heavistone has only a few questions of detail, which might come in handy in argument.

A couple of other PE witnesses come and go, to identify things and people; nothing much before we're back to the Durban Mice.

The first of these is a real beaut, a big sod called Wilberforce Mdwayi, whom as true as God's my father I've never seen in my life before. He's up on the stand with such eagerness he can scarce wait for Cyril Ries to lead him through his evidence-in-chief. He takes the oath.

Ries starts carefully; he's got a layout ready for this evidence, a composition, a strategy. Each bit must fall exactly into place, and at just the right time. He is going to build up to a climax, in which my guilt will be clear, indisputable. Mr Mdwayi, says he, with much narrowing of the eyes, cocking his head the while, and impressive pauses in which carefully to choose exactly the right words. Mr Mdwayi, do you recognise the person before the court?

His name is Jock, says Mr Mdwayi, and his second name is Lundie and he came to a house at Bayview Road number two-forty-eight in Durban at ten o'clock on the tenth of December nineteen sixty-one and Bobby Naicker was there and Ashby Mbanjwe was there and the leader Slim was there and Isaac Mvusi was there and Bhekisizwe Ntuli and Ebrahim...

Yes Mr Mdwayi yes, says Cyril Ries loudly, and quickly because the witness is reeling off the names of all the Durban mice, and Issy Eaglestone is jotting them all down. Sure, when my turn comes to testify the court will give the defence time to go into their backgrounds, but how much better, eh, to spend a few afternoons beforehand in the public library, sifting at leisure through microfilm copies of all the major newspapers of sixty-one for general details of their political lives and, especially, details of any evidence they may have given in other trials. Phone an attorney in Bloemfontein, perhaps, where the records of all previous trials are kept, and get him to sift through all the political ones since sixty-one for this or that name, and note the details of what this or that one said in the witness-box.

Yes, Mr Mdwayi, yes, says Cyril Ries, replacing the expression of dismay on his face with one of great cunning. Mr Mdwayi, he says, will you please tell the court what the purpose of this meeting was?

The purpose was for Lundie to tell us to kill all the white people, go to work and kill them, go to school and kill them, go to the street and kill them, tell the people on the farm to kill all the white farmers, kill the white people in Port Elizabeth, kill them in Durban, kill them...

Yes, Mr Mdwayi, yes, but more slowly, please...

Kill the rich white people, kill...

Mr Mdwayi, Mr Mdwayi! Cyril Ries sort of backs off lest Wilberforce Mdwayi make him #1 even though they have this heavy varnished meranti table between them. Mr Mdwayi, thank you, but not too fast!

There is silence in court, but for the gnashing of the Wilberforce teeth.

Hell, I think, where did they find this baboon?

Sammy Muller and assessors sit agape.

Hell, I think, they should have sent him to the Fraud Squad for education. Sit him down with a fridgefull of beer, get him receptive and sensible. Book him in somewhere with bubbly in a bucket of ice and his missus from wherever, get him relaxed and ready for court, that sort of preparation. They don't seem even to have told him one must be led through evidence. He's made a right bunch of narners of the SB and Cyril Ries so far; but on, on, let's see to what heights he may yet rise.

So then, Mr Mdwayi, will you tell the court whether the accused came to Durban only with messages, or was there something else he had to do there?

He showed us how to make dynamite in a plastic bucket with a stick you mustn't use an iron bucket and an iron spoon you take fertiliser and diesel and you mix it up with aluminium powder then you take some hose-pipe two inches long and you put purple crystals in there with rust and aluminium powder and you pour in glycerine to light the dynamite. You put it in the supermarket and you kill all the white people, and you put it in the church and you kill all...

Yes, Mr Mdwayi, thank you, but not too fast, please. Did the accused demonstrate anything else to you, any other apparatus?

Yes, the accused showed us how to take a plastic jerrycan and fill it with petrol and put the same hosepipe in the top then you pour in the glycerine and put it in the Magistrates' Court and you kill the magis...

Yes, Mr Mdwayi, thank you thank you thank you. Cyril Ries is cutting his losses, that's clear, and cursing himself, or maybe the Security Police if I know anything about human nature, for playing such a stupid hand: Two of a Kind was the best it was worth anyway, corroborative evidence, and then only if presented with great skill, and polish.

Thank you, M'Lud, he says, No further questions, and sits down. He rests his brow upon his hand. He looks chagrined.

Sammy Muller looks incredulous.

The assessors look at Sammy Muller.

Frank Heavistone looks weary. He rises and sighs. I wonder what on earth he'll find to cross-examine in this caucasiocidal mound of mumbo-jumbo, but he's at no loss for words or postures, as usual.

Mr Mdwayi, he asks in a tired paternal voice, but gentle; Mr Mdwayi, do you get on well with your neighbours? I mean, do you like them?

Yes, I like them, says Wilberforce, too much.

Do they like you?

Yes, they like me too much.

Ah, that's good. Are you religious people?

Yes, we are too religious.

Good. Good. Are you all of the same congregation at temple, mosque or church? I mean, do you all pray at the same place?

Yes, we all go to the Lutheran church.

Ah, good, yes. Very good. Would you tell us the name of your pastor, please?

He is Pastor Zulu.

And do you go regularly to church, Mr Mdwayi? Often?

Yes, I always go to church.

So, I take it then, you went to church last Sunday?

Yes, I went to church.

Could you tell the court which of your neighbours sat on your left side at church, please?

Silence.

Well don't worry, perhaps you've just forgotten. Perhaps you can remember who sat at your right side?

Silence.

Well maybe you could take a guess, and we could get those neighbours to come to the court and confirm whether or not they sat on your left or right side?

Silence.

Never mind, Mr Mdwayi, to forget such details is natural. I'm sure you remember the Reverend Zulu's sermon, though, eh? Maybe you would tell us what it was about. I mean, what was the subject of this sermon, Mr Mdwayi, what did he talk about?

Silence.

We could bring Pastor Zulu along, just in case you get mixed up and remember the sermon of the week before last, or another from even longer ago than that. Things do get mixed up in the mind after a few weeks or a month or so; maybe we could get him here to help you?

Silence. A long one.

No riffling. Just caressing the golden links, and patiently looking at Wilberforce Mdwayi this time, friendly, paternal.

Don't you find it strange, Mr Mdwayi, that you can remember in detail what happened three and a half years ago, events at two-forty-eight Bayview Road Durban at ten p.m. on the night of the tenth of December, and that you can remember exactly the names of people who were with you there that night, quite a number of them, that you can remember in detail what the accused explained there, including some chemical recipes, yet you cannot remember what the pastor of your church said last week in the house of God, nor can you remember who from amongst your friendly neighbours sat with you in church?

Permanent silence this time.

No further questions, M'Lud.

This is like the game of cricket: let one man go out at a single-number score and half the team will follow him, one of them for a duck, for sure.

Twenty

I DON'T KNOW WHERE THE WEEK WENT; it's already Friday again with a weekend of lockup looming, without Paddy Furlow. In just these few days I've become used to my daylight hours out in the great wide world; well, just a little bit widish I mean, but great enough when surrounded by people most of the day.

Nu? Do the usual thing, mensch; plan the hours so that none go waste. Saturday I'll spend on overview skieming. I skiem the next prosecution witness will be Top Mouse, Bheki Ntuli, and I know what he's going to say about Durban. But what if some of it turns out to be about PE? I'll need at least one day and a night to rehearse and revise my present plot, and perhaps devise an addendum later on, when he's said his piece.

Sunday, though, will be only for pleasure. Breakfast is late on Sunday. After breakfast, between seven and nine, I shall get in a brisk jog in the cell, though being too brisk about it makes one a little giddy, what with the radius of the circle being so small. I shall then take a quick luxurious shower in my exercise time, they have hot water in this place, would you believe it? and put on the nice crisp clean khakis that come as the weekly change on Sunday, for inspection, and take the day off.

Last week the Super was late; Cruywagen was giving me my exercise when he came along the stoep and gave me the merest perfunctory glance as I stood to attention over there amongst the desperate geraniums, like Ruth amongst the alien corn, and Cruywagen had just left me in the yard afterwards because there's always a great feeling of catharsis after inspection, and relaxation, and why shut me up when there's only half an hour to graze and lock-up at eleven and I seem happy enough between the drooping borders anyway?

So maybe I'll get lucky again. Maybe before returning to Pretoria I'll get two or three more City Hall recitals in the sun, to take back for the long, grey enamel highveld winter.

Meneer Cruywagen, I say, Van môre af is ek verhoorafwagtend, nee, ekskuus tog, as of tomorrow I am awaiting trial, my sentence has expired, I am a remand prisoner. What about getting my street clothes for me? Can I have some writing paper and a pencil, please, so I can write to my mother? Will you get some money from my account in Reception and buy me some tobacco and some sweets please? Today, so I can take them to court with me tomorrow?

Hell, I know he can't do any of these things, it's Sunday, but I can see he feels really mean about that, which is what I wanted, of course. He apologises sincerely, with the verb at the end of the apology. There's not a lot of time between a warder's lunch-time and a bandiet's supper-time, about an hour and a half. I don't have a watch, of course, but judging by the amount of outdoors I get shortly I reckon he must have come back straight after his food, without wiping away the crumbs, poor kindly bloody fool, with a flimsy sort of net over his arm and one of those rubber rings that they use on board cruise liners for a game called tennequoits or something, and he says he will fetch one of the thirty other Awaiting Trials but I mustn't talk about this, he will take a chance because it's Sunday, and we can have a carefree game of deck tennis behind the White Section here where stand a couple of poles for the net. He will stick around while we have this tournament, to keep us segregated.

Hell, it's my turn to feel really mean. He's told me often enough, to the point of irritation, when I've been trying to concentrate on evidence or enjoy a quiet personal reverie, about his pretty wife and their two kids who go to an English-speaking school and put their verbs in the middle of sentences, and I'm quite sure he would rather be with them for the full hour or so of Sunday lunch.

Hey, Meneer Cruywagen, what bad luck! I just this morning sprained my thumb in the shower trying to catch the soap when it slid out of my hand, man, and I dangle my right-hand thumb down there beneath extended fingers, and wobble it about with my left hand to show how unavailable it is for the playing of tennequoits. Shame, I see he's a bit relieved when I suggest some extra outdoors instead, he won't have to vat 'n kans with the not-so-solitary deck games.

Well those who make futile argument against the statistical truth that the Earth is grossly overpopulated tell us that you could accommodate the entire population of the planet standing up on the Isle of Wight, as if anybody would find fulfilment doing this for three score years and ten. As unlikely, that, as it would be for thirty people to enjoy standing up for half an hour on a tennequoit rink, but that's what they now do, like it or not.

The afternoon, I mean, is not divided up for this or that classified whack of exercise, I get the whole lot straight, down the geranium path, an hour and a half of it. It is not for me to dispute the logic of this.

Strangely, the court is ready to start dead on time on Monday. In fact there's quite a hubbub in the corridor outside at nine because none of a dozen or more police pockets contains the keys to my cuffs and irons, and Sammy Muller will not allow these things anywhere near his court. Somebody remembers that they're in the cubby-hole of the police car, but is the car still around? Panic. All rush about, and find the car, and see the keys through the window of the locked door, but where the driver? They find him buying fags down the street and glancing at this and that titty magazine on the tea-room shelf, ewe gerus, and all gallop back with the key to the cubby-hole and me.

Just great, it gives me twenty minutes in the corridor to get my manacled wrists over Jess's head and shoulders and into some serious vryery with many kisses while she ruffles up my hair, and I start to wonder soon enough: If Sammy Muller doesn't like manacles in court, what's he going to say when the accused appears there with an erection like the one I'm getting going right now? I try to think about the binomial theorem, a device I've found helpful in this particular crisis since I was fifteen, on the bus for example, where one would be stricken by that malaise called the Transport Horn, Cornus Transportii, sitting on the nice squashy seat there and one's stop the next coming up, where one would have to disembark tying one's shoelace and bent double, or walk half a mile back from two stops further on when the binomial theorem had done its work.

So I'm working on these mathematicable intricables with scant success when Issy Eaglestone takes over and remedies the dreaded condition straightway, by the same process of distraction expected of the theorem. Jock, he says, shaking my cuffed hand behind Jess's back, congratulations on your bar mitzvah, you are now a Registered Mailbag Engineer, and we are presently going to lay on Sammy Muller some good quality kosher chutzpah and see if we can get bail for you. Don't be bloody silly, Issy, where the hell am I ever going to get bail with the history of estreatment our people have? I say.

But we're interrupted at this point by the cops with the keys, and Issy moves off. The large aesthetic youth moves forward and claps me on the back. Good man! he says. I've brought you these cigarettes and a cheese sandwich. I peer inside the sandwich and see it's cheddar cheese. Bit of all right, that; I haven't seen cheese these years. An armed policeman takes me off to the door of the court; he's not allowed inside with a weapon.

Issy was ever the optimist. Sammy hardly even listens to Heavistone's application; the legal explanation of his refusal amounts in conversational English to no more than Don't be bloody silly, Heavistone, where the hell would I ever give bail to one of you lot?

Bhekisizwe Ntuli may be many things, but there's one thing he's not, and that's a baboon. He is at home in a court of law as is Cyril Ries, indeed they have become a batting partnership with a considerable score; of the five cases in which Bheki has shopped his comrades Ries has prosecuted in three, and got three convictions. Three boundaries, three sixes. Then there were the other two sixes, of course, where Ries did not prosecute, so Bhekisizwe Ntuli has a score of thirty in less than one over. This one will give him thirty-six runs off six balls.

Bhekisizwe Ntuli is at home in a court of law as I am, for I have been tried five times. He has great self-possession, he is not going to be thrown by any of Heavistone's devices into panic or outburst. But then Major Op't Boud had great self-possession too, and plenty of court experience, thank you. Well, we'll see whose confidence and devices work best this time round. As I say, I'm down the chutes anyway, I might as well enjoy the test match. Pity I can't smoke my fags and eat my cheese sandwich up here in the grandstand.... I wouldn't mind a bottle of beer.

Cyril Ries draws back the folds of his gown from his pudgy gut and hooks his thumbs in the armholes of his waistcoat. He rises and descends a few times on the balls of his feet in silence, narrows up his eyes, smiles craftily and chooses with much care some cunning words for his opening question.

Mr Ntuli, he asks, Do you know the accused?

No, replies Mr Ntuli, I know him.

Do you mean no you don't know him or yes you do know him?

Yes I do know him.

Mr Ntuli, says Cyril Ries, Will you explain to the court the circumstances of your meeting the accused, and the date of your meeting?

No, it was on the evening of the tenth of December nineteen sixty-one, says Ntuli; I fetched him from the airport at nine p.m. and took him to Denzil Cohn's flat and we had tea, then we went to a meeting at a house in Bayview Road. He was from the Technical Committee of Umkhonto we Sizwe in Port Elizabeth, and had been sent by the District Committee of the Communist Party there to instruct us about some explosive devices.

I see. Will you explain to the court how, in your view, it comes to be that the Communist Party can send someone from a separate organisation on such a mission?

No, they are all the same people, however they name their organisations. The ANC, the Communist Party and Umkhonto we Sizwe, all the same people.

How do you know all this? Are you one of them?

No, I am one of them, from all three organisations.

And the accused?

No, he was from the Communist Party and Umkhonto we Sizwe.

And his purpose?

No, his purpose was to explain to us how the Armed Struggle would bring liberation, and to teach us about explosives.

Will you now explain these things to the court please, Mr Ntuli.

No, the first phase of the Armed Struggle was industrial sabotage, to make the economy collapse and give morale to the people. The second stage was urban guerrilla warfare to rally the people behind us. We would attack police stations and army barracks, and make the country ungovernable. The third stage would be full field warfare, with victory for the masses over the armed forces of the fascist régime.

So to put it briefly, would you say quite definitely these things were about overthrowing the State by force?

No, we had a long discussion, because it was very daring, and he said definitely we must overthrow the State by force because there was no other way. After that he showed us how to make explosive bombs and incendiary bombs, to overthrow the State.

Bhekisizwe Ntuli gives details of the explosive mixture and all the fine processes of constructing the timing device. Though it is simple, he explains, yet it must be done with great care if it is to be accurate and give one seven and a half minutes exactly.

He is dead right down to the merest minutiae. The police have schooled him well; I wonder how much of it they got in Max's trial, and from Sisa Sigcau. You could go out with this description in court, and make the thing work. I mean you could make the bombs work, the demolition bomb and the incendiary. The unLeninist stuff about the three stages to Liberation nobody could make work with whatever infinite care; it is hortatory crap not worth an air ticket to explain. It might just be worth a bus ticket to escape, if running is too slow.

But I'll tell you what, it's bloody dangerous propaganda to feed those intuitively wise masses of yours. They might just believe it all, and not stop doing it when you think it's time for you to come to power. Making the country ungovernable, I mean. Ungovernable countries with collapsed economies don't get liberation. What they get is tyranny. A Strong Man. Ein grosser Mann. A dictator, and something you really can call fascism.

Cyril Ries does the up and down on his toes again with some more of the Machiavellian look. I wish he would put his forefinger to the side of his nose and wink his eye, but he doesn't. He puts his head right back like a fish eagle and opens his mouth and says Aaaah yes! to the ceiling.

Mr Ntuli, he says with many a furtive and shifty glance, What did you do then?

No, then we had some more tea and the accused told us about theory and the dictatorship of the proletariat and the withering away of the state, all that sort of theory. He said every soldier must have proper theory. We need to have commissars in the people's army.

Much much detail of the rôle of a commissar follows, supplied, says Bheki Ntuli, by me. Did the accused see himself as such a commissar in the people's army? No, he did.

Do you mean no he did not or yes he did?

Yes he did.

And then, Mr Ntuli?

No, then we went to the Bluff to Treasure Beach and we set off a thermite bomb on the sand. The accused made the thermite by mixing up aluminium powder and iron oxide in a jam tin. We ignited it with potassium permanganate and glycerine on top and he showed us how you can also light it with a sparkler, but that makes too much light. We didn't put it on wood to burn it or iron to melt it because it would make extra light and people would come and watch us, so we just put it in a wide hole in the sand to hide the light and you could see how it melted all the sand.

Yes, then?

No, then we helped Ebrahim Patel make some curry and we had some dinner at Bayview Road and we all went to a reservoir on the Berea and we tested the timer which is also the detonator. The accused made it at home and put it on an air vent there and we waited and after seven and a half minutes it went off.

Then?

Many many details of many many circumstances follow, and it occurs to me this might just mean a lot of collars and shirt-tails and trouser legs and things sticking out of the Ntuli bag of evidence, bits for an ugly Jack Russell perhaps to get his mean spiky teeth into, and wrench the neatly packed contents all to shreds.

Mr Ntuli, says Heavistone, what type of car did you use to go to the airport to fetch the accused on the night of the tenth of December nineteen sixty-one?

No, it was a Beetle. A Volkswagen.

I see. Now, Mr Ntuli, did the plane arrive on time, at nine p.m?

No, it arrived on time.

I see.

Mr Ntuli, says Sammy Muller, please try not to say No if it did arrive on time.

Yes it did arrive on time.

Now then, says Heavistone, how long did it take you to get the accused from the plane and into this Beetle?

No, fifteen minutes. I mean fifteen minutes.

And then how long back to your destination in Durban, Mr Cohn's flat?

It took us half an hour, thirty-five minutes maybe.

I see. And there you had tea. How long did it take to make this tea and drink it, Mr Ntuli?

No, another half an hour. I mean another half an hour.

So, then, after tea you went to Bayview Road where the accused explained to you how the armed struggle would bring liberation to the people, eh?, and showed you how to make an explosive substance, an incendiary device, and a timer. Is that correct?

Yes, it is correct.

Mr Ntuli, how long did it take the accused to explain the process of armed struggle?

No, I'm not sure.

As long as a class at school, or a lecture at a college?

Yes.

About an hour?

Yes.

I see. And how long to demonstrate the construction of the bomb, the incendiary device and the timer/detonator?

Half an hour each one.

That's quick, eh? You must have been a very intelligent party. By the way, Mr Ntuli, according to a previous witness Mr Wilberforce Mdwayi, the following persons comprised your party: Bobby Naicker, Ashby Mbanjwe, Slim, whom I believe to be Mr Cohn but correct me if I am wrong, Isaac Mvusi, and one Ebrahim, who I suppose is the Ebrahim Patel whose curry you have just mentioned. Then there were yourself and the accused, of course. Do you agree with that list?

A bit of quick thinking on his feet... Bhekisizwe Ntuli can't remember what he's said previously in other courts, I'll bet, but he doesn't want to contradict another prosecution witness in this one and lose the deal he's done with the police. Yes, I agree, he says.

So all of you understood how to make a bomb after half an hour's demonstration, and an incendiary after another half an hour, and a timer/detonator after yet again half an hour, and then you all went to Treasure Beach for a demonstration of the incendiary device, is this correct?

Yes, it is correct.

And you all went in the Beetle, eight people?

A moment of confusion, and bluster. No, there was another car.

You must forgive me, Mr Ntuli, if I am a little bewildered. You see, testifying in The State versus Bobby Naicker in 1963 you made no mention of a second car for the trip to Treasure Beach. You mentioned only Mr Cohn's Beetle.

Frank Heavistone has the court record of that case in his hand. He riffles it. Bheki Ntuli sees the riffling.

Nobody asked me about it, says Bheki Ntuli.

That doesn't surprise me, Mr Ntuli, since you mentioned only four persons present at the fateful meeting in Bayview Road, and the same four for the fateful journey to Treasure Beach.

No, nobody asked me about anybody else.

But Mr Ntuli, my learned friend Mr Cyril Ries, who prosecuted in that trial also, asked you the following question, and I quote from the record;

"Mr Ries: 'Mr Ntuli, were only you four, Cohn, Lundie, Naicker and yourself, present at this demonstration at Treasure Beach?'

Witness: 'No, we were the only four.'

Mr Ries: 'Do you mean no you were not the only four or yes you were the only four?'

Witness: 'Yes, we were the only four.'

Bhekisizwe Ntuli is silent, and I must say in fairness that he looks genuinely puzzled.

So can we assume, asks Heavistone, that you left four names out because it suited you so to do, and that with equal ease you would have left out the name of the present accused had that suited you so to do?

Ntuli is still at a loss.

And similarly you would include him or leave him out in this case too, according to your convenience?

How indeed can there be an answer?, I think. Ntuli offers none.

So here you all are, then, says Heavistone, leaving Bayview Terrace for Treasure Beach in two cars. Can you tell us approximately how long such a journey would take?

Half an hour, says Ntuli.

I see. And how long did the demonstration of the thermite bomb take? But pardon me! exclaims Heavistone, interrupting himself. Excuse me Mr Ntuli for one moment, and he riffles another document Carstairs happens to have placed in his left hand. Goodness gracious! Here in the court record of The State versus Ebrahim Patel I see that your evidence says very clearly that you went, not to Treasure Beach, but to Addington Beach near the ski-boat base, and I see also that in this evidence the present accused was not amongst the four, his place being taken by one Isaac Mvusi.

It would take very few minutes to Addington Beach, would it not, and quite a while to Treasure Beach, would it not, Mr Ntuli, and which was it?

It was Treasure Beach. Bheki Ntuli looks confused. Addington Beach was another demonstration on another day, he says, and believes it, you can see that.

Frank Heavistone flicks the pages in his hand back to the point in the trial of E. Patel at which B. Ntuli started his evidence. The tenth of December, he says, would you like to look at this document, Mr Ntuli?

Mr Ntuli shakes his head. No, he says.

I see. So then let's go back to the question; you said it took you half an hour to get from Bayview Road to Treasure Beach?

Bheki Ntuli suddenly realises what's going on here, you can tell by the blurting way he's starting to talk that he wants to seem at ease. Twenty minutes, he says, the most.

Let's say twenty, if you so wish, instead of your original thirty, says Heavistone. Or thirty-five. Does that include climbing down the coastal dunes? Do you agree that there are dunes there, and if so would you give an estimate of their height? Would it help you if I were to get from the Surveyor-General's office in Pretoria a topocadastral map of that area, showing contours and elevations at the dunes?

They are about as high as a six- or seven-storey building, and it took us five minutes to climb down through the bushes.

And how much longer to climb up again when your demonstration was done?

No, ten minutes, says Ntuli.

Hmmm, says Heavistone, Now how long did the demonstration take, of the thermite, I mean?

It's hard to say. A couple of hours.

Two hours? That's fast work for such a delicate and dangerous job, isn't it?

No, it is not too fast, in fact it took a bit less.

Oh? About how much less?

Quarter of an hour less. It took about one hour and forty-five minutes. Bheki Ntuli is haggling over every minute.

And at the end of it you climbed back up the dune in ten minutes and went back to Bayview Road where you had Mr Patel's curry for supper?

How long did that take?

It's hard to say.

Well shall we start our bargaining with one hour?

No, much less, you see Ebrahim Patel had everything ready before we left, so we just had to put the curry on the stove then eat it.

But you have just said you helped him prepare it.

No, I mean we put it on the stove for him, says Ntuli.

And that is help in the preparation of food? says Heavistone.

No, wait a bit, I forgot, that was another time he cooked curry at Bayview Road, I got the times a bit mixed up.

Never mind, Mr Ntuli, it's easy to get confused. I myself am a little confused just now. So how long did the cooking and eating of the supper take?

No, it took about an hour, I suppose.

Then at this point you went to the reservoir for another demonstration, of the timer/detonator this time. Is that correct?

No I mean yes that is correct.

You must be patient with my confusion, Mr Ntuli, says Heavistone, there are many things I am puzzled about. For example, if my reckoning is correct you arrived at the reservoir at four forty-five a.m. on the morning of the eleventh of December. I thought you and I had gone into the matter of times pretty thoroughly, you know, but if I have nonetheless made a mistake in my arithmetic please feel free to point this out. You see, I can't imagine anyone in his right mind going to commit so highly unlawful an act as the one in question at a time when early risers from surrounding flats are flinging wide their windows to greet the dawn, early joggers are out on the road, police cars are returning to their stations after a night on patrol, and so on...

No, I think it was another time when we had the curry, says Bhekisizwe Ntuli.

No further questions, M'Lud, says Frank Heavistone.

Twenty-one

NO FURTHER WITNESSES, M'LUD, says Cyril Ries. That concludes the case for the Prosecution.

What? Where is the infestation of mice I have dreaded so in the last weeks? Only three plus O'Bum and his lads and the small fry? I expected at least another three. But maybe Cyril Ries has belatedly caught on; too much evidence may mean even more contradictions, and it's not worth the risk. Maybe he's cutting his losses.

Will the Defence be ready to open its case tomorrow? asks Sammy Muller, and I dare say I am not the only one to detect a small nuance in his intonation there, which tells us this being Thursday we might just make a long weekend of it and some of us will get in a few extra holes at the Royal Durban tomorrow.

M'Lud, says Heavistone, rising to his feet, As I explained to the last witness, the Defence is a little confused by latter evidence, and would appreciate an extra day or so for further perusal of his and other testimony thus far given.

Would the Prosecution have any objection to the Court's reconvening on Monday? asks Sammy.

No, M'Lud, says Cyril Ries, and I think Ja, ou boet, you're going to need some fancy footwork in Argument time, the way your witnesses have cocked things up for you, and you'd better get down in a high-pressure huddle with your police pals tomorrow while some of us are at golf or flying about in a Tiger Moth. You might just suggest that I might just be laughing at them. They could have charged me before Patel and Naicker. Bheki Ntuli's straight story alone, without police embellishments and his consequent self-contradictions, would have put me away for twelve, not a doubt. But you were too greedy, you bastards, you wanted every last available year, every last month, week, day for maximum punishment, maximum revenge. You were too greedy, you bastards, and with a bit of luck I will present my story convincingly and you will get fuck-all.

But there's not really enough doubt going to the benefit of the accused, and the circumstantial evidence is still there, especially that of the Airways booking clerk. The twit who booked my last-minute seat to Durbs used my real name, can you believe it, and there it is; flight records show that the seat was used. Though this doesn't necessarily mean it was used by me, of course, as corroborating evidence it's still powerful stuff. But I do know that there's a small chance now, and I'll have a happy weekend after the regulation one-day's skieming.

The drama rehearsals and the road-running of this regulation day are interrupted at mid-morning by A. Hepburn, there's a visit from Jess with a big tin of toffees and a pipe with snout and raiment of such elegance as to knock Sammy and both assessors all three clean off their majestic thrones on Monday. There is even a coathanger.

So I hook the hanger with this fancy apparel on the window bars and put on the running tekkies and shorts which also Jess has brought, and the T-shirt saying A LUTA CONTINUA on the front, and THE STRUGGLE CONTINUES on the back, and I'm off down the geranium path at exercise time, with my teeth all stuck together with Liquorice Lockjaw, and humming through my nostrils a boep-type soft-shoe melody, a Central-type song where you're not allowed to sing, but softly to hum through the nose. At the bottom where the path widens out a bit in the sunshine everything becomes just too much and I bust out dancing, and enough of the toffee is dissolved to allow real verbal song too;

Sou ief aai kies joe
Ien the gaarden,
Ien the moenlaait,
Woel joe paarden
Mie en tuptouw
Throe the tjoelups
Woeth mie?

......, so help me God, I say, and Frank Heavistone leads me through the story of my life and interesting times in Port Elizabeth, touching also on interesting times in Durban, but way back there in the days of Oxfam and the Congress of Democrats. It would of course be silly to pretend I just didn't know any political personalities around the country. The trick is to show that I knew them all right, but more or less socially, with a bit of political enthusiasm chucked in, perhaps, but no more to it than that.

I relate the engrossing history of explosives invention in Port Elizabeth with Max, and tell of the political connection to Govan, and keep to the straight truth, why not, except that everyone other than those two will have a new identity and a new address, and unless absolutely necessary will not find a place in the story at all.

Col. Nasser is in it, of course, because such a presence was pivotal to the entire PE adventure. He is with us in the round, here in the Natal Supreme Court; I remember everything, all things about him; his legs were skinny I know, because I once paddled with him on the beach, an innocent rendezvous, whilst discussing sabotage strategy. I remember that he always put his specs lens-down on the table, so there were scratch-marks in front of his eyes and he often misread things. All those small personal things I remember, even irrelevant ones, because I was so close to him. But who his associates were I have no idea. Max and I were disciplined Party people, I tell the court, we didn't enquire about anything it wasn't absolutely necessary for us to know.

Telling the story takes all morning and a bit of the afternoon. I think I've told it pretty well. I've pretty well rearranged the City of Port Elizabeth and repopulated it. The only thing I've been unable to reinvent is the weather. In the absence of the person with the pins folks have brought their own, and you can hear them falling all about, plink, plink, and Cyril Ries too you can hear, scritch-scritching his notes down on a piece of paper and pulling diabolic cunning faces for me to notice because he's going to take me apart tomorrow if he can get Sammy Muller to give us all the afternoon off so he can hatch up a Mephistophelean strategy for cross-examination in the morning, and these diabolic cunning faces are to weaken my morale in preparation.

I count my day a great success. Jess has got the dimensions of my duds dead right, what a fit. They're light and cool, and what a colour combination too; dark ochre gabardine pants and an olive-green jacket with a knitted silk tie, brown, so fashionable. My haircut is not the greatest, though, as is to be expected, Cruywagen did it, and my new beard is still a bit wild. There's not quite enough of it yet, at best I look like Yasser Arafat, a middle-aged cactus, but even that by my reckoning is better than looking like a little boy. A desire so to seem I could never understand, especially in big strong men and German generals.

Cyril Ries homes straight in next day to where by his curious logic I must be most vulnerable, the psychological parts, because I'm not a big strong man but a skinny fucker.

He smiles hideously. He screws up his eyes.

Have you always worn a beard? he asks.

No, M'Lud, I say to Sammy Muller, because I'm giving evidence to the court and not to the prosecutor. I face Sammy too, I don't look at Cyril Ries.

No, M'Lud, out of consideration for my mother I was clean-shaven at birth.

If you display once more such a flippant attitude to this trial I will charge you with contempt of court, says Sammy Muller.

Cyril's hideous smile becomes a more hideous smirk, for he has drawn first blood. Not what you'd call a flood of it though, if you know what I mean, not a haemorrhage; the public gallery is suppressing an assortment of giggles by this means and that, and I notice Sammy's assessors one blowing his nose and the other picking up his pen from the floor.

M'Lud, I hold this court in the greatest esteem and respect, I apologise, and will as of now be most proper in what I say. Sammy Muller nods his head.

Cyril Ries is not going to let go of the psychology after such initial success. Cyril Ries has the cunning not of the fox, but of the badger; if he can't get at your throat he will get his teeth in your ankle and work his way up your trouser leg to your scrotum.

Were you brought up by your father? he asks.

No, M'Lud.

I know he is darting the cunning stare at me through his diabolic screwed-up eyes, but I look at Sammy. Do you have any brothers? asks Cyril.

No, M'Lud. I know he's now going to go through my entire family by gender, distant relatives included, maybe neighbours too if he really gets going, and their maidservants and their manservants, and their ox and their ass, and everything that is mine neighbours'. Their camels.

No, M'Lud, a mother, three sisters, a wife and a daughter.

Six females, women and girls, I say, to save the court's time.

Cyril raises his his echinodermal self to its full five foot nine. He pounces! Why do you tell me all this about your women when I didn't ask you for it? Is it perhaps because there is something insufficient in your malehood?

Perhaps, M'Lud. It is not for me to say; one would have to get psychiatric opinion on that. I feel happy enough with my malehood, though maybe I shouldn't.

There's a shortish silence, while he marshals his thoughts. Which way now? But he catches up after a bit.

It dawns on me that he means to do what Heavistone did to the desolate pharmacist, and cosh me proper before the interesting parts of cross-examination. He knows what his community knows, that white people with feelings of inferiority – Inferiority Complexes is the term, hey? – such sub-standard reject whites turn to gatkruip wheedling toady non-whites for easy acclaim and kudos and petty power.

In my evidence-in-chief Heavistone's list of folks I would have been likely to know in liberal circles in Natal was pretty comprehensive, and art circles too, for they overlap a bit. Even the 10th December list provided by Wilberforce Mdwayi, I knew them all except Mdwayi himself. Keep as close to the truth as possible.

Cyril riffles the list while I look at Sammy.

Good old Natal.

Isn't it strange that so many of your friends are Indians? he asks.

Sammy is busy writing. I notice his right eyebrow rise, nothing else, and I look for the first time at Cyril, and I see him looking at this eyebrow too, then quickly looking at me looking at him for the first time, and smiling at him, and he wants to bite off his tongue and spit it out of his mouth, and to step across the court there and then and hit me in the face, and I wish fervently that he would do this, and he knows that I wish it and hates me more than ever before.

He could have said Jews.

So he drops the personality defects and gets to the straightforward evil of my ways, the same evil for which I have pushed my time and Govan is pushing his, and Max got his lot, so what's to hide?

Being confirmed criminal is quite relaxing in its own way; you don't mind standing on a station platform while mum tells Johnny that you are not a cowboy but a crook, and I don't mind now the gasps of disbelief from the woman and man in the street who have come to the public gallery for gasps, as I lay bare our plans for the violent seizure of power in the State, Baai staail.

I give Cyril Ries straight all the lurid revolutionary detail he wants. He has only to ask. It leaves him a bit nonplussed, flummoxed, and when he moves on from there to details in my fabrication I oblige with the same ease and candour. He can't find the dividing line, because I've learned the technique of lying in court from Paddy Furlow and the Fraud Squad, none better, and the first principle is: stay as close to the truth as possible, be candid, and let your lies be few, big and simple. Slide the candour over to the lies, have no change of texture in your evidence, if asked for unrehearsed details say you can't remember that bit and stick with your forgetfulness; don't think on your feet like Bhekisizwe Ntuli, and don't get rattled. Leave nothing loose for the Jack Russells.

Cyril Ries can't crack my evidence. He can't rattle me either, not because I'm smart, but because I have spent some hours in this court or that, by now, and so has Ben, and hours in court are what we spent hours discussing on the Madhouse floor.

He tries the bad manners trick. It fails the first time because I have seen Frank Heavistone use it but recently, and wondered what I would do if it were used on me, so I give the answer to Cyril's question to Sammy while Cyril is busy talking to his mates at his table. But he tries again doggedly, badgeredly. He asks the question and falls to friendly conversation with the police at his table. I remain totally silent. After a bit he snaps Why will you not answer my question?

I have been looking at Sammy hunched over his papers the while, and he at me when he's not writing, it's quite intimate. M'Lud, I say conversationally, this is a very important question, and my personal welfare depends directly on how I answer it. May I take my time in considering my reply?

Take what time you need, Sammy says, and could he properly say otherwise? I take so long Cyril Ries has pretty well forgotten what the question was by the time I do answer it. My answer is No, and he has to do his fish eagle looking at the ceiling thing a good bit, to piece it all together.

I don't mean I'm smart, I'm not really. I'm really not. I mean they could have got a smarter prosecutor. In truth, all of his questions are over in two hours or so, and they could have been in one, but after tea he goes on grinding away, largely repetitiously, until it becomes clear he's boring the court, bad mistake.

No further questions, M'Lud, he says.

Frank Heavistone is almost done in his case for the defence, and I've been his only witness, which doesn't seem a hell of a lot. Not that I've ever seen how he could make up a list of defence witnesses anyhow; the only way really to prove that I hadn't done this thing would have been to establish an alibi, and how to do that after three and a half years? Who to find? Impossible.

The only possibility is to compile a list of witnesses to support a plea in mitigation of sentence after I've been found guilty, and I'm sure he has a good long list there.

But all we're left to count on in the matter of sentence, in fact, is the lack of credibility in some of the State evidence, and the reasonable doubt which might exist in the minds of judge and assessors, which should with a bit of luck go to the benefit of the accused, me. But only by way of diminution of sentence, according to my guess. Things are tilted a lot in favour of the prosecution, and I don't want even to start having hopes after all the months of assuming I'll be found guilty, because I am guilty.

Ask when you get back if they will count this second sentence along with the first, ou Rassie magnanimously suggests, so you can maybe qualify for some privileges and write to your wife once a month.

Stupid. Soos die spreekwoord sê: Lelik is orraait, maar onnosel... Ah well, hou koers, maybe one day they'll get their turn, their chance, to learn how it all really works in boep.

So there are odds and sods on Frank Heavistone's list, to fill in merely technical details here and there. I can't remember who they were, after all these years, except one; the chief met. officer in Durban, to seal off the evidence of Bhekisizwe Ntuli, to provide solid fact for Heavistone when argument comes.

M'Lud, says Heavistone, I submit to the court as exhibit six, I think it is, a report from the Meteorological Station at Louis Botha Airport, if it would please your Lordship to confirm this number, which report will confirm the evidence given by the present witness from the government weather station, also the witness Ntuli, in the matter of time taken by events on the night of the tenth stroke eleventh of December, nineteen sixty-one.

The report says that sunrise was at 04h 45.16 on the morning 11/12/61.

So that's it. All done. Argument now, then Sammy will say the fateful words and I'll be on my way back to the grey enamel and varnished meranti with a nicely reduced little sentence, thank you Cyril Ries for the clumsiness. Nine years, maybe eight. Sorry the holiday's over, but the lieutenant and I will have plenty to talk about in the coming winter nights.

The toffees were a bit of all right.

M'Lud, says Heavistone, I call Ms Julia Shum, and in Julia Shum steps, out of nowhere, and looking as if she does this every day, which is her way. I have known Julia since the old art school days; it was her way then, and ever has been, it seems. She must suddenly have appeared from wherever, unexpectedly, just today, just now, otherwise I'd have been told about her by my team. I stare at her in disbelief.

Unless you work with people, or live next door to them, you tend to lose touch, and I was right out of touch with Julia when we met in the Baai back in sixty-one, that is when she came upon me in Fogarty's Bookshop where I stood contemplating the theft of a book on Japanese military aircraft design in 1941.

Well, well, good Heavens! what are you doing here, of all places? she exclaimed. Jules, good Gracious! I exclaimed. Thinking I am about to steal this book because I have no money, that's what I'm doing here, but tell me what you are doing here.

Lecturing English at the University of PE was what she was doing there, But never mind that for now, said she, first let me tell you why you should not steal this book because you have no money: money comes and goes, but your bad conscience will stay with you forever. I make no moral case against stealing, she said, since most people do it most of the time by other names; it's just that you feel such a shit afterwards, because it's another form of lying.

Lying, said Julia Shum, being a liar, is the worst thing that can happen to you in this life, because it diminishes you in your own conscience. Misrepresentation of truth to the world really means you're deceiving yourself about your own substance, so rather let me lend you some money and you can buy the bloody thing.

I'd happened to be shoplifting in Fogarty's because it was next door to an estate agent's place I'd just been in, with cards in the window and coloured photographs of this place and that for sale and to let, and we with our new ANC money were looking for more private premises than Ma Garbutt's flophouse or the posh Walmer place for the conduct of our fiendish lives.

See how expensive everything is, said I to Jules. I didn't tell her of the source of our rent, naturally, nor of our fiendish lives, and in a subtractive sort of way this was lying too, I suppose; lying by silence, as it were. Anyway, I was glad of her concern and the response it elicited, and felt a surge of old friendship returned when she said But hang on, there's a vacant flat next door to mine, and I'm sure it's the same size as mine so the rent should be the same. It would be good to have an old friend as neighbour, she said.

And that's how we came to be resident in Meyer Mansions, just opposite the English Department of the University, Port Elizabeth.

So then, Julia Shum steps into the witness box as if she does it every day. She is palish of complexion and has cat's eyes, only they're black. A bit slitty and slanty. She has black hair too, and knows what to do about all this midnight pigmentation, so her dress also is black. It is quite long, mid-black-stockinged-calf, with mid-arm sleeves. Her forearms are pale, and the hands elegant. Though she is fortyish she has no belly, and the dress is nice and tight and flat across there. She is lean, but not in the breasts.

243

She wears a soft black cloth hat, well down, level, and the brim turned up in front, where is pinned a vermilion rose. A real rose, bought within the hour from the vendor with his buckets and blooms in the shade of the City Hall opposite, by the Delville Wood cross. It is so fresh, and big, and dewy and all, that you can actually smell it in the court, in small whiffs from time to time.

She has a cat's mouth too, wide, with a grin and nice big teeth, and her lips are not very full, also like a cat's.

So help me God, says Julia Shum.

Sammy Muller maintains his dignified demeanour as always, of course, though I notice he is no longer hunched over his notebook but sitting upright against the padded leather backrest of his throne, chin up. His left hand is extended imperiously on the desk, and the right holds his ballpoint to his mouth between thumb and first two fingers, as one would a cigarette in a holder. I get an impression that in his time he has held many cigarettes thus in rendezvous with women like Julia Shum.

The assessors sit smiling with their eyes, the corners of their mouths held purposefully down.

Frank Heavistone establishes that Julia Shum lived next door to us in 1961. He asks her to describe her employment. He asks her if she can remember the tenth of December in that year.

Not specifically, she replies, but I do remember very clearly the period from the beginning of that month until Christmas.

How so? he asks.

Because there is so little to remember, you see, says Julia. Over that period of each year I am sequestered in my flat with examination papers, marking well into each night. That was my single occupation at the time in question.

And you allowed no interruption during this period of marking, no visitors?

Very few. The accused or his wife would bring me cups of tea, and occasional meals if the marking schedule were getting heavy. I was very appreciative of their care. I did not regard this as interruption, nor them as visitors. They did not feel obliged to stand on ceremony and talk, they did not expect conversation. It is so with close friends.

So you were close to the accused and his wife?

Oh yes indeed, I felt very tenderly towards them because their first baby was due in the first half of December. In fact it arrived on the thirteenth.

So you saw each other often?

Yes, irregularly but often. Daily, at the least, I should say. We shared the floor of one wing of a small block of flats, Meyer Mansions, so it was as if we were living together, in a way.

I see. So then, can you tell the court whether you saw the accused at home on the night of December the tenth, nineteen sixty-one?

No, I cannot; it is too long ago. I am sure he was at home, though.

So? How is that?

The marking of English papers is very laborious, says Julia Shum, especially when the subject is to do with Literature, because of the number of critical essays involved; but one must nonetheless be perceptive and relaxed while doing it, as I was on that evening amongst others. With his wife so near her time I should have been most perturbed if the accused had not been at home with her. I should have felt obliged to act in loco parentis. My marking schedule would have been badly interrupted. It was not.

Thank you, Miss Shum, says Heavistone. No further questions, M'Lud.

Cyril Ries has questions, but very few. The positive part of Julia's evidence is that she was marking, and nothing else; so what is there to cross-examine there? The negative bit is that she didn't see me, and how can you question somebody about something that didn't happen? Okay, so there also is the matter of her sensibilities, but who can examine something so personal? There are no loose ends to her evidence, nothing to worry at, and tug about; it is big and simple.

But Ries is dogged. At least he can score something for his police pals. Would you see any acquaintances of the accused coming to Meyer Mansions at any time?

Any acquaintance would have to pass my door, so yes, I should see him or her if the door were open.

And none of them were your acquaintances too, I suppose? Big sarcasm here.

None of them WAS my acquaintance, says Julia.

Ries gets a bit chary of the singulars and plurals. Yes but some of them – that is – is very interested in you too, isn't he or she, perhaps?

Some of them ARE very interested in me INDEED, recently, says Jules.

Cyril pounces! Ah! Who are they? Will you describe them to the court?

Big head, pink face, orange moustache, says Jules, and the public turns to look at ou Rassie, and laugh. Sammy too, but discreetly.

I think Sammy fancies Julia Shum a bit.

So what is there to argue?

Cyril Ries describes the hair-raising horrors of our revolutionary enterprise, as expected, and much hysterical stuff about the Soviet Union, but the public's hair has been raised but a year or so ago after a similar description at Rivonia, and such horrors pall soon enough. Sammy just now is the least hysterical person I've ever seen, with his cheek resting flat on his left hand as he writes his meagre notes. He is less concerned about the arrival of the Red Army than the departure of the red rose. It seems.

Frank Heavistone almost as a formality points out the poor quality of prosecution evidence, but the claim for its dismissal has to be on record, however apparent such poor quality may be to the court. It appears to him that all witnesses have improperly been told by the police what to say, says Heavistone. This lamentable fact is the cause of the confusion in his evidence of their star witness, Bhekisizwe Ntuli.

I am seriously to be praised, however, for my candour. See how straight I was about my former criminality. It is because I have nothing to hide. He doesn't even bother to refute the Swart Gevaar and Rooi Gevaar stuff, it's such old hat. Yesterday's propaganda is as valueless as yesterday's newspaper, says Frank Heavistone.

But of cardinal importance, now, is the testimony of the witness Julia Shum. Her evidence was forthright and succinct, as indeed one might expect it to be, for the circumstances were so simple. We were in fact a small commune of three, as it were, says Frank Heavistone, each living sensitively to the needs of the other two. She was peacefully going about her academic life at home, while I in the next room was peacefully reading Shakespeare with my pregnant wife; had I suddenly departed this tranquil scene for horrifying revolutionary adventure it would inevitably, one way or another, have disrupted the harmony of this extended family, as it were.

In any case, what cause had she to distort the truth? What would she gain from such distortion? She is not a co-conspirator, there is no charge against her; she has been questioned by the police, but that implies no complicity.

Argument is pretty perfunctory, then, lacking the venom and vituperation I have seen in some trials. But no great interpretation of evidence is involved. The important stuff is factual, from Ntuli, Shum and the accused, me, and all that has to be weighed up is the probability.

It's clear from Sammy's demeanour that weighing it all up is not going to take him too long. It's Thursday again, and he's not going to drag this case out over another weekend. He can work out a summing-up relaxed in his bath this evening with a double whisky on the soap stand, and deliver it and pass sentence before the tea adjournment tomorrow morning, and that will leave too little time to start any new case this week; so we can all be away and shaya igolofo and fly about in biplanes, whatever, nice and early, before lunch.

It's gone on long enough, is what Sammy Muller's body language tells me. The assessors look sleepy.

Well it seems his view of the evidence tallies with mine, pretty well. Of course he has to go through the roll of witnesses, starting with the hollow-eyed chemist and those others before Op't Boud, but staying with them only long enough to point out that their evidence has been rendered redundant, in the main, because my evidence conceded everything theirs was intended to prove. I mean the possession of explosives ingredients, pointing out targets for attack, that sort of thing from PE showing my lawless nature.

Like me he is bollocksed by O'Bum and Wilberforce. What was the purpose of their testimony? Mdwayi was an embarrassment to the whole court, says Sammy, though he may have had some rôle in a strategy abandoned by the prosecution.

O'Bum too seems to have figured in such a strategy, about which we can only speculate. As things transpired, all he did was provide an interesting joust with Senior Counsel for the Defence.

Of course he takes a lot longer to say all these things than I have taken to write them here, and by intonation and careful choice of words in his saying them he makes it pretty clear that he is glad Frank Heavistone won the joust.

Now, he says, we come to the evidence of the witness Bhekisiswe Ntuli. The demeanour of this witness impressed me, says Sammy Muller. He clearly set out to give us the simple truth, whatever his motives may have been, whether or not it was to his material advantage to incriminate his former accomplices. The problem is, he has given so much evidence in so many courts, under cross-examination by senior defence counsel in so many political trials, that he is now punch-drunk, and no longer sure what the truth is that he is trying to tell. Regrettably, I find I must reject his evidence in toto.

Sammy Muller pours a little water with ice in it from a wide-mouthed carafe. Which brings us to the evidence of the accused, he says, and takes a sip.

The demeanour of the accused was impeccable, after a somewhat bad beginning, he says. The presentation of his evidence was most impressive, he says. It was fluent, unhesitating and expressive. I had the feeling at times that he was eager to express the truth.

Not many times, though. It is just a pity that such an artistic story contained so little of it.

I picture Sammy at his ablutions there on the first evening after my taking the stand, calling his missus from the kitchen so he can tell her about my evidence: Oh Honey, bring us some more ice, please, and the syphon from the fridge? Come sit on the edge of the bath here for a moment and I'll tell you a tale of prime codswallop, the best. What a load of bullshit! Absolute crap, but beautifully packed and delivered.

He now goes piecemeal through the ironclad yarn Frank Heavistone gave me to remember and rehearse.

The evidence of the accused sounded as if it had been rehearsed, says S. Muller, except at the beginning when he was repeating evidence given in an earlier court in which he was tried and found guilty and sentenced, which sentence he has now served, which means he has nothing to lose by repeating that earlier evidence. He did enlarge on details, however, which is to his credit. Thereafter we move into invention.

The degree of inventiveness displayed by the accused, he says, is such that one might see the person Vette, for example, as a character in a novel. A novel by Dostoyevsky, that is.

He picks out exactly the point at which the factual history of my behaviour ends and the fantasy starts. Maybe that's why he's a judge and Frank Heavistone isn't quite, not yet.

I suppose I look a little aghast at this deflation of my ego. The assessor on the left, the one with the melancholy eyes and the pendulous jowls, starts tinily smiling at me and making with his eyebrows, and nodding small nods, to console me a little bit.

In fact, says Sammy, the evidence of the accused says nothing other than that he was not in Durban on the night of December the tenth, nineteen sixty-one. It simply repeats what he said in his plea: that he is not guilty. But I am not at all sure about that.

It is to the credit of the accused that he elected to give evidence where he had the choice not to do so, but in fact it has little substance of any value to this court. Sammy falls silent. It looks as if he feels there ought to be more to say, but there isn't.

Fuck, I think, all you've done is talk about doubtful evidence, why don't you just have done, man, and give me the benefit of all this doubt, according to the fundamentals of Roman Dutch law?

It is fundamental to our system of Roman Dutch law, says Sammy, that doubt must accrue to the benefit of the accused, and yet the evaluation of evidence in this case has not been easy for me. Even after giving the matter much thought I was by no means convinced of his innocence, all evidential doubt notwithstanding.

I look glumly at him, and the droopy-jowled assessor looks at me now with a smile unconcealed if small, and nods his old pate.

I am, however, says Sammy Muller, relieved of this quandary by the evidence of the witness Julia Shum. Her evidence was brief, to the point and very convincing. Though she did not, of course, provide a positive alibi for the accused, she did convince me, very positively indeed, that no person of her sensibilities could ever have left unnoticed the abandonment to her own devices of a pregnant woman so near her time.

This places such severe doubt on the guilt of the accused that I can only pronounce a verdict of Not Guilty.

Twenty-two

I STAND THERE NONPLUSSED. The Court will Rise! calls the policeman usher, and all rise, but I have to sit down. It seems unnatural that I can just walk out of here. Bandiete don't walk about like that, just as they please. Just when they feel like it.

Sammy and his team gather up their goeters and exit right, and Jess takes hold of my hand and leads me from the little raised corral where accused people sit, down to the well of the court where everybody's smiling and congratulating somebody else, and my ma and sister are weeping, and Jess too a bit. We get into another good hug while folks shake my hand behind Jess's back and the large aesthetic youth claps me on the back again and says Good man! Issy Eaglestone is there saying I told you we could do it, and behind him grinning at me I spy Julia Shum, dea ex machina.

I beckon her over and include her in the family hug, and give her a schmoo on the cheek, and we look at each other with nothing to say amongst the general mill of bodies, but after a bit it all calms down a little and I am able to ask her Jules, why did you do it?

I hate fascists, she says.

Well, she has a point there. We may not have fascism, but we sure enough have a police state, and there are plenty of fascists running it.

As congratulation eases off we drift outdoors to the autumn sunshine of the great wide world. W/O Wessels, he of the double-manual harpsichord keyboard with Dadaist fur lid, moves over from a police car with another Security boer from Durban. I notice ou Rassie and MacBackside at this car, but whatever is going to happen now is Natal business; they're just up here for the giving of evidence. And advice, it goes without saying, from a father-figure.

Er, says Wessels. Er, man, ah. Would you mind coming with us, it won't take long? Blimey, this is the first time I've been INVITED to enter enter a convivial SB motor-car. Depends where we're going, doesn't it? I say. No, says Keyboard, with the lower half of his face smiling, We just going to the prison for a bit. Oh THERE, I say. No, I don't really need to go there, I've got my bag with me, and I show them this bag with toilets and a jersey in it; They always make you take your property with you when you go to court, I say, in case you're acquitted.

The way Wessels speaks he lowers his upper lip only for pronouncing plosives. There aren't any in his next sentence, so he doesn't have to spoil the smile; No we just going to see, he says, whatever that might mean.

Carstairs steps briskly over. Don't speak to these people unless I'm present! he says to me. To them he says What do you want, are you detaining my client?

Noooo, oh no nooooo! exclaims Keyboard, like that has never before happened in our history, and both boere are smiling with both halves of their faces now.

Never to worry, Nigel, I say, they have invited me to go to the prison to see, and I think I'll go along, just to say farewell, sort of. I'll be at Lola's flat in a couple of minutes, see you there.

To tell you the truth, however eager I am to get to the wine in my sister's fridge it really intrigues me to see what this lot is going to behold at the boep. I turn to Jess; Want to come along? Ja, she says, but I don't want to be with these men. I'll follow in your ma's car with Lola.

So we pile into the Chevy, the Natal contingent in front and me in the back with the PE lads. O'Bum is on the right, and Rassie opens the left-side door for me. No thanks, I say, I think I'll sit by the window. Not so much a matter of sucks, this, for the last time when I was all draped about with wrought-iron artwork and the door was strapped up with the belt from ou Jorrie's broek, as for the fact that I sure as hell don't want to sit next to somebody who hates me as much as ou Poephol does. We move off in silence, but for the clacking of the Erasmus choppers. In the driver's mirror I see v. Gat making stereo Morse code with his eyelids.

Shakespearean shouts greet us from the other side of the big boep door as Wessels' underling thumps his great beef bones on the studded oak and clangs the electric bell. In Afrikaans, these shouts, about being keeper of the gates of Hell.

Here's a parcel of politick knaves, i'Faith! We go straight into the reception office where a new bloubaadjie from Central sits poised to enlist fellow miscreants. Is jy gestraf? barks Head Warder Delport. Nee, wat, I reply, ek is onskuldig gevind. Het jy nie jou eiendom hof-toe saamgeneem nie? Did I not take my property to court? Ja, natuurlik, hier's hy, and I show him my bag.

Nou ja, vok af, man!

I'm ready enough to fuck off, but the SB stand and stare at Delport and he stares vacuously back at them. They don't know what to say. We all about turn and fuck off. I get in my ma's car next to Jess and we're off to the champers in the fridge. It is the damnedest thing I've ever seen.

I wasn't the only one who couldn't believe I was free.

We park the Morris in Longmarket Street and stroll arm-in-arm to Lola's flat in Timber Street. People seem to amble all over the pavements without discipline, they drift from the left to the right side and back again without purpose. All of these people doing things in the same place must be somehow connected, and the complexity of the relationships between them is beyond comprehension. And what a lot of women all about. Everywhere.

We sit on soft unmeranti chairs and drink wine and chat. People's goings-on seem so urgent and complicated. I wonder what all the energy's about, but half a bottle or so of Stein fixes all that and I fall asleep on the couch. At eight Jess wakes me and we're off to the Morris and the drive home to Durbs and bed. Being out at night is really the weirdest. I want to look at shop windows but hurry on. Especially when we come to a jeweller's shop with fluorescent lighting and silver all over every shelf: bracelet, trophy, teatray and twenty-first birthday key, I feel just so guilty, and hurry on.

I wake at the usual time, the very first of first light. I am not awakened by any electric bell, nor in fact by the first light; I am unused to sleeping with a pillow under my head and two of them are now on top and all is dark.

I am awakened by birdsong.

Lift up Your Heads! calls a toppie, again, again and again.

Lift up Your Heads, Oh Ye Gates, and be Ye lift up, Ye Everlasting Doors... I remember it as I worm my way down deeper into the billowy bedclothes. The King of Glory shall come in...

I am close up against Jess, and my arm is still over her. I get that strange feeling I'd forgotten about, that women can't be made of the same stuff as men. Men are like bags of coal. Jess feels more like Muis van der Kombuis. The delicate skin under the supple enfolding sheets and the hair in my face and warm breath, and our bodies in the lush feathery well of bedclothes still odorous of lovemaking; I'd forgotten about these wonders. My memory of sex in jail was sentimental enough but coarse compared to the reality. It is total. Peace and Heaven.

But the increasing din makes unlikely any dozing off again. It's the plangent duet of a brace of barbets now, and as if they're not noisy enough two hadedahs have landed on the roof like a couple of old umbrellas, and they're yelling their heads off as if they're on fire: Water! Water! In Goddes name, Water! What the other small peeps and gossiping noises are about I can't imagine, so I've got to heave out of bed my frogs, snails and puppy-dogs' tails, to find out.

I remember how to get out of a bed you're sharing with someone; don't roll in the direction of your leaving, roll the other way and move this way, then you don't pull the blankets off your pal.

The room faces east; I open the curtains and window straight on to the rising sun behind a cassia tree, speciosa, in full gaudy cadmium-yellow bloom, yellow of star and speciosa filling the frame, the showy petals brushing against the panes and packed end to end with small socially chatting white-eyes, and yellow-bum bulbuls, and malachite sunbirds working on the flowers. A paradise flycatcher is cartwheeling about catching flies in the vivid paradise and doves are at their puffed-up courtship gurgling along the branches. A pied crow in SS uniform is chasing mynahs off the grass and redwings are whistling on a telephone wire. Sparrows twitter.

Seynt Valentyn, that art ful hy onlofte,
Thus singen smale foules for thy sake;
Now welcom, somer, with thy sonne softe,
That has this wintres wedere overshake,
And dreven away the longe nightes blake!

But memories of tea prevail, and I'm off to the kitchen for a cuppa. I peep in at Susie who looks as kids look in bed: as if they fell asleep standing up and landed just any old how. She's a pretty thing, to be sure. A complete stranger, though. I think I'll take the morning off to get to know her; the Botanic Gardens are more or less over the road and we'll go there and feed bread to the fishes in the duckpond and take the air in the deep greens of exotic glades. Hell, that's a long time ahead! The clock says it's only five. The Haripersadh rooster next door is still crowing.

Looking for the sugar bowl I find a packet of lime jelly in a cupboard. While my tea is brewing I mix this up with only a cup or so of boiling water, so the gelatin's going to be bouncy-firm when it sets. I take two eggs from the fridge and poke a small hole in each end of both, with a needle from the sewing-machine drawer. I stir up the insides of the eggs with the needle and blow them out into the cat's bowl. I suck in the hot green jelly, and make red spots on the shells with a felt pen from Susie's drawing box, and put the eggs in the ice-tray of the fridge to set.

The mug I've chosen for my tea is actually a soup-bowl with handles on it. It holds nigh a litre, I reckon. I take it with me for an exploration of the garden. Up at the back are two huge avocado trees, the one on the right a fairly usual cultivar, small and rich fruit, the Bos'n's Butter, and the one on the left one of those Australian things with fruit the size of your head, literally, big sods, man, but a bit watery to the taste. It occurs to me one of these things landing on Susie would brain her for sure; we must give some thought to that. But under this tree is a fine place for a wendy house. I'll make a real one, of good packing-case timber from a big Scandinavian crate, and a proper door with a mortise lock and handle, and a glazed window on hinges, and I'll paint it red and green, with a dark green asbestos roof, double pitch. It will have a real wooden floor on beams, too, and later I'll make some furniture.

Down here I'll grow bananas, right opposite the bath outlet pipe; they like soapy water Tony Gomes told me when I shared digs with him in London, and he should know, he was from Barbados, a Bajan, and he used to harvest bananas. Plant them eight feet apart, he said, cut all small shoots away so the main one gets plenty of light. Dig a little dam around each one to take the bathwater and dig your kitchen peelings and tea-leaves in there too. You'll get a bunch of fat fruit so big and heavy you'll have to prop the plant up to hold it.

When they're ripe, grab up the purple prepuce at the bottom of the bunch and cut the whole plant down with a left sweep of your machete, said Tony, demonstrating this technique in front of Mrs Pitt's miserable gas heater in our mouldy digs in Paddington, then cut the bunch loose from the plant, the lily, with the return sweep, so it's all one rhythmic action. You should have two hundred and fifty on the bunch, roughly, he said. At this point he fell silent, and looked out over the grey snow.

Well, I'm in a bit of a reverie too, now, as Susie comes up quietly behind me and takes my hand. Hullo, she says, are you looking at my garden? Yup, I say, I'm going to grow bananas. Okay, I'll show you around, she says, and we're off. She seems very self-possessed, which I quite like in kids, I hate them to be in awe of adults. Would you like to go to the bot gardens? I ask. Okay, she says, and turns about there and then to go and get into the Weetbix before we set forth.

When I catch her up I find Jess is up and about and in the bathroom cleansing and rearranging and clothing herself for the day. I remember that this usually takes a couple of hours on a Saturday, so I tell her Look, I'm going to shoot across to the bot gardens with Susie, to feed the fishes, hey, we'll be an hour or so. I get Susie into her tracksuit and myself in mine, I put a half loaf in a slingbag for the fish and when Susie isn't looking I slip the eggs in too, and we're off!

These fish are plenty smart, they live right under the lilies and grass overhang of the bank, starting off as survivors, I suppose, of a couple of raids by a bloody big pelican that got in amongst them and swallowed just about the entire ancestral line. They all come shooting across to us when we loom over the water though, because they know the pelican is afraid of people.

I break off a piece of bread and give it to Susie to throw to the fish. She eats it. I tweak off another piece and throw it to the fish, and they heap themselves up in a mound above the surface, like piranha, in their eagerness to get at the bread. Interesting. I give another piece to Susie and she chucks it in and the fish do the same thing. Interesting. I give her another piece and she thinks hard about things. She raises it to her shoulder for throwing. Interesting, but not interesting enough. She eats it. The next piece too. In fact she eats her half of the half loaf. She is happy to watch me waste mine. Some woman, this, I tell you.

Just wait here a minute, I say, and don't fall in. I'm just going to see if Jess is coming, hey? and I nip over to a display of smallish bromeliads growing on a log artistically placed on the ground. I look to make sure Susie isn't watching and put the two eggs in the leaf vases of two of the plants, there where the mosquitoes breed if you don't watch out, and I stroll back to Susie, nonchalantly whistling. No, Jess isn't coming, I say, but let's walk around a bit and see if maybe we can see a nest of the Bootootoo Bird.

We walk away from the bromeliads. A Bootootoo Bird? Well, it is about as big as a chicken, but it's got these big long legs, you see, because it doesn't actually build a nest, it stands over a certain plant which looks like the top of a pineapple, you know?, and lays its egg in there. You know what a pineapple top looks like? Susie nods eagerly. So now we're going to look for those plants, and maybe we'll be lucky if a Bootootoo Bird has been along. But you don't often find their eggs.

By this time we're right around the duck pond and I say to her I'll tell you what, you look on that side of the path and I'll look on this, and after a bit I think For Chrissake, child, is there something wrong with your eyes? but as I think it she tugs at my fingers and she's looking at me speechless and her eyes are wide, circular, and she's afraid to look round again in case what they've just seen is illusory.

Hey, lucky us! I say, Usually you find these eggs only in the forest. You can tell they're Bootootoo eggs all right, by the spots. Can we take them? she asks. Oh I'm sure we can, they've laid some more in the forest, I'll bet. We'll take them home and cook them, says she. No, no, these you eat just like that, straight away, and we sit on the log while I crack open my egg and peel it and bite into the green insides. She stares dumbfounded; she's never seen anything like it. Go on, I say, crack it open, peel it, it's nice. Nor has she ever tasted anything like it.

Our wanderings take us right across the gardens to the Sydenham Road side, and there I espy seven maids with seven mops busily bustling about small tables and chairs and wiping things down at the little tea kiosk some charity ladies run over the weekends. I say to Susie Just sit on this bench for a bit, I'm going for a wee, and I stroll off behind this tearoom where I find the lady in charge opening up so she can start baking the scones, and I ask her if it is too early to buy ice-cream? and she says Never too early, Luv, so I'm over to the freezer chest and get a couple on sticks from right down the bottom where it's extra cold.

While I'm about it I get a tube of fruitgums too, and run like the clappers over to the pod mahogany with its broad branches down down to the ground, and in a couple of little cracks in one of these I plant the ice-creams on their sticks, and the gums I plant in the loose curly bark of a squat-looking eucalypt. I run back, changing pace as I come round the tearoom. I stroll up to Susie. Hey, how about looking for other birds' nests?

And so, by various subterfuge, unhurried for verisimilitude, we come upon the fruit of the Icecream tree, that the Antarctic Roomys Bird takes for its chicks, it's a bit like a flying penguin, but all white. Also some of the material that the Vrugtegommetjie Bird uses for building its nest; the fruit of the Gum tree. The chicks as they grow up don't need feeding, for they just eat the nest, but chicks and mum are all out of luck this time, because we have got here first and scored the gums.

There is no limit to future nature study. There is a cedar here with facsimile biltong bark, and I reckon vienna sausages would be dead right as bean-pods on a certain species of the family Leguminosae. But it's teatime now, and I'm in need of more of the stuff, would you believe it? Come on ducky, home time. I hope it hasn't all done too much harm for a career in biology one day, perhaps. But then again I've known successful enough biologists who believe some people can walk on water, and come alive again to moralise at us after they've been dead.

When we get home the artistical youth is there, doing something at the desk. Rodney is writing a thesis for a Master's Degree in Fine Art, says Jess; tell us about your thesis, Rodney.

Rodney tells us his thesis is on certain aspects of socialist sensibility, that's why he's chosen for interpretation certain aspects of the art of Siqueiros and Rivera. I notice that he is busy with my big fat book on the Mexican muralists. Ja, interesting fellows, I say, the way they were able to pick up the fresco technique again after hundreds of years, without anybody to teach them the little tricks of it. Only the recipes they had, yet they painted stuff as good as Giotto's.

YYYess... says Rodney, though I must say I'm less interested in the mere technology of it, or the mere physical materials, than in the symbolism. Take note that by symbolism I do not mean imagery, the story told, as it were, with the human figure set in an historical panorama, the imagery of an ideological overview, if you get my drift. No, I am interested in the rôle of culturally liberated woman in socialist art in terms of formal symbolism, by which I mean symbols conceived as monumental tactile form (interesting that you should mention Giotto) and of course the symbolism of colour (here I might mention as a typical example of cultural condescension the colour range used by Raphael in his depiction of the Madonna – all pinks and blues in his soft rendering of drapes and female flesh, suggesting a mindlessness in Womankind). No; in brief, I mean to examine in formal terms whether the Mexican painters allowed room in their cultural hegemony for their supposedly liberated women. Are they positioned compositionally as the men are, importantly, powerfully? Are their features portrayed as people of equal social substance? (I am naturally not talking of the Soviet style of painting, where men and women are presented as of equal brutality.) No, others enough have examined the Mexican murals, but none in terms of the liberated woman, her presentation in terms of simple formal symbolism.

Ja, I say.

Rodney's thesis is going to have a good symbolic title too: Frida Kahlo's Other Eyebrow, something like that. But I'm not sure, it's a long time ago.

But enough of Me, now! he exclaims. I should like to drink a toast to Us, though it is I suppose a little early in the day. He looks at his watch. But it's ten o'clock! the bar's open! He! He! He!

He's into the kitchen where stands our special bottle of French brandy from the night before. I hear him at the ice-trays from the fridge. He emerges with three glasses and cubes in a bowl, and the brandy. Glug glug glug, three times.

Well, it's great to see you back in circulation, he says, Cheers!

What on Earth does he mean? I must confess at this point that I'm a little slow in the uptake in these things. What on Earth do you mean by circulation? I ask. I never was in it.

No, I mean, he says with an uncomfortable laugh, huh, huh, huh, because something is going a bit wrong, and the best way out is to make a civilised little joke, I mean I'll move over a bit now you've rejoined us.

Silence.

The civilised little joke is that he changed the bedsheets the last morning, very symbolically. The morning before the evening on which I got into the bed.

I go into cold immobile shock, clenched solid, all of me, pumped full of adrenalin, because I know that I might kill at this moment. I'll find a weapon in the kitchen. What little of my rational mind is still functioning tells me that if I do it now, NOW, the matter will not even come to court, and if it were to I would be acquitted. Such is the mind of a true bandiet, who thinks always in terms of evidence, who thinks fast, who understands the equations. A bandiet is not nice. I'd be surprised if he were.

Don't do it like Koelie, do it NOW!

I went to the laundry basket, M'Lud, and found there bedsheets with semen of the deceased on them; his love-puddles.

No, los the kitchen. It won't effect my evidence much if I take time to get to the Indian shops just here in Berea Road, and find a lino knife, short, stubby, recurved, the thin sheeny steel of the broad blade tempered keen to cut a surgical edge on a plastic tile, nor will it affect this evidence if take hold of this Rodney's body somewhere and soon enough lock my marathon legs around his thorax from behind and crush out the breath of his life, and pull his chin back in the crook of my arm, and split through skin with the hiss of slitting vynide, and slice through sterno-masoid muscle and carotid artery and over thyroid cartilage to the great vein, the jugular, and feel the heat of him draining through my clothing, feel him die in my grip.

I can do it, I know how to use my body, it's still taut from obsessive exercise and sheer rage is in me. I'm ready.

Rodney is easy meat.

Silence.

What about Susie, then? What afterwards to say of this execution, and the blood all down my body, and what about the smell of the shitting when his body knew it was dying?

As she stands with the Bootootoo egg in her hand?

My gaze is fixed on him. It is all within an ace. If I move at all, a single muscle, I will not stop moving until catharsis. I notice that he is wearing my green corduroy trousers, lengthened in the leg and widened at the waist, and my leather belt.

Listen well, my China, I say, with difficulty for lack of breath, Get your stuff out of my desk and fuck off. You can keep the trousers, and thanks for the cheese sandwich.

Yes, I understand, but...

PISS OFF NOW, BOY, or you're DEAD!

There's an ugly sustained silence after he's gone. I wouldn't mind an outburst, a confrontation, but I don't get one.

What do you think, then?

Silence.

I walk about the garden a bit more. Down at the street boundary I find there is a brick retaining wall, a couple of metres high, so I look a bit downwards on my neighbours across the way. We're a mixed bunch around here, in spite of the Group Areas Act; Mauritians who count as white, coloured folk down at the corner, who don't of course, Hindu Indians next door, Natal English working-class pigeon-fanciers beyond them, Afrikaner railway workers on the left and a real Prog lady up at the back, just about everything except plain black. I sit on the retaining wall and think about all this because I don't want to think about what's behind me. The birds have stopped singing.

It is eleven o'clock. A bloke in a jalopy pulls up opposite and gets out to open the gate. Howzit? I call, and give a salute. I see he has a couple of rods on a roofrack, a big one for garrick and a shorter shad stick, nicely tapered, with a wooden reel on it. This bloke knows about surf angling, that's clear.

Any fish? I ask. Ja, a couple of snoek on a spoon at the Rocket Hut, he says, but I hear they're taking shad at Pattie's Groyne. Can I borrow your stick and fetch a few? I ask. Sure, he says, if you bring it back before tomorrow. The line's a bit heavy for shad, he says, twenty pounds, and I don't know if you can use a centre-pin reel, but you're welcome. His name is Joe Simonson. No, that's okay, Joe, I think my reel is around somewhere, it's like yours, but I'll take yours just in case. He hands me the rod, with the snoek spoon still on it, hooked back on the first runner.

Where are you from? he asks. Back from the Transvaal, I say, and I've missed the fishing. Try sardine and a bung, he says. That's what I had in mind, I say.

We'll go together when I've made up a rod.

So I rummage about in various old boxes and bags in a wall cupboard, and good luck, there are my reels, still with bits of bait and stuff on them four years old, but they spin as when new. The shad reel is jacaranda; I remember turning it on Mr Bettleham's lathe when I was sixteen. I think I'll line it with fibreglass one of these days. I squirt some sewing-machine oil on the bearings. I take it outside and tie the line on a nail in the big avo and unreel it to the other end of the garden and pull on it until it breaks. We've still got good line here, it's been out of the sun these years, and the breaking strain is still ten pounds or so.

I make a hefty sandwich, the thing they called a wad in the army, with white bread for the hell of it, plus another pint of the tea, in a jam jar with a screw-top lid; there's no thermos around and it'll be fine cold. Hey Jess, I think I'll take a hike down to Pattie's and fetch a couple of shad for supper, I say. Shouldn't be too long.

Silence.

Ciao! I say.

The hike to the beach is four kays or so, along Alice Street and Old Fort Road, and I'm a fast walker, so by the time I get to Paul Gauguin's Pandanus palms and the coconuts and the casuarina grove just back from the beach I'm glowing healthily and all my senses are sharp.

Long before that, though, I can smell what seamen call the land breeze, and landsmen call the sea breeze: the iodine vapours of seaweed and the fanny tang coming off the mussels and invertebrate rock growth of the intertidal zone, and little bubblies from sea-lice, and u/v blocker suntan lotion, and old greasy bags left over from fish and chips and meat pies. Roasted monkeynuts.

From the shadows of the casuarina grove I see it; Oh dear God the sea, my lovely place, thumping and hissing away as if it has had some purpose these three thousand million years, but why did I think it would look any different from the last time I saw it through the window of the risible Chev? That's Lal too, way out there, I'll wager, with his million-year-old predatory purpose. If it is Lal, he's changed his ways, he is not alone. But his small small laaitie may have got big; maybe he doesn't just sit with the mealie-bag any more, he's after the protein too.

I sit on the mat of casuarina needles and tiny cones and eat my sandwich, tomato and onion and lettuce, with plenty of pepper and some lemon juice, and idly wonder how a conifer has come to populate the world's beaches. They're supposed to grow in Alaska, aren't they? Finland, and so on.

Idly also, why is all sound dampened so at the beach? Up in the mountains it isn't. Kelp gulls land nearby and squawk, and I can scarce hear them. They eye my sandwich. Small chance, my mates, this salad is my salad, after four years without. Anyway, I'm more interested in the sandpipers running where the sand is wet down there, their titchy feet going about a thousand to the minute, and why does the whole multitude now and then start to hop on one leg, suddenly, as if at a signal?

I lie down a bit with my head on the tackle bag with the raincoat in it, and relish the salt breeze puffing about my face, and the small scudding fairweather cumulus above the conifer wisps.

Ande in a launde, upon an hille of floures,

Was set this noble godesse Nature;
Of braunches were hir halles and hir boures,
Y-wrought after hir craft and hir mesure;
but the nobility bit doesn't mean Nature is some judgmental old Tory matron decorously dressed in curtains like Mrs God, up there in Her corset amongst Him and His incorporeal dignitaries in their undimensional Supreme Court, reciting Her recondite rules of ecological behaviour, punishing us with hothouses because we haven't kept Her things in balance, but gone squirting chlorofluorocarbons all about and the like.

Nature is a Music Hall queen, lightly touching the arm of a young admirer in her feathery dressing-room, smiling a little flirtatiously her gorgeous smile with that sidelong glance of her painted eyes, and if she appears to hate us at times because we chop down rain forests and piss in rivers and unbalance things, it isn't because she's cross at all, it's just that her favourites on this earth are the species Felis domesticus and the family Columbidae, the cat among the pigeons, with Homo sapiens a bit down the list.

She hates balance, Natura abhorrat equilibrium, it would mean no evolution and none of the delights we want to save for our kids.

It's Lal, right enough. It's his laaitie too, right enough. I do one of the standard deals that unemployed anglers do. I borrow a sardine from him and give him my second shad; the first I cut up for bait. He lends me a traced three-oh hook and a cork bung, and I'm in business.

He's made room on his rock for his son, though it's a bit cramped. I'm on the next one, a sort of sloped-over pyramid. Your small small laaitie got big same time hey? I say after a bit. Lal nods, but doesn't go as far as an actual smile. Very bold rascal fellow that laaitie, he says.

After a long while he says to me Where you went last time, you?

No, I went to boep, I say, came out yesterday. Lal nods again. He doesn't ask what for, or say bad luck and all that rigmarole; everybody he knows, pretty well, has been in and out of boep for a bit. Well, the men, that is. It's nothing new. It's part of being unwhite, and unemployed.

After an even longer while he turns to me again. Came back this place one shot hey? He really smiles now, with all his decrepit teeth; I've never seen it before, in ten years. It's horrible.

There's a lull, and suddenly I nearly lose balance on my slopy stone as a good strong six-pound shad drags down the tip of the rod and I strike back at him. I feel with my feet to a flatter rock and let him sprint about until he's quiet, and haul him out. I get my fingers in his gills and grip the shank of the hook and free it from amongst the furious teeth, and drop him in my shoulder-bag. We fish on, half an hour or so.

Hey Lal, I call, How many you got, you?

Twenty-seven, me, says Lal.

Harold Strachan published his first book,
Way Up Way Out: A Satirical Novel,
seven years ago at the age of 72.
A South Africa Air Force pilot during World War II,
he became an art teacher in the 1950s and was active
during the 1960s in the Communist Party and
Umkhonto we Sizwe (MK), the armed wing of the ANC.

He was imprisoned for four years and held under house
arrest for ten years after that. He eventually left the
CP and ANC, but refused to leave South Africa,
and after 16 years' unemployment set himself up as an
art restorer and renowned columnist for *Noseweek*.
This is his second book.

First published in 2004 by Jacana Media (Pty) Ltd.
5 St Peter Road
Bellevue, 2198
Johannesburg
South Africa

ISBN 1-77009-033-9

Cover design by Orange Juice
Printed by PTN Print
See a complete list of Jacana titles at www.jacana.co.za